A NEW ECONOMIC
GROWTH ENGINE FOR CHINA
Escaping the Middle-Income Trap
by Not Doing More of the Same

A NEW ECONOMIC GROWTH ENGINE FOR CHINA

Escaping the Middle-Income Trap by Not Doing More of the Same

Editors

Wing Thye Woo *(Fudan University, Shanghai; Columbia University, New York City; Penang Institute, George Town; University of California, Davis; & Central University of Finance and Economics, Beijing)*

Ming Lu *(Fudan University, Shanghai)*

Jeffrey D. Sachs *(Columbia University, New York City)*

Zhao Chen *(Fudan University, Shanghai)*

 Imperial College Press

 World Scientific

Published by

Imperial College Press
57 Shelton Street
Covent Garden
London WC2H 9HE

and

World Scientific Publishing Co. Pte. Ltd.
5 Toh Tuck Link, Singapore 596224
USA office: 27 Warren Street, Suite 401-402, Hackensack, NJ 07601
UK office: 57 Shelton Street, Covent Garden, London WC2H 9HE

British Library Cataloguing-in-Publication Data
A catalogue record for this book is available from the British Library.

A NEW ECONOMIC GROWTH ENGINE FOR CHINA
Escaping the Middle-Income Trap by Not Doing More of the Same

ISBN 978-981-4425-53-7
ISBN 978-981-4425-54-4 (pbk)

Printed by FuIsland Offset Printing (S) Pte Ltd Singapore

Foreword

Shangli Lin

Vice-President, Fudan University

Although China has become the second largest economy in the world and a middle-income country in the process, the challenges that China faces are more daunting than ever. From all aspects of the domestic and foreign situation, China has now reached a critical juncture in its development. Unless China is able to overcome the difficulties in undertaking further reforms in the next ten years, China would be caught in the middle income trap and be unable to become a modern country. The future course of China's economic development is also of great concern to the rest of the world because the socio-political-economic conditions in China will have significant impact on global economic prosperity and on global political harmony.

Fudan University is one of the best universities in China, and has deep research strength in the social sciences. Because Fudan University is located in Shanghai, which is a pioneering city in the reform of China's economy, Fudan is dedicated to conducting pioneering research on all the important issues in China's development. Among the major efforts by Fudan in this direction is the current building up of the Fudan Institute of Development Studies to promote creative research in the social sciences and to provide better analytical support to accelerate China's reforms and development.

The year 2012 is a critical year in determining the overall strategic direction of China's future policies. It is therefore most timely that the School of Economics at Fudan University and the Earth Institute at Columbia University have worked closely together to prepare this comprehensive report on China's economic priorities. This team of leading international economics experts is led by Wing Thye Woo (Distinguished

Professor at Fudan University, Director of the East Asian Program in the Earth Institute of Columbia University, Executive Director of the Penang Institute, and Professor at the University of California, Davis), Ming Lu (Professor of Economics at Fudan University), Jeffrey D. Sachs (Professor of Economics and Director of Earth Institute at Columbia University, and Special Advisor to the United Nations Secretary-General), and Zhao Chen (Professor of Economics at Fudan University). This report contains an integrated economic policy agenda that achieves optimality in economic management by ensuring consistency among short-term demand management, medium-term supply growth, and long-term sustainable development. This economic action plan encapsulates the ambitious objective of Fudan University to promote development studies in China through the mobilization of wisdom from a worldwide network of the best scholars on each topic.

As the Fudan University's Vice-President in charge of the Institute of Development Studies, I am especially pleased by the high quality of this book. I am confident that the simultaneous publication of this book in English and Chinese will spread the valuable achievements of the Columbia-Fudan research team and improve the economic development practices in China.

Contents

List of Contributing Authors and Editors

Sarah Brennan
Associate Director
Lenfest Center for Sustainable Energy, Earth Institute
Columbia University, New York City, USA
sarahannebrennan@gmail.com

Ximing Cai
Associate Professor
Ven Te Chow Faculty Scholar in Water Resources
Civil and Environmental Engineering Department
University of Illinois, Urbana-Champaign, USA
xmcai@illinois.edu

Zhao Chen
Professor and Deputy Director
China Center for Economic Studies
School of Economics
Fudan University, Shanghai, China
zhaochen@fudan.edu.cn

Gang Fan
Director, National Economics Research Institute, Beijing, China
Professor, HSBC Business School, Peking University, Shenzhen, China
Secretary-General, China Reform Foundation, Beijing, China
Professor, Graduate School of Chinese Academy of Social Sciences, Beijing, China
fangang@neri.org.cn

Jin Feng
Professor
Department of Economics
Fudan University, Shanghai, China
jfeng@fudan.edu.cn

Liping He
Professor
Department of Finance
Beijing Normal University, Beijing, China
liping@cei.gov.cn

Lixin He
Associate Professor
Department of Public Economics
Fudan University, Shanghai, China
lixinhe@fudan.edu.cn

Klaus S. Lackner
Ewing-Worzel Professor of Geophysics
Department of Earth and Environmental Engineering,
Director, Lenfest Center for Sustainable Energy, Earth Institute
Columbia University, New York City, USA
klaus.lackner@columbia.edu

Upmanu Lall
Alan & Carol Silberstein Professor of Engineering
Department of Earth and Environmental Engineering and
Department of Civil Engineering and Engineering Mechanics
Director, Columbia Water Center, Earth Institute
Senior Research Scientist, International Research Institute for
    Climate & Society, Earth Institute
Columbia University, New York City, USA
ula2@columbia.edu

Ming Lu
Professor
Department of Economics
Fudan University, Shanghai, China
lm@fudan.edu

Jeffrey David Sachs
Director, Earth Institute
Quetelet Professor of Sustainable Development, School of International and
    Public Affairs
Professor of Health Policy and Management, School of Public Health
Professor, Department of Economics
Special Adviser to United Nations Secretary-General Ban Ki-Moon
Chief Strategist, Millennium Promise Alliance
Columbia University, New York City, USA
sachs@ei.columbia.edu

Xiaofen Tan
Associate Professor
School of Finance
Central University of Finance and Economics
Beijing, China
xiaofent@163.com

Guanghua Wan
Professor, Yunnan University of Finance and Economics, Kunming, China
Principal Economist, Asian Development Bank, Manila, Philippines
guanghuawan@yahoo.com

Wing Thye Woo
Professor, School of Economics, Fudan University, Shanghai, China
Director, East Asia Program, Earth Institute, Columbia University,
    New York City, USA
Executive Director, Penang Institute, George Town, Malaysia
Professor, Department of Economics, University of California, Davis, USA
Professor, Central University of Finance and Economics, Beijing, China
wtwoo@ucdavis.edu

Jingjing Ye
PhD candidate
Southern Methodist University
Dallas, USA
jye.consultant@adb.org

Yongding Yu
Academician
Senior Fellow, Institute of World Economics and Politics
Chinese Academy of Social Sciences, Beijing, China
yongdingyu@gmail.com

Yuxin Yu
Post-Doctoral Fellow
School of Economics
Fudan University, Shanghai, China
jadeyyx@163.com

Zhigang Yuan
Dean, School of Economics
Director, Employment and Social Security Research Center
Fudan University
Advisor, Shanghai Municipal Government
Shanghai, China
zgyuan@fudan.edu.cn

Liqing Zhang
Dean
School of Finance
Central University of Finance and Economics
Beijing, China
zhlq@cufe.edu.cn

Yan Zhang
Associate Professor
China Center for Economic Studies
School of Economics
Fudan University, Shanghai, China
yanzhang_fd@fudan.edu.cn

Juzhong Zhuang
Deputy Chief Economist
Asian Development Bank
Manila, Philippines
jzhuang@adb.org

PART I

A New Economic Growth Engine for the 21st Century:
Change Out Not Scale Up the Present Policy Regime

The Major Types of Middle-income Trap That Threaten China

Wing Thye Woo

1. A New Stage in China's Economic Development but Will This be the Permanent Stage?

The World Bank reclassified China as an upper middle-income country in July 2011. The deductive character of logic leaves no doubt about what is the next stage in this classification scheme: a high-income country or, to be exact but awkward, a lower high-income country. The international experience with economic growth, however, advises strongly against the temptation to predict the date of China's advent into high-income-hood by making a straightforward projection from China's growth path in the past 33 years. By straightforward projection, we mean a prediction that is based on the assumption that future growth rates of China's GDP per capita would resemble its past growth rates in a predictable way, with the straight-line projection being an extreme example. The more common straightforward projection is to build in an incremental slowdown to the average growth rate of the recent period such that the Chinese growth rate would converge to the U.S. growth rate by the time that China achieves parity in the standard of living with the United States.

The case against the straightforward projection is summarized in Table 1 which shows the GDP per capita (in 1995 PPP US$) of 65 countries in 1913 (the eve of World War I), 1964 (the year of the Tokyo Olympics, which marked the entry of the first Asian economy into high-income status), and 2008 (the last year in Maddison's, 2010, dataset on historical statistics); and the income ranking of these countries in the

Table 1. GDP per capita: Level and Rank in Selected Years for 65 Economies.
1913 = eve of World War I, 1964 = Year of Tokyo Olympics,
2008 = latest year in Maddison (2010)

	GDP per capita			Rank out of 65 countries			Annual growth rate in 1870–1913 period
	1913	1964	2008	1913	1964	2008	
Albania	811	1,616	4,149	56	49	52	1.83
Algeria	1,163	1,806	3,520	40	46	55	1.49
Argentina	3,797	5,926	10,995	10	18	28	3.28
Australia	5,157	9,849	25,301	2	7	6	1.39
Austria	3,465	7,567	24,131	13	15	13	1.90
Belgium	4,220	8,341	23,655	7	13	15	1.37
Brazil	811	2,472	6,429	55	44	42	0.39
Bulgaria	1,534	3,657	8,886	29	29	34	1.84
Burma	685	612	3,104	61	65	57	0.94
Canada *	4,447	9,999	25,267	5	6	7	2.97
Chile	2,988	4,638	13,185	16	23	26	2.58
China	552	645	6,725	64	63	40	0.12
Colombia	1,236	2,675	6,330	37	39	43	NA
Czechoslovakia	2,096	5,372	12,925	22	20	27	1.80
Denmark	3,912	10,560	24,621	9	4	10	2.05
Egypt	902	1,166	3,725	48	59	53	1.00
Finland	2,111	7,307	24,344	20	17	12	1.88
France	3,485	8,819	22,223	12	12	17	1.89
Germany	3,648	8,822	20,801	11	11	19	2.10
Ghana	781	1,414	1,650	57	53	62	1.76
Greece	1,592	4,141	16,362	28	27	24	1.81
Hong Kong	1,279	4,327	31,704	33	26	1	1.92
Hungary	2,098	4,388	9,500	21	25	33	2.00
India	673	821	2,975	62	62	58	0.71
Indonesia	874	993	4,428	51	60	51	1.26
Iran	1,000	2,526	6,944	44	42	39	1.00
Iraq	1,000	3,115	1,049	45	35	65	1.00
Ireland	2,736	4,986	27,898	17	21	5	1.32
Italy	2,564	7,487	19,909	18	16	20	1.64
Jamaica	608	2,904	3,668	63	38	54	0.39
Japan	1,387	5,668	22,816	30	19	16	1.93
Jordan	1,000	2,981	5,702	46	37	45	1.01

Table 1. (Continued)

1913 = eve of World War I, 1964 = Year of Tokyo Olympics,
2008 = latest year in Maddison (2009)
Only these 65 countries in Maddison (2009) had GDP per capita data in 1913

	GDP per capita			Rank out of 65 countries			Annual growth rate in 1870–1913 period
	1913	1964	2008	1913	1964	2008	
Lebanon	1,350	2,534	4,453	32	41	50	1.43
Malaysia	900	1,728	10,292	49	47	30	0.93
Mexico	1,732	3,594	7,979	26	32	38	2.90
Morocco	710	1,381	3,465	60	55	56	0.71
New Zealand	5,152	10,418	18,653	3	5	23	1.55
Nepal	539	626	1,134	65	64	63	0.93
Netherlands	4,049	9,437	24,695	8	10	9	1.17
North Korea	869	1,253	1,122	53	57	64	1.11
Norway	2,447	8,316	28,500	19	14	3	1.80
Peru	1,032	3,465	5,388	43	33	46	NA
Philippines	988	1,600	2,926	47	51	60	1.40
Poland	1,739	3,622	10,160	25	31	31	1.86
Portugal	1,250	3,718	14,436	35	28	25	0.76
Romania	1,741	2,258	4,895	24	45	47	1.91
S. Korea	869	1,390	19,614	52	54	22	1.11
Singapore	1,279	2,541	28,107	34	40	4	1.92
South Africa	1,602	3,450	4,793	27	34	49	1.91
Spain	2,056	4,515	19,706	23	24	21	1.63
Sri Lanka	1,234	1,320	4,895	38	56	48	1.13
Sweden	3,073	10,618	24,409	15	3	11	2.50
Switzerland	4,266	14,191	25,104	6	1	8	2.17
Syria	1,350	3,637	8,360	31	30	36	1.43
Taiwan	732	1,679	20,926	58	48	18	0.87
Thailand	841	1,249	8,750	54	58	35	0.99
Tunisia	883	1,589	6,103	50	52	44	1.02
Turkey	1,213	2,496	8,066	39	43	37	1.18
UK	4,921	9,568	23,742	4	8	14	1.32
Uruguay	3,310	4,858	9,893	14	22	32	1.27
USA	5,301	12,773	31,178	1	2	2	2.37
Venezuela	1,104	9,562	10,596	41	9	29	2.03
Vietnam	727	895	2,970	59	61	59	1.11
W. Bank & Gaza	1,250	1,603	2,178	36	50	61	1.56
Yugoslavia	1,057	3,019	6,686	42	36	41	1.74
World	1,524	3,130	7,614				1.71

Memo: The unweighted average of the growth rates of the above 65 countries in 1870–1913 is 1.53%

three years. The GDP per capita data in 1913 were available in the Maddison (2010) dataset only for these 65 countries. The average annual income growth rates of these 65 countries in the 1870–1913 period (in the 43 years prior to 1913) are also reported in Table 1.

While the United States and Australia topped the ranking in living standard in 1913, the undisputed country to watch in 1913 was 10th-ranked Argentina, whose growth rate of 3.28 percent was the highest growth rate in the 1870–1913 period, and more than double the group average of 1.53 percent. Since Argentina was also "a land of recent settlement" like the U.S. and Australia, the general expectation was that Argentina with its much faster growth rate would soon catch up with them. This was, however, not to be. Argentina's income rank dropped from 10th in 1913 to 18 in 1964 and then to 28 in 2008.

Argentina's failure to catch up is not unique.[1] Four of the top 10 countries in 1913 are not in the top 10 group in 2008 — New Zealand, U.K., Belgium and Argentina were replaced by Ireland, Norway, Hong Kong and Singapore. The point that the past is not a reliable predictor of the future is also illustrated by Taiwan. Taiwan, which had grown at 0.87 percent annually in 1870–1913, achieved the biggest rise in rank within this group of 65 economies over the 1913–2008 period. Taiwan's income rank jumped from 58 in 1913 to 48 in 1964 and to 18 in 2008. The interesting questions for China from Table 1 is that, while it is clear that Argentina has failed to catch up with the richest countries, but in what sense could we say that Argentina (the star growth performer in the 43 years before 1913) spent the 20th century inside the middle-income trap? And how could China (the star growth performer in the 33 years before 2013) escape this same fate?

---

[1] Of course, the optimistic expectations about Argentina on the eve of World War I were typical of the *joie de vivre* of that time. Norman Angell (in *The Great Illusion*, 1910) had famously predicted that deep economic integration had rendered war among the European powers obsolete because of the huge costs that would be incurred by the victors and the losers. Angell was awarded the Nobel Peace Prize in 1933.

2. Defining the Middle-Income Trap

Possibly the most important consideration in defining the analytical metric to classify a country as high-income, or middle-income, or low-income[2] is that the definition of income categories must have a built-in dynamic element to take into account that the income of the world's richest countries has been rising steadily over the last two hundred years. In the context where the highest potential level of income (output per person) internationally is increasing, due to factors like technological progress and institutional innovation, the boundaries of the income categories should not be drawn on the basis of absolute levels of income. This is because we believe that most countries that are not severely geographically-disadvantaged (e.g., a landlocked desert with no mineral resources) could come to attain an income level that is close to the highest international level of potential income after they have adopted and adapted the appropriate policy regimes in the various socio-economic-political spheres. For example, a country that denies education to its women is unlikely to ever achieve the income level of the rich countries because this country is running on one leg — actually, hopping on one leg — to catch up with the moving finishing line.

So to assess whether a country has been making substantial progress in catching-up during the 1960–2008 period, we follow Woo (2011) in defining high-income, middle-income and low-income by the ratio (expressed in percent) of the income level of the country to the income level of the United States, which is commonly accepted to have been the economic leader of the world at least since 1920. We call this ratio of a country's income level to the U.S. income level as the score of the country on the Catch-Up Index (CUI).[3]

For the task of benchmarking income levels, we use the GDP (measured in 1990 international Geary-Khamis dollar) and population data from the Maddison (2010) dataset that covers the 1 A.D. to 2008 A.D.

---

[2] We will use the three terms "income," "GDP per capita," and "standard of living" interchangeably in this paper.

[3] To minimize noise in the ranking, the value of CUI in any year could be replaced by a moving average centered on that year. In the graphs, we will use a 5-period moving average centered on the designated year.

period. After matching the CUI with the common notions that most Western European countries are high-income countries, and that most sub-Saharan countries are low-income countries, Woo (2011) defined:

- high-income countries as countries with CUI > 55%
- middle-income countries as countries with 55% > CUI > 20%
- low-income countries as countries with CUI < 20%

In thinking about the probability of China stumbling into the middle-income trap, we keep in mind that because China is a continent-sized country with a large proportion of its territory without easy access to cheap water-based transportation unlike the Netherlands, Ireland and Denmark, we should look more at the growth experiences of the largest regional economies, and less at small economies that have caught up.

Figure 1 captures the essence of Latin America being in the middle-income trap by graphing the 5-period moving average (centered on the year indicated) of CUIs for 1962–2006 for the five large Latin American countries: Argentina, Brazil, Chile, Mexico and Venezuela. There is convergence within the group as shown by the narrowing of the spread of CUIs from about 60 percentage points in 1960 to about 20 percentage points in 2006 but the mean value of the group in 2006 is about the same as the mean value in 1960, i.e. the group is stuck at CUI = 30 percent. It is in the sense that that these five Latin American countries are showing no signs of catching up with the living standard of the United States after 50 years when we say that they are caught in the middle-income trap.

Figure 2 shows the CUIs of the *developing* members of the Asian group: China, India, Indonesia, the Philippines, Thailand and Malaysia. Other than for the Philippines, every developing Asian member has a higher CUI in 2006 than in 1962, moving the average CUI of the group from 7 percent to 16 percent. Unlike in Figure 1, the end result is a widening in the spread of CUIs rather than a convergence because there were three countries that had very high growth: Malaysia, Thailand and China. By growing at more that 4 percent annually, Malaysia and Thailand are the star performers in this group, joining the richer half of the Latin American countries by 2008.

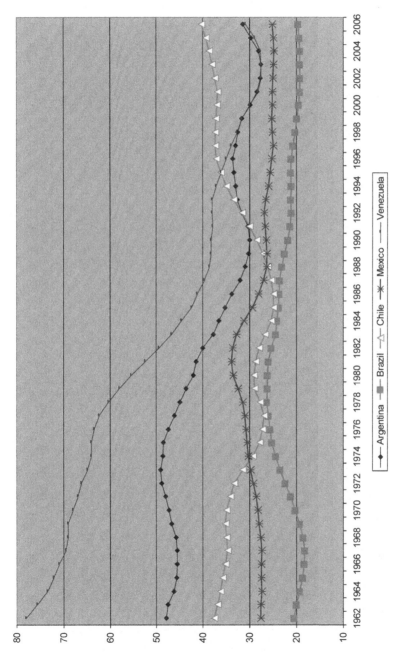

Figure 1. GDP per capita (PPP) of Latin America as % of U.S. Level.

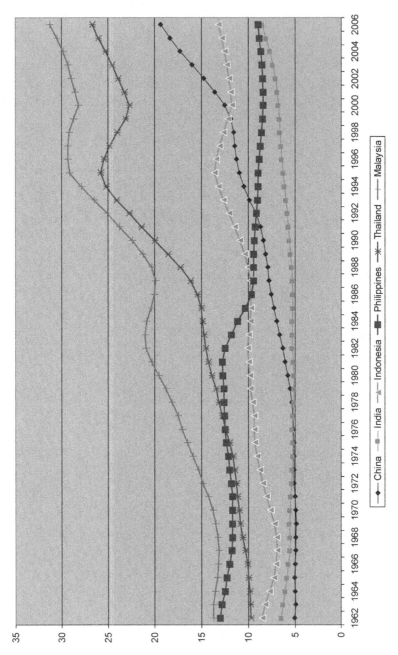

Figure 2. GDP per capita (PPP) of Developing Asia as % of U.S. Level.

China had the lowest CUI (5%) in group in the 1960–1975 period for very understandable reasons: the Great Leap Forward economic strategy created a famine in 1960–1962 that killed 25 million people, and the Great Proletarian Cultural Revolution in 1966–1976 virtually closed all high schools and universities, and disrupted production and normal government functions off and on. China started its catch-up process in 1978, and accelerated its catch-up speed twice (1992 and 2000) to reach middle-income status in 2007. China's living standard overtook India's in 1978, the Philippines' in 1993, and Indonesia's in 2000. China's income piped Colombia's in about 2007–2008 and joined the middle-income club.

The growth record of the above developing Asian economies depicted in Figure 2 might have overstated the impressiveness of the catch-up growth in Malaysian and Thailand, however. To be reminded of what is truly impressive economic catch-up, Figure 3 shows the CUI of Malaysia with the CUIs of Japan, South Korea and Taiwan. Malaysia was actually richer than Taiwan until 1965 and richer than South Korea until 1970. And when Malaysian growth accelerated in 1971, its new growth rate was still considerably lower than those of Korea and Taiwan. Furthermore, Malaysian CUI stagnated from 1981 to 1988, and stagnated again from 1997 until the present. Korea and Taiwan experienced only a slowdown, not a stagnation, in the rise of their CUIs upon the onset of the Asian Financial Crisis; and this slowdown was short-lived.[4]

With the perspective of the broader canvass in Figure 3, we can recognize that Malaysia has had respectable, but not outstanding, economic growth, and that Malaysia is now muddling in the middle-income trap. The issue is which set of its neighbors China is likely to resemble when it nears the CUI = 35 mark: Malaysia-Thailand or South Korea-Taiwan?

---

[4] The movement of Japan's CUI is very much what we expected based on the behavior of the CUIs of the large high-income countries. Although Japan's CUI value in 2008 (73.2) was the same as in 1973, it is still higher than that the 2008 values of the CUIs of France (71.3), Germany (66.7), and Italy (63.9).

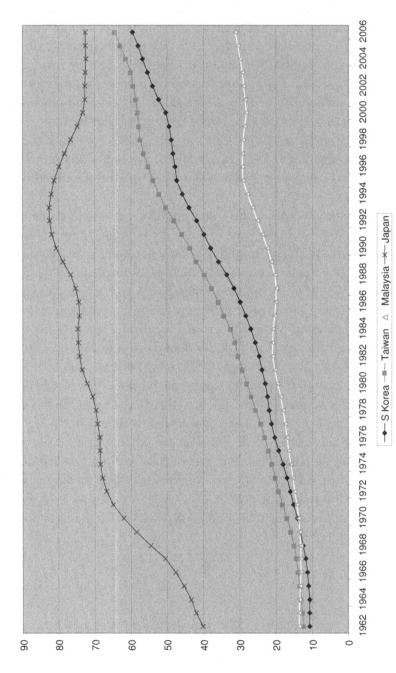

Figure 3. Japan, S. Korea, Taiwan and Malaysia: Living Standard as % of USA Living Standard.

3. What Could Cause China to Fall into the Middle-Income Trap?

Predictions of gloom and doom for China have a long tradition amongst China economists. For example, in the mid-1990s, Nicholas Lardy of the Peterson Institute for International Economics started highlighting the de facto insolvency of the Chinese banking system with the implication that a bank run leading to financial sector collapse (which would then be likely to send the economy into a tail spin) was a strong possibility in the medium term. The 21st century began with the claim by Gordon Chang (2001) that China's imminent accession to World Trade Organization (WTO) would cause such widespread unemployment within China's already alienated population that China's economic and political systems would collapse.

These two dire predictions have turned out to be wrong. China, in fact, accelerated its annual GDP growth to double-digit rates after 2001. Nicholas Lardy was wrong because while the banks were indeed bankrupt, the Chinese government which owned them was not bankrupt and could hence afford to bail out the banks when necessary. The fiscal strength of the government made it irrational for depositors to contemplate a bank run. Gordon Chang was wrong because the WTO membership quickened the pace of job creation in China by greatly increasing the volume of FDI inflow. The WTO membership made China more attractive to FDI because it guaranteed the access of Chinese goods to the U.S. market by eliminating the need for China to get the most-favored-nation (MFN) status annually from the U.S. Congress; McKibbin and Woo (2003).

A good guide on how one should assess the probability of continued high growth in China is to be found in the discussions of the annual Plenum of the Communist Party of China (CPC) that concluded on October 11, 2006. From 1978 through 2005, every Plenum had ended with the resolution that the primary task of CPC in the following year was "economic construction," i.e., increase GDP. The 2006 Plenum broke with tradition and, instead, passed a resolution to commit the CPC to establish a harmonious society by 2020. The obvious implication from this new resolution is that the present major social, economic and political trends within China might not lead to a harmonious society or, at least, not lead to a harmonious society fast enough.[5]

What is the origin of the CPC's decision to change its primary focus from "economic construction" to "social harmony"? To use the analogy of China's economy being like a speeding car, the CPC saw that car could crash in the near future because there were several high-probability failures that might occur and trap China in middle-income status. To be specific that there are three classes of failures that could occur hardware failure; software failure; and power supply failure.

A *hardware failure* refers to the breakdown of an *economic mechanism*, a development that is analogous to the collapse of the chassis of the car. Probable hardware failures include a banking crisis that causes a credit crunch that, in turn, dislocates production economy-wide, and a budget crisis that necessitates reductions in important infrastructure and social expenditure (and also possibly generates high inflation, and balance of payments difficulties as well).

A *software failure* refers to a flaw in *governance* that creates frequent widespread social disorders that disrupt production economy-wide and discourage private investment. This situation is similar to a car crash that resulted from a fight among the people inside the speeding car. Software failures could come from the present high-growth strategy creating so much inequality, and corruption that, in turn, generates severe social unrest, which dislocates economic activities; and from the state not being responsive enough to rising social expectations, hence causing social disorder.

A *power supply failure* refers to the economy being unable to move forward because it hits either *a natural limit or an externally-imposed limit*, a situation that is akin, respectively, to the car running out of gas or to the car smashing into a barrier erected by an outsider. Examples of power supply failures are an environmental collapse, e.g., climate change, and a collapse in China's exports because of a trade war.

---

[5] The proposed harmonious socialist society would encompass a democratic society under the rule of law; a society based on equality and justice; an honest and caring society; a stable, vigorous and orderly society; and a society in which humans live in harmony with nature.

I will limit my discussion to one or two of the most likely precipitating events in each class of failures.

4. The Likely Hardware Failures: Fiscal Stress from the State Banks and Low Productivity Growth from the State Enterprises

China began the recapitalization of the state-controlled banks (SCBs) in 2003 and brought the capital adequacy ratio (CAR) of the four largest SCBs to about 8 percent at the end of 2004. The important question is how many more rounds of bank recapitalization can China afford without generating a fiscal crisis? The simple fact is that fiscal sustainability lies at the heart of whether a banking crisis would actually occur. As long as the state is perceived to be able and willing to bail out the SCBs, depositors would retain their confidence in the SCBs regardless of the actual state of their balance sheets. Since the stock of publicly acknowledged government debt in 2011 is only about 20 percent of GDP, it is usual to hear official assurances that the current fiscal deficits of less than 4 percent of GDP do not pose a problem for debt servicing by the state.[6] However, the current value of the debt-GDP ratio is not a good indicator of the sustainability of the existing fiscal policy regime, a better indicator would involve working out the evolution of the debt-GDP ratio over time.

To put the issue formally, the evolution of the debt-GDP ratio as given by:

$$d(\ln[\text{Debt}/\text{GDP}])/dt = r + [\text{GDP}/\text{Debt}] \cdot [f + b] - y$$

where

r = real interest rate on government debt

f = primary fiscal deficit rate

= [state expenditure excluding debt service − state revenue]/GDP

---

[6] One should really use the consolidated debt of the state sector because it includes at least some part of the contingent liabilities (e.g., foreign debts of state-controlled enterprises and banks, and unfunded pension schemes in the state sector) that the state might have to assume responsibility for when the state-owned units default on their financial obligations.

b = non-performing loans (NPL) creation rate
= [change in NPL in SCBs]/GDP
y = trend growth rate of real GDP

As long as $y > r$, then the Debt/GDP ratio will have a steady-state value that is nonzero when sum of $(f + b) > 0$. Specifically,

$$(\text{Debt}/\text{GDP})_{\text{steady-state}} = (f + b)/(y - r) \text{ when } y > r.$$

China appears to belong to this case because its post-1978 annual growth rate has averaged 9.8 percent, its growth rate in the next ten years is likely to be above 8 percent; and the real interest rate has been about 4 percent. For the generation of likely future scenarios, I will make the conservative assumptions that y is 8 percent, f is 1 percent, and r is 6 percent.[7] It is difficult to predict b, the rate that banks would generate NPLs, because it depends on the type of banking reform undertaken. If no meaningful reforms are undertaken, then b is likely to remain at the historic value of 6 percent.

Therefore conditional on the effectiveness of reforming the SCBs, the steady-state ratio is:

$$(\text{Debt}/\text{GDP})_{\text{steady-state}} = 350 \text{ percent when } b = 6 \text{ percent}$$
$$(\text{Debt}/\text{GDP})_{\text{steady-state}} = 200 \text{ percent when } b = 3 \text{ percent}$$
$$(\text{Debt}/\text{GDP})_{\text{steady-state}} = 100 \text{ percent when } b = 1 \text{ percent}$$

The noteworthy finding from the above scenarios is that China will produce a level of $(\text{Debt}/\text{GDP})_{\text{steady-state}}$ that is high by international experience despite the optimistic assumptions that long-run growth rate is 8 percent, that b will be lowered from 6 percent of GDP to 1 percent. The most optimistic outcome is still two-thirds larger than what the European Union has set to be the "safe" debt-GDP target (60 percent) for its members. The banking system has made China vulnerable to a

---

[7] f has been above 1.5 percent for the past seven years. r was 4 percent in the past only because the interest rate was regulated. I think that the implementation of financial deregulation that is necessary for normal healthy development of the financial sector will render r to be at least 6 percent because, one, according to Solow (1991), the stylised fact for the real interest rate in the United States is that it is 5 to 6 percent; and, two, both the marginal rate of return to capital and the black market loan rate have been more than 20 percent.

fiscal crisis even though there is a theoretical steady-state level for the debt-GDP ratio. Of course, the creation of NPLs cannot be attributed entirely to the SCBs, their chief customers, the embezzlement-ridden and inefficiency-ridden state-controlled enterprises (SCEs), deserve an equal share of the blame.

The important point from this second fiscal feature is that the 2004 recapitalization of the SCBs was the last time that the government can afford to recapitalize the SOBs, and possibly the last time that the government can do so without upsetting confidence in the financial markets about the soundness of China's fiscal regime.

When the Global Financial Crisis (GFC) erupted in full force in September 2008, the central government fought the fast slowdown of the national economy in November 2008 by introducing a two-year four trillion RMB stimulus package, which is equivalent to about 14 percent of China's GDP. The central government would fund only 1.18 trillion yuan (29.5 percent) of the total stimulus spending, and the local governments would finance the rest of the cost of the stimulus program by raising funds from wherever. The fact that the central government would fund only one-third of the proposed expenditure might prompt one to think of the stimulus program as a work agenda for the government to create the incentives to induce investment to reach the stated level, but such an interpretation would be wrong. The stimulus should be properly understood as permission by the central government to allow additional investments up to the stated level.

This different understanding is based on the reality that a large part of China's economy is still state-controlled,[8] and that this segment pursues other objectives besides the ideal of profit-maximization. Because state-controlled enterprises (SCEs) are usually bailed out when investment decisions turned out to be over-optimistic or are derailed by bad luck, this soft-budget practice has created the well-know interest-inelastic phenomenon of "thirst for investment" which makes the economy inflation-prone; see Woo (2006). An expanded SCE yields its state-appointed manager three major benefits: higher likelihood of pro-

---

[8] State-controlled firms include state-owned firms and publicly-listed firms where the state and its intermediaries hold the controlling share.

motion based on the proven ability to handle bigger things, greater patronage power to build a political base; and more resources that could potentially be diverted for personal gains.[9] Equally important is that the leaders of the local governments share the enthusiasm of SCE managers for growth for the same three reasons.

The central government has two lines of defense to maintain macro-stability in China's partially-reformed economy. The first line is that all large projects need the approval of the National Development and Reform Commission (formerly, the State Planning Commission). The second line of defense is that all banks are assigned credit quotas.

So when Premier Wen Jiabao approved the stimulus program and covered only a third of its cost, he was giving permission, (1) to the SCEs to invest more in order to offset the spending slump in the private sector; and (2) to the state-controlled banks (SCBs) to extend the necessary loans to fund the approved projects. Herein lies the mechanism for the success of the stimulus program: the use of non-profit-maximizing state-controlled production and financial units to boost aggregate demand. Because the SCEs and the SCBs are implementing a state-assigned mission, their managers cannot rightly be held responsible should the assigned projects turn out to be financial busts in the future.

Not surprisingly, the public media carried occasional anecdotes about new investments in industries plagued by overcapacity (e.g., steel, cement, and aluminum); trophy investments (e.g., grand town centers, high-speed rail and stately administrative buildings); and spontaneous privatization of project funds (e.g., massive purchase of cars by state bodies).[10] Many of these industrial and infrastructure investments were undertaken by the 8,000 local investment companies established by the local governments. It has been estimated that at the end of 2009, the

---

[9] "China Finds Huge Fraud by Officials," *The New York Times*, December 30, 2009.

[10] See, for example, "Is China's Economy Speeding Off the Rails?" *The New York Times*, December 23, 2009; "China: No one home," *Financial Times*, February 21, 2010; "China audit finds misuse of funds tied to stimulus," *Financial Chronicle*, Dec 29 2009, http://www.mydigitalfc.com/news/china-audit-finds-misuse-funds-tied-stimulus-821; and "China boosts auditors' power as stimulus package spending prompts corruption concerns," *People's Daily*, February 21, 2010, http://english.peopledaily.com.cn/90001/90776/90785/6898354.html

loans of these investment vehicles amounted to 51 percent of GDP in 2009 and the debt of the central government amounted to 20 percent of GDP.[11] There is thus concern in some quarters that much of the bank loans to the stimulus program would end up as non-performing loans (NPLs), and that the resulting financial crisis would cause China to crash just like the U.S. and U.K. did in 2009.[12] Or alternatively, the bailout of the SCBs by the government would cause a fiscal crisis that would require large cutbacks on important infrastructure and social programs.

A second common concern about China's stimulus program is that the SCBs were channeling the flood of liquidity to the SCEs and *further*[13] neglecting the increased financing needs of the private sector brought on by the GFC. Pressed for working capital, two well-known large private companies, Rizhao (a steel firm) and Mengniu (a diary), agreed to be acquired by their state-owned counterparts. As SCEs are generally less efficient and innovative than private firms, the expansion of the role of the state firms has rightly raised the issue of whether Premier Wen's way of imparting the needed boost to capacity utilization during the GFC would become a drag on future productivity growth.[14]

While CPI inflation in 2009 was reassuringly low at −0.7 percent, "land prices ... doubled in 2009 on a nationwide basis."[15] The first quarter of 2010 saw even more rapid increases in land prices, especially

---

[11] The 51% figure is from combining information in Shih (2010) who reported the debt of the central government to be 20% of GDP, the information in the *Financial Times* ("China warned of growing 'land loan' threat," March 28, 2010) that the combined figure was 71%.

[12] For example, "China is heading for a Japan-style bubble," *Financial Times*, November 2, 2009; and "Contrarian Investor Sees Economic Crash in China," *The New York Times*, January 8, 2010.

[13] Risto and Jia (2012) found that bank loans to non-state firms were drastically curtailed from 2004 onward.

[14] "Communist Party Needs to Loosen Its Grip on China," *The New York Times*, March 2, 2010. This debate over the growth of the state firms at the expense of private ones is conducted over the heading of *guojin mintui* (the state sector advances, and the private sector withdraws).

[15] "China Tells Banks to Restrict Loans to Local Governments," *The New York Times*, February 25, 2010.

in the major coastal cities.[16] As a real estate bubble is inevitably socially-alienating (by disappointing new home buyers on the way up and dismaying existing home owners on the way down), the government sought to stabilize property prices in mid-April 2010 by making it harder to buy houses, e.g., requiring first-time home buyers to put a minimum of 30 percent downpayment for houses larger than 90 square meters; and increasing the mortgage rate on second homes. The roaring real estate market and the use of non-market means (e.g., ban on purchases) to tame it are symptoms of some deep economic problems that China will have to address in order to sustain growth over the long-run.

The real estate boom was, of course, only part of a generalized investment boom unleashed by the 400 trillion RMB stimulus program. The November 2008 stimulus program ultimately resulted in strong inflationary pressures appearing in 2010. China applied its monetary brake sharply in 2011, accentuating the financing difficulties that the private sector had faced since 2004. The result, it appears, could be a sharp slowdown in GDP growth on the eve of the CPC Congress at the end of 2012,[17] which would see a large-scale change in the top political leadership, unless a new round of stimulus is hurriedly implemented right now.

To summarize, there are two hardware failures that are likely at present. The large dose of SCE-cum-SCB-based macro-stimulus in 2009–2010 have (a) created future NPLs that could cause either the SCBs to collapse or a fiscal crisis from the bailout of the SCBs, and (b) lowered productivity growth in the future by enabling the state sector to crowd out of the private sector. China's current instruments of macro-stimulus have thus created a potential trade-off between maintenance of full capacity utilization in the short-run and sustenance of high rate of capacity expansion in the long-run. The important task for Chinese policymakers now is to eliminate this tradeoff. This task will require the

---

[16] In 2009, land prices had gone up 200% in Shanghai, 400% in Guangzhou, and 876% in Wenzhou; "China: No one home," *Financial Times*, February 21, 2010.

[17] Wlliam Kazer, "China PMI Falls, Points to Need for Stimulus," Wall Street Journal, 21 June 2012; Reusters, "China Data Show Drops in Exports and Prices," *International Herald Tribune*, 22 June 2012; and Keith Bradsher, "Chinese Data Mask Depth of Slowdown, Executives Say," *New York Times*, 22 June 2012.

state to replace the usual macro-stimulus with new market-friendly instruments to maintain an adequate level of aggregate demand; a topic that we will take up in Section 8 of this chapter.

5. The Likely Software Failures Are from Flaws in Governance

The satisfactory functioning of a market economy requires a wide array of regulatory institutions that range from straightforward law-and-order administration to complicated legal adjudication. An example of the latter would be possessing the prerequisite scientific understanding to determine whether a patent case involves real technological innovation or not. China's strategy of incremental reform combined with the fact that institution building is a time-consuming process meant that many of its regulatory institutions are either absent or ineffective. The results have been governance failures on many fronts, of which the most well-known are the violations against the welfare of consumers, e.g., the addition of poisonous substitutes into toothpaste, cough medicine, and animal feed; the application of lead paint to children's toys; and the over-employment of antifungals and antibacterials in fish farming. Most of these above abuses had received enormous attention only because these items were exported to other countries and their harmful effects were reported widely in the international press.

Inadequate institutions of governance are not the only cause of social tensions in China, however. The present economic development strategy, despite its ability to generate high growth, also generates high social tensions. In the last ten years, it has had great difficulties in reducing extreme poverty further and in improving significantly the rural-urban income distribution and the regional income distribution; see Woo, Li, Yue, Wu, and Xu (2004). An Asian Development Bank (2007) study on income inequality in 22 Asian countries over the 1992–2004 period found that for 2004, only Nepal had a Gini coefficient (47.30 percent) that was higher than China's (47.25). However, in 2004, China's income ratio of the richest 20 percent to the poorest 20 percent (11.37) was the highest in Asia; significantly higher than the next highest income ratio (9.47 for Nepal). China is probably the most unequal country in Asia today.

Table 2. Disposal Income per Capita in Each Income Category in 2008

Category	% of urban residents	Official income (RMB)	"True" income (RMB)	Distribution of hidden income (%)
Lowest income	10	4,754	5,350	0.4
Low income	10	7,363	7,430	0.0
Lower middle income	20	10,196	11,970	2.3
Middle income	20	13,984	17,900	5.1
Upper middle income	20	19,254	27,560	10.9
High income	10	26,250	54,900	18.8
Highest income	10	43,614	139,000	62.5
All urban dwellers	100	16,885	32,154	100.0

Hidden Income = Total True Income − Total Official Income
Source: Tables 5 and 6 in Wang and Woo (2010).

Furthermore, the present mode of economic development also generates immense opportunities for embezzlement of state assets, seizure of farmlands for industrial development, and corruption because of the absence of effective mechanisms to supervise government employees. These features certainly make social harmony hard to sustain. Wang and Woo (2011) have found that urban residents have substantial unreported (hidden) income. Table 2 reports their estimates of official income and true income in each income group. The official income per capita and true income per capita in the richest 10 percent of households in 2008 was 43,614 RMB and 139,000 RMB respectively; official income being one-third of true income. Total household disposable income in 2008 was RMB 14.0 trillion according to the official data but RMB 23.2 trillion according to the Wang and Woo estimate. And as 63 percent of the total unreported income went to the richest 10 percent of urban households, the income of the richest 10 percent of Chinese households is really 65 times that of the poorest 10 percent instead of the 23 times reported in the official data. In short, the Gini coefficient is clearly much higher than the Asian Development Bank's (2007) figure of 0.47 for 2004.

The data on social unrest are consistent with the hypothesis of rising social disharmony. The incidence of public disorder, labelled "social incidents," rose steadily from 8,700 in 1993 to 32,500 in 1999 and then to 74,000 in 2004; and the average number of persons in a mass incident has also risen greatly, from 8 in 1993 to 50 in 2004. Clearly, the number of mass incidents would have been lower and governance would have been better if the government's actions had been monitored closely by an independent mechanism and the government had also been held more accountable for its performance. The embrace of the Harmonious Society program by CPC is acknowledgment that democracy, the rule of law, and a more equal income distribution comprise an indivisible combination that is necessary to ensure the social stability that will keep the economy on the high growth path to catch up with the United States.

6. The First Type of Likely Power Supply Failure Is Environmental Collapse in China

The present mode of economic development has given China the dirtiest air in the world, is polluting more and more of the water resources, and, is, possibly, changing the climate pattern within China. The unexpurgated version of a 2007 World Bank reported that "about 750,000 people die prematurely in China each year, mainly from air pollution in large cities";[18] and a 2007 OECD study has estimated that "China's air pollution will cause 20 million people a year to fall ill with respiratory diseases."[19]

Water shortage appears to pose the most immediate environmental threat to China's continued high growth. Presently, China uses 67 to 75 percent of the 800 to 900 billion cubic meters of water available annually, and present trends in water consumption would project the usage rate in 2030 to be 78 to 100 percent.[20] The extended period of semi-drought in northern China combined with the economic and population growth have caused more and more water to be pumped from the aquifers, leading the water table to drop three to six meters a

---

[18] "750,000 a year killed by Chinese pollution," *Financial Times*, July 2, 2007. 350,000 to 400,000 died prematurely from air pollution in Chinese cities, 300,000 from poor air indoors, and 60,000 (mostly in countryside) from poor-quality water.
[19] "OECD highlights Chinese pollution," *Financial Times*, July 17, 2007.
[20] "Top official warns of looming water crisis," *South China Morning Post*, November 7, 2006.

year.[21] And a study using measurements from satellites (the Global Positioning System) has established that the part of China north of the 36th parallel latitude has been "sinking at the rate of 2 mm a year."[22]

While northern China has been getting drier and experiencing desertification, nature as if in compensation (or in mockery) has been blasting southern China with heavier rains, causing heavy floods which have brought considerable deaths and property damage almost every summer since 1998.[23] The sad possibility is that the northern droughts and southern floods may not be independent events but a combination caused by pollution that originates in China.[24]

Clearly, without water, growth cannot endure. And in response, the government begun implementation in 2002 of Mao Zedong's 1952 proposal that three canals be built to bring water from the south to the north: an eastern coastal canal from Jiangsu to Shandong and Tianjin, a central canal from Hubei to Beijing and Tianjin, and a western route from Tibet to the northwestern provinces. Each canal will stretch over a thousand miles.[25] This massive construction project will not only be technically challenging but also extremely sensitive politically and fraught with environmental risks. The central canal will have to tunnel through the foot of the huge dyke that contains the elevated Yellow River, and the western canal will have to transport water through regions susceptible to freezing and earthquake.

---

[21] "Northern cities sinking as water table falls," *South China Morning Post*, August 11, 2001.

[22] "Northern China sinking… as the south rises," *The Straits Times*, March 18, 2002.

[23] The National Development and Reform Commission (2007) reported: "The regional distribution of precipitation shows that the decrease in annual precipitation was significant in most of northern China, eastern part of the northwest, and northeastern China, averaging 20~40 mm/10a, with decrease in northern China being most severe; while precipitation significantly increased in southern China and southwestern China, averaging 20~60 mm/10a .."

[24] There is now persuasive evidence that China's voluminous emission of black carbon (particles of incompletely combusted carbon) has contributed significantly to the shift to a climate pattern that produces northern droughts and southern floods of increasing intensity; Streets (2006).

[25] "Ambitious canal network aims to meet growing needs," *South China Morning Post*, November 27, 2002.

The enlargement of the Danjiangkou Dam (in Hubei) to enable it to be the source of the central canal has already displaced 330,000 people; and many more are expected to be displaced.[26] Moving people involuntarily is certainly potentially explosive politically. The project could also be politically explosive on the international front as well. One plan for the western canal calls for "damming the Brahmaputra river and diverting 200 billion cubic metres of water annually to feed the ageing Yellow river," a scenario that is reportedly "giving sleepless nights to the Indian government ... [which is concerned that this Great Western Water Diverson Project] could have immense impact on lower riparian states like India and Bangladesh."[27]

The general point is that effective policy-making on the environmental front is a very difficult task because much of the science about the problem is not known. The uncomfortable reality for China is that unless ecological balance is restored within the medium-term, environmental limits could choke off further economic growth. And the uncomfortable reality for the rest of the world is that the negative consequences of large-scale environmental damage within a geographically large country are seldom confined within that country's borders. The continued march of China's desertification first brought more frequent sand storms to Beijing and then, beginning in April 2001, sent yellow dust clouds not only across the sea to Japan and Korea but also across the ocean to the United States. China's environmental management is a concern not only for China's welfare but for global welfare as well.

There is no doubt, however, that the Chinese government is trying to improve its performance in sustainable development. The 12th Five-Year Plan for 2011–2015 that was passed by the National People's Congress in March 2011 has identified "Green China" as one of its core objectives. But it is still hard to call China's green targets ambitious, e.g., energy intensity is to decline by 17 percent in the forthcoming 5-year period when it fell 20 percent in the last 5-year period, and non-fossil

---

[26] "Massive scheme aims to quench China's thirst," *Financial Times*, July 26, 2004; a lower estimate of 300,000 is given in "China Will Move Waters to Quench Thirst of Cities," *New York Times*, August 27, 2002.

[27] "China's river plan worries India," *Times Of India*, October 23, 2006.

fuel will account for 11.3 percent of overall energy use in 2015 up from 8 percent in 2011.[28]

7. The Second Type of Likely Power Supply Failure Is Trade Protectionism

It was no April Fool's Day joke when the *Wall Street Journal* of April 1, 2011 carried the headline "China Meeting Highlights Currency Conflict." The list of grievances against the U.S. economy caused by the large U.S.-China bilateral imbalances has now expanded from the loss of U.S. jobs to the meltdown of the U.S. financial market in September 2008.[29] The "bad China" feeling is so strong that even *The New York Times* (March 17, 2010) stooped to oxymoronic rhetoric, calling the *fixed* RMB-Dollar exchange rate "a textbook example of the beggar-thy-neighbor competitive *devaluation*" (emphasis added). The English language is not the only casualty in the discussion of the U.S.-China economic relationship: history has also been given the wrong twist. According to Lardy:

> "The United States is the addict. We are addicted to consumption … China is the dealer. They're supplying the credit that makes it possible for us to over-consume."[30]

It is hard not to see this reference to the Opium War of the 19th century with the identities of the aggressor and the victim reversed as a transmogrification of history that is quite over the top. What should be very clear from the above recent rhetoric is that China-U.S. trade tensions have reached a dangerously high level now that the United States is experiencing intractably high unemployment from the Global Financial Crisis.

---

[28] 12th Five Year Plan Hailed as 'Greenest FYP in China's History' (Posted Tue, 2011-04-12 14:54 by China Briefing); http://deltabridges.com/news/prd-news/12th-five-year-plan-hailed-%E2%80%98greenest-fyp-china%E2%80%99s-history%E2%80%99

[29] Krishna Guha, Paulson Says Crisis Sown by Imbalance. *Financial Times* (January 1, 2009): http://www.ft.com/cms/s/0/ff671f66-d838-11dd-bcc0-000077b07658.html

[30] Winter Institute: China and U.S. joined at the hip, St. Cloud State University news release, Monday, March 2, 2009, http://www.stcloudstate.edu/news/newsrelease/default.asp?storyID=28126

There are quite a number of China-centric explanations[31] for China's chronic trade surplus, and we will discuss the two that seems the most important (a) the *financial market theory* that attributes the imbalance to the inability of China's largely unreformed financial system to intermediate all savings into investment, and (b) the *industrial policy theory* that attributes the trade imbalance to China's promotion of exports and suppression of imports.

The *financial market theory* focuses on the aggregate-level accounting identity that the overall current account balance is determined by the fiscal position of the government, and the savings-investment decisions of the SCEs and the private sector. Specifically:

$$CA = (T - G) + (S_{SCE} - I_{SCE}) + (S_{private} - I_{private})$$

where   CA = current account in the balance of payments

CA = (X − M) + R
  X = export of goods and non-factor services
  M = import of goods and non-factor services
  R = net factor earnings from abroad (i.e. export of
    factor services)
  T = state revenue
  G = state expenditure (including state investment)
  S_{SCE} = saving of the SCEs
  I_{SCE} = investment of the SCEs
$S_{private}$ = saving of the private sector
$I_{private}$ = investment of the private sector

Because the Chinese fiscal position (T-G) has nearly always shown a small deficit, the current account surplus reflects primarily the savings of SCEs and the private sector being larger than the sum of their investment expenditures. Why has China's financial system failed to translate the savings into investments? Such an outcome was not always the case. Before 1994, the voracious absorption of bank loans by SCEs to invest recklessly kept the current account usually negative and the creation of NPLs high. When the government implemented stricter controls on the

---

[31] "China-centric" because they ignore the obvious fact that the current account balance is also determined by U.S. conditions.

SCBs from 1994 onward (e.g., removing top bank officials whenever their bank lent more than its credit quota or allowed the NPL ratio to increase too rapidly), the SCBs slowed down the growth of loans to SCEs. This cutback created an excess of savings because the SCB-dominated financial sector did not re-channel the released savings (which were also increasing) to finance the investment of the private sector.

This failure in financial intermediation by the SCBs is quite understandable. Firstly, the legal status of private enterprises was, until recently, less secure than that of the state enterprises; and, secondly, there was no reliable way to assess the balance sheets of the private enterprises, which were naturally eager to escape taxation. The upshot was that the residual excess savings leaked abroad in the form of the current account surplus. Inadequate financial intermediation has made developing China a capital exporting country and put it in conflict with its trade partners![32]

The *industrial policy* explanation for China's chronic trade surplus views this anomalous situation as the unintentional outcome of, (1) of the over-riding economic and political priority in China to create jobs for its underemployed (surplus) labor force; and, (2) the widespread belief in the efficacy of infant industry protection — ambiguously labeled as the "promotion of indigenous innovation" — in accelerating China's movement up the value-added ladder. The resulting export subsidies, import barriers, and undervalued exchange rate worked together to accelerate the simultaneous growth of export firms (which increased exports) and import-competing firms (which decreased imports), and hence kept the trade balance in surplus.

The industrial policy theory has been challenged on the grounds that its microeconomic plausibility is at odds with economy-wide constraints. Specifically, in a 2-sector general equilibrium model of exportables and importables, there could not have been simultaneous growth

---

[32] See Woo (2008). Savings behavior is not independent of the sophistication of the financial system. An advanced financial system will have a variety of financial institutions that would enable pooling of risks by providing medical insurance, pension insurance, and unemployment insurance; and transform savings into education loans, housing loans, and other types of investment loans to the private sector. *Ceteris paribus*, the more sophisticated a financial system, the lower the savings rate.

of the exportable sector and the importable sector because labor would flow from one to the other depending on the relative size of the effective export subsidy rate and the effective import tariff rate — and, hence, the trade balance would not be affected by the industrial policy. However, this above theoretical reasoning about industrial policy does not hold for China because of the existence of surplus labor in the countryside that could move into both the exportable sector and the importable sector, and because of the existence of a sizeable non-tradeable sector (e.g., low value-added service activities, and subsistence agriculture) that would release labor to the "policy-favored" tradeable sector.

Clearly, the prevention of a trade war with the U.S. would require that China accelerates the development of its financial sector if the financial market theory is correct; and removes the export incentives and import barriers from rent-seeking industries with low potential to generate dynamic externalities. However, regardless of which theory is right, both actions should be undertaken because they both enhance China's economic welfare, with one of them also lowering the probability of a trade war with the United States. We will discuss the details of each action in Section 11 of this chapter.

8. The Hardware Reform Agenda

We had identified earlier the deleterious consequences of the administration of the emergency-room medicine of large-scale SCB-funding of hastily approved SCE projects. We would like to recommend that the present slowdown in June 2012 be dealt with by unleashing two new inter-related growth drivers that would minimize the tradeoff between full utilization of existing production capacity and viable long-term growth of production capacity, and they are (1) creation of more new private entrepreneurs; and (2) urbanization according to the principle of future home ownership.

The state can partly offset the expanded state sector by mobilizing the inland migrant workers (*nongmin gong*) laid-off from the coastal provinces into an entrepreneurial force. Many of the *nongmin gong* have sufficient work experience to start their own factory-workshops to take advantage of the increased cost competitiveness of the inland provinces created by the explosive extension of the national transportation network during the GFC. Because the primary barrier to the emergence of this group of owner-operators is the availability of credit, the government should legalize small and medium private banks as they have comparative advantage over the four large state banks in catering to the needs of these new entrepreneurs.[33] Farmland should also be privatized so that the new businesses can have the collateral to access credit from the new private banks. The creation of a new large group of private entrepreneurs will bring three major benefits: (1) expenditure by this new group will substitute for the present macro-stimulus program in keeping aggregate demand high; (2) private firms are likely to have higher productivity growth than SCEs; and (3) these small and medium private enterprises will be more labor-intensive than SCEs.

The second new growth driver would be urbanization based on the principle of affordable future home ownership. The fast growth of the real estate sector, not only recently but also over the last decade, reflected not just speculative demand but also genuine pent-up demand for housing and genuine accommodation of the high rate of the joint industrialization-urbanization process.[34] The bulk of the new arrivals from the countryside cannot qualify for bank mortgages, and so many investors have been buying multiple housing units to rent to the new arrivals with the intention of raising the rents over time in line with the income growth of the renters. In this sense, much of the recent housing demand has been speculative.

We propose that China studies the low-cost public housing schemes in Hong Kong and Singapore and establishes a national housing program where the new arrivals would rent homes for seven years and then have the first right to buy these units at a price based on construction costs. China can afford a massive public housing program because the expen-

---

[33] The system of prudential supervision must also be strengthened, and interest rate be deregulated.

[34] If speculative demand had been the overwhelmingly dominant cause for the property boom, then house rents would not have risen substantially (because the speculative investors would tend to rent out their extra units). Instead, rent in Beijing in March 2010 was 19.6% above March 2009; see "Survey shows house prices still too high," *China Daily*, May 12, 2010: http://www.chinadaily.com.cn/metro/2010-05/12/content_9839054.htm

sive part of such programs in other countries is the cost of land and not the cost of the structures, and land in China is mostly owned by the state.[35]

Our proposed "future-ownership" form of urbanization will support China's growth in three ways: (1) the maintenance of real estate investment to supply the needed housing and to help maintain existing level of aggregate demand; (2) the redirection of bank loans to new rural migrants, with the new housing agency as the intermediary, to prevent the appearance of NPLs; and (3) this housing scheme will redistribute income to the rural migrants (which helps in reducing the threat of software failure), with the positive side effect that consumption would rise to help offset the elimination of the macro-stimulus program.

We note that the first new growth driver and second new growth are mutually-reinforcing. The new enterprises of the former rural migrants would inevitably be located in or near towns and cities to take advantage of infrastructure and positive spillovers from agglomeration. We also note that the main institutional adjustments that must be made to enable the working of the second new growth driver are the same that would help the development of the first new growth driver: privatization of farmland, termination of the household registration system, and liberalization of the financial system.

9. The Software Reform Agenda

We think that the probability of a software failure is higher than the probability of a hardware failure. The former is easier to deal with because, for most hardware problems, China can learn from the experiences of the rest of the world, especially those of the richer countries in East Asia, as long as ideological constraints on methods of economic management continue to wither. The 1868 insight of the Meiji reformists that success in economic catch-up largely involves a willingness to adopt and adapt to "best international practices" will continue to apply to

---

[35] It should be noted that housing construction is relatively labor-intensive, and that home decoration is highly labor-intensive.

China until its per capita GDP converges with that of Japan and Western Europe.

Dealing with software failure is harder than dealing with hardware failure for two major reasons. The first is that development policymaking in China has become more challenging because popular expectations of administrative performance have risen dramatically with income growth and, more importantly, with increasing knowledge of the outside world. In this new situation, the greater use of democratic procedures, the establishment of an independent judiciary, and the restoration of a free press might be inevitable if China is to successfully accommodate the rising social expectations and mediate the emerging differences in social expectations. A Chinese government that consistently fails to deliver progress toward the Harmonious Society vision fast enough to catch up with the rise in social expectations runs an increasing risk of social instability.

The second reason is that successful reconfiguration of the administrative software requires not just highly developed political skills but favorable circumstances in the domestic political arena and a benign international environment — both of which are normally beyond the reach of most politicians. What happens in the future will depend on whether the CPC is politically skilful enough to lead the transition to the democratic, equitable, and law-based harmonious society and emerge afterwards as the most important political force. The practical issue is whether the CPC can do a better job in political transition than the Kuomintang did in Taiwan during 1983–1988.

10. Dealing with Power Supply Failure Caused by Environmental Degradation

Effective policy-making on the environmental front is a very difficult task because much of the science about the problem is not known. For example, if the change in China's rainfall pattern is indeed due to China-emitted air pollution, then China must no longer select its water strategy and it energy strategy separately. A systems approach to policymaking is necessary because the interaction among the outcomes from the different sectoral policies can generate serious unintended environmental damage. A sustainable development policy would require a complete rethinking about the location of population centres and the types of enhanced international cooperation on global environmental management.

In discussing the environmental aspects of the water transfer plan, it is important to note that there is now an open controversy in China involving a key government infrastructure project, and that this controversy is not limited to members of the technocracy. The very public nature of the controversy, and the involvement of more than just scientists, engineers and economists in it, reveals how very far social attitudes have progressed. The important point is that this change in social expectations will require any government in China to live in harmony with nature. However, any government will have great difficulties in doing so even if it wants to because a green-growth policy involves a systems approach, and scientific understanding of many ecological sub-systems and the nature of their interactions is still rather incomplete.

The global environment is an important area in which China can help to build a harmonious world system.[36] Specifically, China should be mobilizing international consensus to form an international research consortium to develop ways to burn coal cleanly because China is now building a power station a week and is hence able to facilitate extensive experimentation on prototype plants to burn coal cleanly. Furthermore, given the growing water shortages in China (especially in the north) and in many of its neighboring countries, China should start a regional forum on the joint use of water from the Tibetan plateau before the situation gets too critical. China should also be mobilizing an international scientific research effort on the desalination of seawater for drinking. If global cooperation on clean energy research and desalination research is successful, it will unleash sustainable development in the whole world.

---

[36] See McKibbin, Wilcoxen and Woo (2008) for an example of an efficient global CO_2 emission compact that China and the rest of the world could adopt.

11. Dealing with Power Supply Failure Caused by Trade Protectionism

Finally, we consider how to reduce the probability of the speeding car (that is China) crashing into a road block that takes the form of foreign trade sanctions. It should be immediately noted that a trade imbalance reflects the economic situation in two countries: China could not have over-saved if the U.S. had not under-saved. U.S. profligacy is just as much to be blamed for the trade tensions as Chinese thriftiness, e.g., even today, the U.S. government does not have a credible plan to reduce its budget deficit upon the recovery of the economy. The straightforward implication is that a fair solution to any desired reduction program in the trade imbalance would require corrective measures to be implemented by both China and the U.S.

Given that the trade imbalances are produced by a host of factors, another straightforward implication is that the efficient solution will employ more than one policy instrument for the task. There would not just be an appreciation of the RMB against the USD but also equally large changes in policy measures such as the lowering of Chinese trade barriers, the adoption of a budget deficit reduction program by the U.S., and expansion of the trade credit facilities of the U.S. ExIm Bank.

What is to be done in China? It is most unfortunate that the trade imbalance issue has focused overwhelmingly on the amount that the Chinese yuan ought to appreciate.[37] It is now forgotten that the now much-praised Plaza Accord of September 1985, which engineered a sharp appreciation of the Japanese yen, caused so much instability in global financial markets that it became a museum piece after only 17 months (!) with the hurried signing of the Louvre Accord in February 1987. As the world is currently only beginning to get over the trauma of

---

[37] The only economically meaningful definition of the equilibrium exchange rate is the market-clearing exchange rate produced in the absence of intervention by any central bank. This market-clearing exchange rate is characterized by the balance of payments position being zero and not by the trade account balance (or the current account balance) being zero or being at some a priori value. This means that the notion of exchange rate misalignment that is based on the proposed concept of the Fundamental Equilibrium Exchange Rate (FEER) is analytically vacuous because the FEER is not identical to the market-clearing exchange rate.

the global financial crisis of 2008–2009, it verges on irresponsibility to now push China to impart a Plaza Accord-type of shock to the financial markets.

More importantly, the effectiveness of a large appreciation of the RMB-USD exchange rate in reducing the U.S. trade deficit is suspect outside of the textbook situation of a 2-country world. When the yen-USD exchange rate went from 238.5 yen/USD in 1985 to 128.2 yen/USD in 1988 (an appreciation of 86 percent by the IMF definition), the overall U.S. and Japanese trade imbalances saw only small improvements. The U.S. trade deficit improved very little when direct Japanese exports became drastically more expensive in the U.S. market after 1985 because, (1) U.S. customers reacted by switching their purchases to similar imports from third countries; and, (2) Japanese businesses relocated their production to other Asian countries in order to service the U.S. market from there.

Since over 60 percent of Chinese exports are produced in factories with foreign investment, many of these foreign investors would relocate their operations to other parts of the world if the RMB were to duplicate the dramatic 1985–1988 appreciation of the yen. Unless accompanied by U.S. actions to raise its low private savings rate and to cut its budget deficit, a second Plaza Accord is unlikely to diminish the U.S. trade deficit adequately and its primary consequences would be a reconfiguration of the sources of U.S. borrowing from abroad, and a new round of global financial market instability.

We had outlined earlier the financial market theory and the industrial policy theory about China's chronic surplus. We are persuaded that because the development of the financial sector and the elimination of subsidies-tariffs motivated by rent-seeking would increase economic efficiency independently regardless of the impact of each on the trade balance, we should implement both actions. We propose a policy package with three components. First, the steady process of yuan appreciation that begun in July 2005 should be continued, and should also be used more aggressively as an anti-inflation instrument.

Second, import liberalization should be accelerated and expanded beyond WTO specifications because China's simultaneous promotion of export and suppression of imports is the likely basic reason behind the trade surplus. China should also increase imports by enabling new types of imports, e.g., educational services and tourism. With its humongous foreign exchange reserves, China should have expanded its scholarship and student loan programs tremendously to enable the large number of qualified Chinese to go abroad to receive better university-level training. It has been a failure of the imagination that China has not increased this type of import prodigiously for productive purposes.

Furthermore, China should recognize that its large indigenous innovation program to incubate high-tech industries has, in fact, been an inequitable mechanism that transfers income from the customers to the makers of the products covered in the program. The global experience with indigenous innovation programs has mostly been a negative one. Most of the industries they spawned never became internationally competitive, showing that most indigenous innovation programs are based either on a misguided sense about the possibilities from "learning-by-doing" or on rent-seeking motives. Given this global experience, China could drastically reduce the size of its extensive indigenous innovation program without hurting its capability in technological upgrading.

The third component of China's trade-imbalance-reduction package is to establish an improved mechanism for coordinating private savings and private investments. The establishment of a modern financial system will not only achieve the objective of intermediating all of domestic saving into domestic investment, it will also enhance welfare and lower the savings rate by pooling risks through vehicles like medical insurance and pension insurance. We note that financial sector development will also help the two new growth drivers of the hardware reform package (new entrepreneurs and urbanization) to work better.

So far, we have stressed that U.S.-China trade tensions would be lowered much more if both countries undertake corrective policies rather than if China acted alone, and that a wider range of policy instruments should be employed (e.g., budget deficit reduction in the U.S., and import deregulation in China) rather than relying just on exchange rate adjustment alone. We now want to stress that the U.S. and China should also work together to prevent the GATT-WTO free-trade regime from weakening. Specifically, China has benefited immensely from the WTO system, and yet it has, up to this point, played a very passive role in pushing the Doha Round negotiations forward to completion. By default, Brazil and India have assumed the leadership of the developing economies camp in the trade negotiations. According to Susan Schwab, the U.S. Trade Representative, at the G4 (U.S., EU, Brazil and India) meeting in Potsdam in June 2007, Brazil and India retreated from their earlier offers to reduce their manufacturing tariffs in return for cuts in agricultural subsides by the developed economies because of "their fear of growing Chinese imports."[38]

With the U.S. weakening in its resolve to protect the multilateral free trade system, China should now become more active in the Doha Round negotiations to deregulate world trade further. Such a role will be very much in China's interest because Brazil is now bypassing multilateral trade liberalization by entering into FTA negotiations with the European Union. The fact is that a growing number of nations like Brazil "are increasingly wary of a multilateral deal because it would mandate tariff cuts, exposing them more deeply to low-cost competition from China. Instead, they are seeking bilateral deals with rich countries that are tailored to the two parties' needs."[39] It is the time for China to show that it is a responsible stakeholder by joining in the stewardship of the multilateral free trade system. Such an international stance would also reduce the threat of this type of power supply failure to China's own growth.

12. Final Remarks

China has now achieved middle-income status through the marketization and internationalization of its economy. China will stand in 2013 where Argentina had stood in 1913 — the launch pad for high income-hood. Our assessment is that the continued high growth rates that will enable China to catch up with the rich economies can be generated only if China adopts a new development strategy. This new development strategy is based not only on the recognition that the marketization and

---

[38] "Schwab surprised by stance of India and Brazil," *Financial Times*, June 22, 2007; and "China's shadow looms over Doha failure," *Financial Times*, June 22, 2007.

[39] "Brazil, others push outside Doha for trade pacts," *The Wall Street Journal*, July 5, 2007.

internationalization processes have to be deepened and made more comprehensive, but also on the recognition that China has now become an important shaping force of the global economy, and Chinese civil society has come to possess more and more of the middle-class aspirations common in the industrialized world.

China must not only build a stronger economic hardware with measures like labor market deregulation, land privatization, future-ownership-based urbanization, and financial sector development, China must also create a harmonious society and help establish a harmonious world. The administrative software that will allow the achievement of a harmonious society will require an increasing use of free elections, monitoring by a free press, and adjudication by an independent judiciary. China must start adopting the global perspective that it is required of a world leader who will work for the protection of the global environmental commons, the global trading system, and global security in order to ensure that China's convergence to high income-hood is not foiled by the physical environment or the international political environment. In short, the national strategy to prevent China from falling into the middle-income trap has to be undergirded by the broad understanding that Chinese social harmony is required for Chinese economic prosperity and vice versa, and that both cannot exist in isolation from the rest of the world and cannot be independent of the health of Mother Nature.

References

Asian Development Bank, 2007. *Key Indicators: Inequality in Asia.*

Chang, Gordon, 2001. *The Coming Collapse of China.* Random House.

Lardy, Nicholas R., 1998. China's Unfinished Economic Revolution. Washington, D.C.: Brookings Institution.

Maddison, Angus, 2010. *Statistics on World Population, GDP and Per Capita GDP, 1–2008 AD.* Excel spreadsheet downloaded from: http://www.ggdc. net/MADDISON/oriindex.htmthat (accessed January 7, 2011).

McKibbin, Warwick J. and Wing Thye Woo, 2003. The Consequences of China's WTO Accession on Its Neighbours. *Asian Economic Papers*, 2(2): 1–38.

McKibbin, Warwick J., Peter J. Wilcoxen and Wing Thye Woo, 2008. China Can Grow and Help Prevent the Tragedy of the CO2 Commons. In Ligang Song and Wing Thye Woo (eds.), *China's Dilemma: Economic Growth, the*

Environment, and Climate Change. Asia Pacific Press–Brookings Institution Press–Social Science Academic Press, pp. 190–225.

National Development and Reform Commission, 2007. *China's National Climate Change Programme.*

Herrala, Risto and Yandong Jia, 2012. Has the Chinese Growth Model Changed? A View from the Credit Market. Bank of Finland's Institute of Economies in Transition (BOFIT) Discussion Paper No. 5/2012.

Shih, Victor, 2010. China's 8,000 Credit Risks. *The Wall Street Journal*, February 8.

Solow, Robert, 1991. Sustainability: An Economist's Perspective. 18th J. Seward Johnson Lecture to the Marine Policy Center, Woods Hole Oceanographic Institution; published in Robert N. Stavins, 2000, *Economics of the Environment: Selected Readings, 4th edition.* New York: W.W. Norton, pp. 131–138.

Streets, David, 2005. Black Smoke in China and Its Climate Effects. *Asian Economic Papers*, 4(2): 1–23.

Wang, Xiaolu and Woo, Wing Thye, 2011. The Size and Distribution of Hidden Household Income in China. *Asian Economic Papers*, 10(1): 1–26.

Woo, Wing Thye, Shi Li, Ximing Yue, Harry Xiaoying Wu and Xinpeng Xu, 2004. The Poverty Challenge for China in the New Millennium. Report to the Poverty Reduction Taskforce of the Millennium Development Goals Project of the United Nations.

Woo, Wing Thye, 2006. The Structural Nature of Internal and External Imbalances in China. *Journal of Chinese Economic and Business Studies*, 4(1): 1–20.

Woo, Wing Thye, 2008. Understanding the Sources of Friction in U.S.-China Trade Relations: The Exchange Rate Debate Diverts Attention Away from Optimum Adjustment. *Asian Economic Papers*, 7(3): 61–95.

Woo, Wing Thye, 2011. Understanding the Middle-Income Trap in Economic Development: The Case of Malaysia. Invited World Economy Lecture delivered at the University of Nottingham, Globalization and Economic Policy (GEP) conference, *Globalization Trends and Cycles: The Asian Experiences*, Semenyih, Selangor, Malaysia, 13 January 2011. Available at http://www.nottingham.ac.uk/gep/documents/lectures/world-economy-asia-lectures/world-econ-asia-wing-thye-woo-2011.pdf

PART II

Short-term Demand Management:
Working the Hardware Correctly

A Prediction of China's Economy in 2012: Soft Landing and Back to the Normal

Gang Fan and Liping He

Shortly after the outburst of the global financial crisis in 2008, the Chinese government swiftly switched to an expansionary fiscal policy stance, which was supported by a large easing in monetary and credit policies. China's economy escaped from recession, and its GDP growth started to accelerate from the second half of 2009. The Chinese economy was growing at a high pace again in 2010. Signs of inflation soon emerged. Whilst the issue of "exit" was being debated in many economies, China began the process of soft landing. That would put the Chinese economy back to a normal growth path.

In this paper, we will provide a brief assessment of China's macroeconomic performance in recent years. Section 1 traces the background and origins of the current macroeconomic readjustment. Section 2 pinpoints newly surfacing problems in the current macroeconomic movement and their implications. Section 3 highlights the likely scenario of the outlook of China's economy and summarizes our policy recommendation.

1. Background and Origins of the Current Macroeconomic Movement

There have been several changes in China's macroeconomy from 2011 to 2012: deceleration in fixed asset investment growth, the weakened momentum in CPI inflation, and large downfalls in trade growth where the trade surplus shrunk considerably. The root causes of these movements are all related to the global financial crisis in 2008 one way or another.

Before the outburst of the global financial crisis, the Chinese economy was on the downward adjustment in its earlier business cycle. As can be seen from Graph 1, the upward movement of the earlier cycle began in 2005, when the GDP growth rose from 10% — a level that had been high already. At its peak, GDP growth exceeded 13% in 2007. Of which, the year-on-year growth was as high as 13.8% in Q2 2007. In response, macroeconomic policy shifted to a contractive stance in the first half of 2007, when the Central Bank started to raise the baseline interest rates on 1-year bank deposit and 1-year bank loan, together with repeated hikes on bank deposit reserve requirement ratio.

By mid-2008, the momentum of overheating in the economy showed signs of being under control, with GDP growth falling back to 10%. China had achieved a largely successful soft landing.

The global financial crisis was a major shock to the world as well as to China. The trend of domestic economic movement took unexpected turns, and macroeconomic policy had to reverse in direction accordingly. Impacts of economic shifts and policy changes have been so immense that several years later their effects are still almost everywhere.

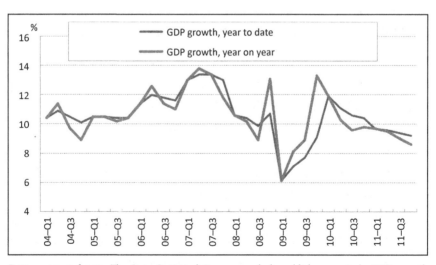

Data source and note: The State Statistical Bureau regularly publishes quarterly GDP growth that is in year-to-date. The year-on-year series are derived from the published ones by simple extrapolation. The two series are identical for the first quarter in each year.

Graph 1. Quarterly Growth in GDP, 2004:Q1–2011:Q4.

In China, policy makers swiftly switched their stance when the tides of the global financial crisis hit the shore of the country. There was a good deal of fear that the domestic economy would be severely dragged into a deep recession. At the end of 2008, the State Council initiated a huge policy package of fiscal stimulus, targeting investment, consumption, income and employment support, and trade support.

As a result, China's fixed asset investment began to surge once again in 2009. Its growth exceeded 30% during the year in real terms. Construction of high-speed railways, investment in infrastructures, as well as urban reconstruction, all appeared to be in a wave looking like another "Great Leap Forward." The excessively expansionary trend in investment prompted policy makers to introduce contractive policy measures from the second half of 2010.

In tandem with fiscal stimulus, monetary policy was also eased. The baseline interest rates were cut several times during the last few months in 2008, which was also accompanied by cuts in the bank deposit reserve requirement ratio. Earlier restriction measures on money and credit expansion were suspended, and there were some new encouragement to money and credit expansion. The broad money supply (M2) rose 27.7% in 2009, and loans outstanding at all financial institutions increased 31.7%. Liquidity was pervasive in the economy and domestic financial system. Against this backdrop, it became inevitable that inflation reemerges. Graph 2 shows the movements in CPI inflation and broad money supply. In order to control the rising trend in inflation, the Central Bank had to adopt a contractive stance. The bank deposit reserve requirement ratio was raised from the first half of 2010, and the baseline interest rates from the first half of 2011 (Graph 3 shows the two series for recent years).

Internationally, in the early stage of the global financial crisis the problems were mainly concentrated in the private sector because of its debt accumulation in earlier years. Bailout measures undertaken by many governments in crisis-ridden economies absorbed the private sector debt risks into the public sector. The late evolution is thus to become a source of sovereign debt risks that have surfaced considerably in recent post-crisis years. In turn, the world economy begins to slide into a downward adjustment in 2011. The "double dip" has brought negative impacts on external demand for Chinese products. China's total exports in goods,

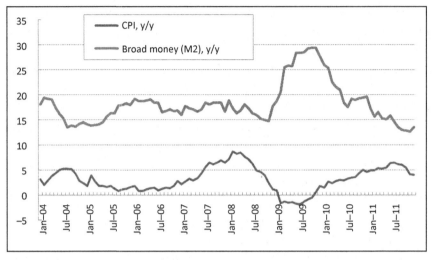

Data source: State Statistical Bureau and the People's Bank of China.

Graph 2. Change in Consumer Price Index and Broad Money Supply, %, 2004.1–2011.12.

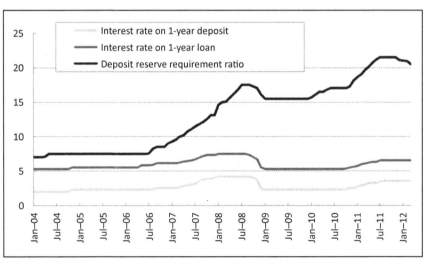

Data source and note: The People's Bank of China; As changes in interest rates and deposit reserve requirement ratio often took place at a single date in the month, the monthly series shown in the graph are a result of weighing the dates of change and non-change during the month in concern.

Graph 3. Baseline Interest Rates and Deposit Reserve Requirement Ratio, %, 2004.1–2011.12.

in dollar terms, plummeted to −16% in 2009, from 2008's 17.2%; and the growth recovered to be as high as 31.3% in 2010, which decelerated to 20.3% in 2011. In the fourth quarter of the year, China's exports in goods in dollar terms further slowed to 14.3%. These figures are very much a reflection of the rhyme in the world economy in recent years.

We may draw several lessons from the above discussion. First, the impact of the world economic crisis on domestic growth should not be overestimated. As it well known, China is a populous economy with a huge domestic market. Its macroeconomic movements are primarily determined by factors that are within the country. Many China watchers agree that the growth pattern in China over many years since the 1990s was set by fixed asset investment The growth in export and trade balance are also important, but they not as important as domestic factors. An implication of this view is that policy making should become more "domestically oriented."

Second, one should not underestimate the growth appetite in the China's domestic economy. Economic overheating is largely a result of China's economic system where there are large quantities of funds in the state sector. Those who have access to finance and conduct fixed asset investment on large projects are mainly state-owned enterprises and state institutions, e.g., government agencies. Credit and capital supply through banks and securities markets is greatly influenced by government approval on investment projects and the relationships of business entities with the government, regardless how the assessment on feasibility and riskiness is being conducted. For all these reasons, investment behavior has had intimate relation with government behavior. Government departments and agencies in China are usually not risk averse, they have strong appetite for growth and expansion.

Third, it is much better that adjustment in macroeconomic policy is quicker, in order to avoid policy actions that are stronger than otherwise. Both domestic and international experience has shown that many macroeconomic variables, such as aggregate output and general price level, have a tendency of inertia, i.e., they may display a certain trend of self-sustaining, with or without a change in parameters and policy variables. Given this, a better policy should be a one that adjusts faster. The main benefit that quickly adjusted policy would bring about is that policy shocks should be more moderate than that to belatedly adjusted policy. In other words, the promptness of policy adjustment tends to reduce the magnitude of policy adjustment. One may ever believe that lowering the variability in policy would itself contribute to the stability in macroeconomic movement.

2. 2011: Soft Landing Is in Progress

There have emerged several outstanding issues in China's economic and macroeconomic policy adjustments in 2011. Some are types of "historical leftovers" and some others new. To name a few, they are rising inflation trend, bubbles in the property market, regional government debt, and credit shortages facing many small businesses.

A widely discussed issue is of course whether China's economy would be able to avoid hard landing in the process of downward adjustment. In the case of China where two-digit growth rates are quite common, a reduction in growth rate during a year that is greater than 5 percentage points would qualify as a hard landing. Usual understanding of hard landing would also involve fast disinflation like headline CPI inflation rate quickly approaching zero. As can be seen from Graph 1 earlier, the first quarter of 2009 might be regarded as a one that China's economy had accidently fallen into a "hard landing," when GDP growth dropped more than 4 percentage points (ppts) — the year-on-year rate down by 7 ppts and year-to-date rate by 4.6 ppts.

There are several reasons to believe that the scenario of hard landing is unlikely to occur in China in 2012. First, external shocks now are much smaller than the earlier one. The biggest risk in the world economy at present is the sovereign debt problem in the eurozone. It is clear however, that the major powers are seeking ways to prevent the risks from exploding. Second, international oil prices in the first few months of 2012 are far lower than that in the first half of 2008. Third, at home, China's macroeconomic policy has in fact shifted toward the contractive stance from 2010 and partly thanks to that the magnitude of overheating in the current cycle appears to be more moderate than the earlier one.

In China's property market, there are several episodes when property prices surged. One had occurred in 2004–2008. At the end of 2008 when the global financial crisis happened, property prices and fixed asset investment in real estate development turned to a sharp downfall. At one time there was virtually no growth at all in fixed asset investment in real estate development in 2009, which also indicates that the inventory of housing property was approaching exhaustion. It was apparently an excessive downward adjustment. As a result, when the economy began to recover in 2010 and entered a new fast-growing phase, the surge in property prices was even greater than before. The real estate boom has been particularly strong in large cities. Many of the local authorities in these cities introduced policy measures of various kinds in 2011 to deter the growth in demand for housing property. From the second half of 2011, the rising momentum of property prices began to weaken, and from early 2012 there are signs that property prices in many large cities have began to fall. Nonetheless, fixed asset investment in real estate development continues to grow steadily, and its pace still exceeds the pace of overall FAI growth.

It is likely that the downward adjustment in the property market in 2012 would be relatively moderate compared to the one that occurred in late 2008 and early 2009. A key variable to watch is the change in investment growth in real estate development. In any case the possibility of collapse in FAI in the sector or that in inventory of new homes for sale is rather small this time around.

The problem of regional government debts began to surface in the first half of 2011. The problem is in some way a side result of large-scale fiscal stimulus that was implemented in 2009 and also a reflection of imperfection in China's government system, particularly the fiscal system. There have been several estimates about the total size of debt accumulation for all regional and local governments. A general view is that the situation of debt expansion in subnational governments has been put into control from 2011, and the level had reached to its peak in 2010. The total amount was believed to be some 25% of China's gross domestic product in 2010, and probably fell to 21% in 2011. Of the total local government debts, there is about one third that sees revenue and cash flows quite normal, and another one third that may encounter certain problems with cash flows but is basically under adequate collateral or guarantees. The last third might lack of capacity to generate revenue.

Policy makers should reform China's budget system by clarifying the "division of labor" for governments at various levels as well as for government departments and their agencies.

3. The Outlook of China's Economy and Policy Guidelines in 2012

It looks almost certain that China's economy would undergo downward adjustment in 2012. We think that GDP growth would be about 8.3%, i.e., a successful soft landing. There are several factors that would support this scenario.

First, China's commodity exports would be able to grow no less than 10% in 2012. The eurozone is in the process of overcoming the sovereign debt crisis and is likely to avoid a deep recession in 2012. Meanwhile, despite some setbacks encountered in the last few months of 2011, the American economy has shown encouraging signs of stabilization and recovery. It should not be a surprise to see U.S. GDP growth exceeding 2% in 2012. Moreover, emerging market economies excluding China would possibly achieve a total growth of 5–6% in 2012. Overall, the external demand for Chinese exports will continue to grow fairly steadily, and the 10% growth rate should not become a difficult task.

Second, as pointed out earlier, fixed asset investment in real estate development is expected to decelerate considerably in 2012, even more remarkably in some large cities. Nonetheless, it is unlikely to see a similar situation to that in early 2009 when such investment almost collapsed. On balance, it is possible for FAI in real estate development to grow at about 20% (the growth rate for January to February in 2012 was 27.8%).

Third, consumption would play a positive and increasingly important role in sustaining GDP growth in 2012. As shown in Graph 4, the pace of consumption growth was relatively low in the past years, especially relative to that of investment. But there are signs that the role of consumption has tended to rise in the recent years. Retail sales of consumer goods increased 15% in 2009, up 5 ppts from 2008. The growth rate was a little lower in 2011, but its difference with FAI growth also narrowed in the year. There are several developments that would support consumer spending to grow steadily in the current year, or at least would prevent it from sliding. Urban population in China has just exceeded the number in rural areas, and this would in principle help to raise the consumption level in the country as the capacity to consume in urban population is significantly higher than in rural population. Purchases of automobile decelerated considerably in 2011, but the demand is expected to recover in 2012. The general willingness to spend for Chinese people appears to be strengthening in 2012 as it is culturally a year of self-enhancement (the year of dragon in the lunar calendar). Preliminary figures show that the number of marriages and births have been increasing since the beginning of the year, and that would be followed by proportional rises in consumer spending.

Fourth, in the backdrop that inflation begins to fall and overall fiscal deficit being brought into control, the room for macroeconomic policy maneuver is effectively enlarged. The ability to make fine tuning in macroeconomic policy has been improved, and decision makers appear to be willing to undertake prompt policy adjustment — all of which should help ensure a soft landing in economic growth.

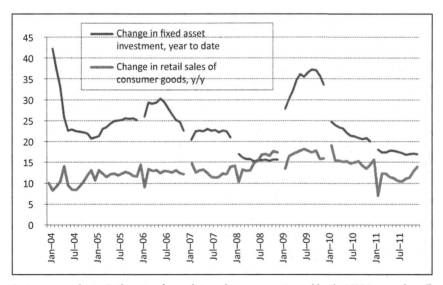

Data source and note: Both series of growth in real terms are estimated by the NERI research staff, and raw data are from the China Monthly Bulletin of Main Economic Indicators. As a data-release practice, some January figures are not available, especially for the recent years.

Graph 4. Growth in Fixed Asset Investment and Retail Sales of Consumer Goods, in real terms, %, 2004.1–2011.12.

In short, China's macroeconomic trends are shifting toward the normal paths. It is displaying several notable developments: the difference in pace between investment and consumption is becoming smaller; and the reliance on external demand has also become smaller. In addition, macroeconomic policy, especially monetary policy, is moving to a neutral stance, i.e., neither easing nor restricting.

There are certain challenges to policy making in 2012. Internationally, trade protectionism appears to be gaining momentum as more countries have been targeting Chinese goods and firms. China needs to face up to the challenges of trade protectionism. Efforts should be made in all dimensions and levels (global, regional, and bilateral) to safeguard the smooth development of multilateral trading system.

International financial markets have also seen some irregular movements since late 2011. Large amounts of funds have been withdrawing from several emerging market economies and causing some unexpected impacts on exchange rates and local money markets in those countries. Regulatory changes and developments in the eurozone financial markets are chief reasons for the recent international financial flows, and they are believed to be largely a medium-term phenomenon. In the longer term, international financial markets should become more stable. In this situation, the RMB will have space to continue to appreciate, and this should also help ease pressure from trade protectionism.

At home, policy makers will have to address several problems in addition to the bubble burst in the property market and regional government debts. Output and prices in some heavy industrial sectors have been falling in recent months, and many small businesses are facing difficulties in getting financing and some are even cutting back on production. Setbacks in some heavy industrial sectors are mainly caused by rapid price disinflation and inventory adjustment. Perhaps there is some overreaction in industrial firms as they cut inventories when facing price falls. It is largely a short-run, cyclical phenomenon. For financial difficulties facing small businesses, the main problem is not due to a low level of aggregate credit supply, the problem is the ineffective credit service provided to small businesses by domestic financial institutions. The government needs to pay more attention to institutional barriers that cause the inadequacy in financial services to small businesses. In dealing with the bubble in property market, the government should adopt market-based approaches rather than direct administrative means.

Soft landing and returning to the normal growth path will provide new opportunities for China to pursue further reform and opening, and will also help reinforce the foundation for more sustainable and balanced economic growth in the future.

The Correction of China's Twin Surpluses

Yongding Yu

After thirty years of breakneck growth, China overtook Japan to become the world's second largest economy in 2010. There is no doubt whatsoever that China's achievement is a miracle.

However, China's growth as seen by Premier Wen Jiabao, is "unstable, unbalanced, uncoordinated and ultimately unsustainable." The reason for this statement is that China's growth pattern over the past thirty years has now almost exhausted its potential. China has reached a crucial juncture: without painful structural adjustments, the momentum of its growth could suddenly be lost.

One of the most important features of China's growth pattern is its persistent current account surplus and capital account surplus. In fact, China has run twin surplus consecutively for 20 years (except for 1993). In 2008, the current-account surplus ballooned to US$426.1 billion, accounting for 9.6 percent of GDP. After the Global Financial Crisis, China's current account surplus-to-GDP ratio has been falling rapidly. However, China is still running twin surpluses, and there is still a lingering question about whether the fall in its current account-to-GDP ratio is structural or cyclical.

This paper first gives a brief introduction to the debate on the causes of China's twin surplus in China. Then the paper argues that, the saving-gap alone cannot explain China's current account surplus. Rather, China's trade promotion policy to a large extent is the cause of the existence of the saving-gap. The implication of this argument is that while China should adopt policy measures to reduce the saving gap, it should also use policy measures such as exchange rate policy to address the twin surplus directly. The paper gives particular attention to an important cause of China's twin surpluses: FDI's crowding effect, which has rarely been touched upon in the literature.

Running current account surplus persistently for decades is nothing new, and is not necessarily an abnormity. For example, the U.S. started to run trade surplus since 1874. This process lasted almost uninterruptedly until late 1979. Since the middle of the 1970s Japan has run trade account and current account surplus for four decades. The same is true of Germany.

According to economics of development, a country will experience different stages of development with different gaps in saving-investment and hence different patterns of external balances in different periods of time. The different patterns of external balances are results of cross-border inter-temporal maximization of utility functions of different countries. A developing country usually would first experience a period of current account as well as trade account deficits, then a period of trade account surplus and current account deficit, and finally a period of trade account surplus and current account surplus. Only by running current account deficits, can developing countries run capital account surpluses, so as to utilize foreign capital inflows from developed countries to supplement the shortage of domestic capital for economic growth. When a developing country becomes a high-income country, its saving-investment gap probably will turn positive, meaning its saving will be larger than its investment. As a result, it will start to run current account surplus and at the same time becomes a capital exporting country.

Generally speaking, because countries in the world are at different stages of development with different income levels and age structures, some countries would run current account deficits, and others would run surpluses. If desired surpluses and deficits of different countries cancel out each other, "global imbalances" in principle should not be an issue.

However, the present global imbalances situation is perverse. On the one hand, the richest country in the world — the United States — has been running current account deficit persistently over thirty years. On the other hand, the much poorer emerging economies as a whole have been running current account surplus since the Asian financial crisis. This pattern of international imbalances represents a serious misallocation of resources on a massive scale. Corrections should and will happen sooner or later, and hence the current global imbalances are not sustainable.

The imbalances situation in China has been even more perverse because China runs both large current account surpluses and large capital account surpluses persistently. As can be seen in Figure 1, until 2005, China's capital account surplus was larger than its current account surplus. As a result of the so-called "twin surpluses," China now has accumulated more than US$3.1 trillion foreign exchange reserves, the bulk of which is in the form of U.S. Treasury instruments.

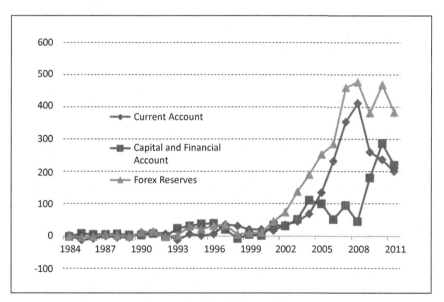

Sources: State Administration of Foreign Exchanges, the PBOC.

Figure 1. China's Twin Surpluses and Increase in Foreign Exchange Reserves (Billion USD).

The most commonly used analytical framework for identifying the causes of the current account imbalance is based on the identity:

$$S - I = X - M$$

where S, I, X and M represent savings, investment, export and import, respectively.[1]

The above identity states that excess saving is equal to current account surplus. Basically there are two strands of thinking about the causes of China's current account surplus. For one school, the cause of China's current account surplus is China's positive saving-investment gap. In other words, The Chinese consume too little and save too much. This school of thought can be labeled as "structural school." For another school, the cause of China's current account surplus should be found in China's policies aimed at promoting trade surplus over the decades as well as external shocks that impact on China's external sector directly. The latter school of thought can be labeled as "policy school." It is worth mentioning that $S - I = X - M$ is just an identity which can say nothing about causality. Causality based on this identity can be verified or falsified only by empirical analysis.

The structural school attributes China's high savings rate to be the most important cause to China's current account surplus. The most commonly attributed causes of China's high savings in turn include[2]:

- Lack of social safety net, as a result, people have to save for retirement, medical care and their children's education in the future.
- High enterprise saving,[3] which in turn is attributable to high share of industry in the economy and hence large share of interest and profits, instead of wages to labor in national income.

---

[1] To simplify analysis, in the lecture, I use the concepts trade balance and current account balance interchangeably.

[2] According to a World Bank study, savings is driven by higher output growth, fiscal consolidation, increases in private sector credit, favorable changes in age structure, improvement in terms of trade. It is worth mentioning that to explain high savings is not equivalent to explain current account surplus. Hence, there is a methodological problem with the structural school.

[3] Corporate saving increase is a global phenomenon. In Asia, savings reached a record high level in 2004, a substantial part of the saving comes from public saving. Marco Terrones and Roberto Cardarelli: Global saving and investment: the current state of play, *World Economic Outlook*, September 1, 2005, p. 93, the World Bank.

- Low dividend payments. In the case of State-owned Enterprises (SOEs), the state, the largest shareholder, receives no dividend at all from most SOEs until recently.
- Increase in profitability since the mid-1990s, due to rapid industrial growth and restructuring of SOEs.[4]
- A favorable age structure: low dependence ratio and high working-age-to-population ratio in the past two decades
- The widening of income gap: share of the rich that have higher saving propensity in GDP increases significantly.

However, according to some other economists, "China's saving is high but not exceptional. As a share of GDP, China's corporate saving at best rivals Japan's, its household saving is below India's, and its government saving is less than Korea's."[5] Hence, attempts to identify any one single explanation for China's exceptionally high aggregate saving rate will almost surely be less than convincing.

While not denying the merits of the arguments presented by the structural school, I tend to emphasize the importance of the contributions of policy factors to China's trade surplus and current account surplus. It is not an exaggeration to say that since the beginning of the opening up in the late 1970s and early 1980s, until recent years, China's export policy, FDI policy and exchange rate policy were mainly, if not exclusively, aimed at achieving current account surplus and accumulating foreign exchange reserves. Correspondingly, saving and investment have to be adjusted one way or another, so that current account surplus can be achieved. It can be said also that to a certain extent, both the positive saving-investment gap and current account surplus are consequences of these policies.

---

[4] Bert Hofman and Louis Kuijs: A Note on Saving, Investment, and Profits of China's Enterprises, World Bank Office, Beijing. This note is written in their personal capacity. A version of this note was published in the *Far Eastern Economic Review*, October 2006. Since 2006, the share of enterprises in total saving has fallen, while that of household saving has increased. Now household saving has returned to be the largest contributor to total saving.

[5] Ma Guonan and Wang Yi, China's high saving rate: myth and reality, BIS Working Papers No. 312, June 2010.

It is worth mentioning that when Chinese economists were debating bitterly in the late 1990s on whether China should continue to pursue current account surplus while having attracted large capital inflows, no one noticed, let alone mentioned, whether there was a positive saving-investment gap in China at all.

Why was China so keen on promoting export and accumulating foreign exchange reserves until the middle of the 2000s?[6] There are five main explanations:

- Shortage of foreign exchange reserves in the 1980s
- Need for self-insurance in the 1990s
- Parking the excess saving abroad (a structural cause) mainly in the 2000s
- Crowding out of domestic investment by FDI
- Promoting aggregate demand (a cyclical factor)

China's main export promotion policies, some of which have been disused in the 2000s, include:

- Self-balancing of foreign exchanges and local contents requirements for important foreign investment projects. This policy was scrapped after China's WTO entry.
- *Undervaluation of the exchange rate.* Before the Asian financial crisis, China set the value of exchange rate was set according to the production costs of exports with the aim of maintaining the competitiveness of exports. During the Asian financial crisis, the RMB was pegged to the US dollar. The peg was dropped in 2005. However, the pace of appreciation is slow.
- *Tax rebate.* This is a very important policy instrument. When the tax rebate rates were correctly calculated, they do not constitute subsidies. However, in practice, the policy provides undue incentives for enterprises to produce for external markets and enables uncompetitive exporting enterprises to survive.

---

[6] There is abundant literature arguing for further accumulation of foreign exchange reserves in China.

- Preferential policies to encourage domestic enterprises to participate in international production networks, and to attract foreign enterprises that can bring Chinese enterprises into the international production networks to invest in China. Preferential treatments take forms like better infrastructure, preferential loans, and cheap land.

It is self-evident that, if China's current account surplus is a natural result of excess saving, why on earth has China bothered itself to design and implement so many export promotion policies over the decades? Hence, it is needless to say, to reduce China's current account surplus, China needs to adjust its export promotion policies.

Now, let's turn to China's capital account surplus. China is a high saving country, and since the 1990s there has been no shortage of foreign exchanges in China. Why does China still wish to attract some $50 billion foreign capital a year? In my view, a country can run current account surplus and capital account deficit, like Japan and Germany. Alternatively, a country can run current account deficit and capital account surplus, like most East Asian countries before the Asian Financial Crisis. Only under special condition countries may run both current account and capital account surpluses to build up foreign exchange reserves. The sudden appearance of twin surpluses in East Asian countries in the aftermath of the Asian Financial Crisis is a case in point. To run twin surpluses persistently for two decades is absolutely an abnormality.

It is worth mentioning that when China was just opening up in the early 1980s, a debt crisis struck Latin American countries. Based on Latin American experience, the Chinese government imposes tight control over foreign borrowing from the beginning. On the other hand, FDI was regarded as the safest form of foreign capital and hence extremely preferential policy towards FDI was put in place. China's success in attracting FDI is the envy of its fellow developing countries. There is nothing wrong with attracting FDI, the question is why China has wanted so much FDI over the past three decades, while it has been running current account surplus (meaning it has not suffered from shortage of saving and foreign exchange reserves)? The answers can be summarized as follows.

First, the twin surpluses are a result of the implementation of an extremely generous preferential policy towards FDI within a fragmented financial system.

When China was just opening up in the early 1980s, a debt crisis struck Latin American countries. Based on Latin American experience, the Chinese government imposes tight control over foreign borrowing from the beginning. However, on the other hand, preferential policy towards FDI was put in place.

Due to the fragmentation of the financial system, it is difficult for many enterprises to raise funds domestically and efficiently, though funds are available domestically. However, due to the preferential policy, to attract FDI as a way to raise funds is much easier. Therefore, the enterprises attract FDI first and then sold their foreign exchanges thus obtained to the central bank, and use RMB to buy capital goods produced locally.

Under normal circumstances, export earnings should be used for imports. Now because imports are financed by FDI, export earnings cannot be spent for imports, other things being equal, current account surplus will increase. Exporters have to sell their earnings to the central bank.

First, in China's efforts for introducing FDI, local governments have played a key role and their excessive intervention is a major cause for the massive FDI inflows into China. Local government officials have very strong incentive to attract FDI, because the amount of FDI they are able to attract is one of the most important, if not the single most important, performance measurements in their work (*Zheng Ji*). It is a common practice in China that all chief officials at all levels of governments are assigned targets for FDI attraction. Those who attract the largest amount of FDI are the most likely candidates for further promotion. Despite the fact that the returns required by foreign investors on FDI are high, from the myopic point of view of officials of local governments, FDI is a "free lunch." Important thing for them is that in the initial stage they do not need to pay hard currency and bear investment risks. They do not care too much about paying large dividends in 5 to 10 years' time, if the investment has proven successful. What they need to do is to commit to pay dividends to foreign investors in future, which will not be their responsibility anyway.

Most emphatically, the local governments are responsible for creating favorable environment for foreign investment, such as acquiring lands that are state-owned or community-owned and hence are cheap; building roads; laying water-supply pipes; erecting power grid; and so on. Chinese officials are competent and effective in achieving these objectives and the costs of achieving these objectives are affordable for them. Furthermore, China's fiscal system and institutional arrangements characterized by the value-added tax and a sort of fiscal federalism, also give local governments great incentives to attract FDI. Therefore FDI has become indispensable for increasing tax revenues at local levels. From the point of view of foreign investors, on top of political and macroeconomic stability, temptation of cheap but skilled workers, low tax rates, long tax holidays, hidden subsidies in emerge use, lax regulations on environmental protection, free infrastructure and low or negative rents on land uses is just too hard to resist. So the interests of local governments in attracting FDI and foreign investors in investing coincide perfectly.

Second, in recent years, in order to give new impetus to the reform of state-owned enterprises and commercial banks, the central government has encouraged the merger and acquisition of Chinese firms by foreign investors and the acquirement of shares by "international strategic investors" in China's commercial banks. Consequently, even though capital flows in domestic capital markets have more than enough funds to be raised for these purposes. In 2005 alone, USD 32 billion of foreign capital flowed in as a result of selling bank shares to international strategic investors even though China had already piled up more than USD 800 billion of foreign exchange reserves. In 2010, some Chinese commercial banks launched successful IPOs abroad, and billions of U.S. dollars flew into China, even though these banks did not need foreign exchange. As soon as they obtained the dollars, they sold the bulk of them to the PBOC for RMBs and the PBOC had to use the dollars to buy more U.S. government securities.

Third, the single biggest FDI provider is Hong Kong and the second largest is the Virgin Islands. The latter accounted for more than

19 percent of China's FDI in 2005. Though difficult to verify, anecdotal evidences show that a very large proportion of China's FDI is rent-seeking-round-tripping FDI.

Having explained why China has attracted so much FDI, while it is a country with excess saving. A related but different question we need to enquire here is why China fails to translate capital inflows (in the form of FDI) into current account deficit.

Theoretically speaking, the answer lies in the prevalent price distortion. It can be shown that without market distortion in the form of preferential policy towards FDI, the inflows should have been translated into current account deficit. Assuming a country initially runs a balanced current account as well as balanced capital account, and further assuming that there is no market distortion of any forms, if capital flows increase suddenly, asset prices will rise and interest rates will fall. At the same time, the exchange rate will appreciate and perhaps the general price level will rise. All these changes in prices will lead to the rebalancing of international balance of payments with surging current account running deficit to balance the capital account surplus. In China, due to interest rate inflexibility and exchange rate inflexibility, capital inflow may continue to increase and current account will not turn to deficit to balance the increase in capital account surplus. Through the central bank intervention, the twin surpluses end up with the increase in foreign exchange reserves.

There is a specific form of price distortion: preferential policy-led FDI crowded out effect. Recent studies[7] have found that, because of China's highly concessional policy to attract FDI, FDI has crowded out a large proportion of Chinese investment. As a result, Chinese capital has to settle for the second best, namely, to invest in U.S. government securities. In recent years, great efforts have been made in promoting outbound FDI. Hopefully, the outbound FDI will be able to replace investment in U.S. treasuries and other financial assets to become the main outlet for China's excess saving and reduce the accumulation of more foreign exchange reserves.

---

[7] Lu Feng and Yu Yongding. *China's Imbalances: A Microeconomic Perspective: Social Sciences of China. Journal of 'Social Sciences of China,'* No. 6, June 2012.

The reason why FDI crowding-out effect contributes to China's current account surplus can be explained in Figure 2.

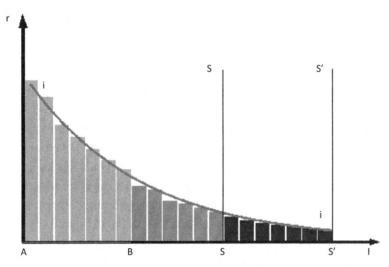

Note: Vertical axis r represents investment return and horizontal axis *I* represents the amount of investment. Each rectangle bar represents one investment project with the width of the bar representing the scale of the investment project. Vertical line SS represents saving which is assumed given and will not be subject to the influence of the interest rate. SS' is China's investment in U.S. government securities.

Figure 2. FDI Crowding Out and Current Account Surplus.

Basically, the figure shows that because China's FDI policy is already extremely generous at the national level, and, owing to market as well as wider institutional distortions, many local governments will go even further to attract FDI regardless of costs, FFEs are able to capture a great proportion of the more profitable projects (AB), China's resources available for investment, which is AS, cannot be fully utilized within China. Assuming that without FDI, China's saving-investment gap would be zero: Saving = Investment = AS. Now, as a result of FDI crowding out, positive saving-investment gap appears, which is equal to AS – BS = AB. The excess resources represented by AB has to be translated into current account surplus, and this surplus is invested in U.S. government securities AB = SS'. Authentic FDI inflows should translate into current account deficit. However, due to the price distortion-led crowding out effect, this translation fails to happen. According to U.S. Conference Board, in 2008 U.S. firms' average investment return in China was 33 percent, and, according to the World Bank, multinationals' investment return in China was 22 percent. In contrast, China's investment return on U.S. government securities is less than 3 percent. The crowing-out effect is serious indeed. It is worth mentioning that there is no denying that the reason why FDI can capture a large proportion of domestic firms' investment opportunity is because many FFEs are more efficient and have better technology.

To summarize the causes of China's twin surpluses, let's return to $S - I = X - M$. Now you can see that it is difficult to say whether the left hand-side of the equation determines the right-hand side or it is the other way around. In fact, in the early stage of development, China's export promotion policy was the dominant contributing factor to China's current account surplus in the 1980s and 1990s. It can be said that excess saving during this period of time was mainly a result of China's current account surplus. Either savings had to be increased or investment had to be cut, so that resources could be used for running current account surplus and accumulating foreign exchange reserves. However, during the 2000s, as a result of the establishment of the domination of FFEs in exporting sector and China's position in the IPNs, trade surplus has become more and more structural. The consolidation of the domination of processing trade in China's trade coincides with the changes such as an increase in precautionary savings, which work on the left-hand sided of the identity $S - I = X - M$. As a result, China's current account surplus looks increasingly like a structural problem. This means that even if the government abandons its trade promotion policy, and the RMB is allowed to appreciate significantly, it is still possible that China will continue to run current account surplus for a certain period of time. However, this does not mean that the change of policy is useless. On the contrary, in order to correct the export-biased economic structure, many policies, including exchange rate policy should be adjusted and changed. Of course, efforts should also be made to reduce the positive S-I gap, so that the pressure on running current account surplus can be reduced. In short, in order to correct imbalances, a comprehensive policy package should be implemented.

Is there anything wrong with China's twin surpluses? In my view, there are at least four problems. I call them the Dornbusch problem, the Williamson problem, the Krugman problem and the Rogoff problem. The late Professor Rudiger Dornbusch pointed out in the 1970s that running current account surplus means exporting capital. It is irrational for a developing country to lend money to rich countries, because domestic resources should be used for domestic investment which will bring in higher returns and improve the people's living standards. The phenomenon of China, one of the poorest countries in terms of per capita GDP, lending money to the United States, one the richest countries in the world, is surely irrational.

Dr. John Williamson pointed out in a 1995 speech that capital inflows should be translated into current account deficits. The twin surpluses outcome implies that China fails to buy foreign capital goods and technology with the borrowed money. Instead, in aggregate terms, China is "lending" the money back to the original creditors at lower interest rate.

Professor Paul Krugman points out that the devaluation of the US dollar in terms of the dollar index means that China's foreign exchange reserves are facing serious capital losses.

Finally, according to Professor Kenneth Rogoff, the ballooning U.S. budget deficit may provide too strong a temptation for the U.S. government to inflate away its debt burden that it becomes irresistible. As a result, the purchasing power of China's accumulated savings in the form of U.S. government securities may evaporate quickly. In 2003, China's foreign exchange reserves totaled just above US$400 billion. Now the forex reserves stand at $3.2 trillion, an 800 percent increase. However, in 2003, the price of crude oil was generally under US$30 a barrel, and the price of gold was less than US$400 an ounce. Now prices for crude oil and gold are more than US$120 a barrel and US$1,600 an ounce, respectively. In fact, from 1929 to 2009, the US dollar has devalued by 94 percent in terms of purchasing power. It will devalue even further in the future.

It is crystal clear that running twin surpluses and continuing to accumulate foreign exchange reserves are not in China's interests. China has taken actions to correct external imbalances, but the progress has been painfully slow and the economy is sinking even deeper into the "dollar trap." Last year, China's trade surplus, capital account surplus and total balance of payments surplus were still as high as US$180 billion, US$100 billion and US$475 billion, respectively. The bulk of the balance of payments surplus has again translated into U.S. government securities.

The policies that the Chinese government has used to try to correct the imbalances include simulating domestic demand, allowing the yuan to appreciate gradually, diversifying foreign exchange reserves away from U.S. treasuries, creating sovereign wealth funds, participating in regional financial cooperation, promoting the reform of the international monetary systems and internationalizing the yuan. However, all these efforts, though useful and necessary, have failed to address the direct cause of the rapid increase in foreign exchange reserves. Due to the continuous worsening of U.S. fiscal position, the possibility of an attempt by the U.S. government to inflate away its debt burden, as pointed out by Rogoff, is increasingly likely. One unfortunate thing is that losses in financial assets will not be realized, until the holders have decided to cash out. If the U.S. government continues to pay principals and interests on its public debt, and China continues to pack its savings in the U.S. government securities, the game may continue for a very long time indeed. However, this situation is ultimately unsustainable. The longer the delay in the adjustment, the more violent and destructive the adjustment will be.

Stopping further accumulation of foreign-exchange reserves is becoming a more urgent issue than rebalancing China's current account. Actually, China's current account surplus-to-GDP ratio has fallen significantly since 2008. However, to stop the accumulation of foreign exchange reserves and thus minimize China's welfare and capital losses, the simplest solution would be for PBOC to call a halt to its intervention in the currency market. But this implies that China must allow the yuan to float freely, and thus to appreciate.

Ending central bank intervention in currency markets is a complex issue. The devil is in the details. But, under any circumstances, the economic and welfare costs of China's slow pace in adjusting exchange rate are too high and will increase by day. It is time for China to consider allowing the yuan to float freely, while reserving the right to intervene when it must, and tighten the management of cross-border capital flows (permissible under last November's G-20 agreements).

The Long-run Growth and Short-run Fluctuations of the Chinese Economy

Zhigang Yuan and Yuxin Yu

Introduction

China became the world's second largest economy in 2010, and was classified as a middle-income country by the World Bank in 2011. However, the recent subprime crisis and the European debt crisis have reduced the demand for China's exports, one of the most important drivers of China's growth. This external development along with the internal shock of rising labor cost show that the Chinese economy is now in the process of an important historical structural transition.

This paper analyzes the future of the Chinese economy from both long-run and short-run perspectives. Figure 1 summarizes our conceptual approach to understanding long-run growth trend and short-run fluctuations. Basically, changes in supply side factors are essential for long-run economic growth, while changes in exports, government policies, investments, and consumptions are responsible for short-run fluctuations.

1. Long-Run Trend of Economic Growth in China

1.1. Changes in labor supply

The reduction in under-employed labor and growth in labor supply have been important drivers of economic growth for more than thirty years. The share of working-age population (people aged between 15 and 64) has been rising ever since 1978 to help provide a nearly unlimited

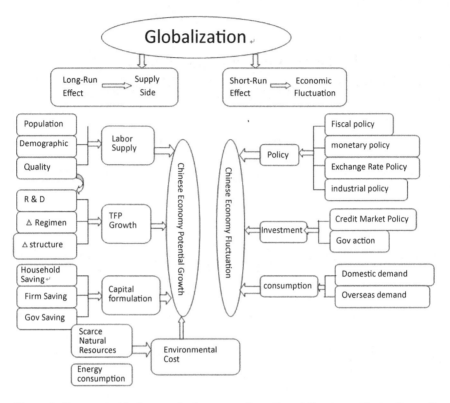

Figure 1. Factors that Influence the Long-run Growth and Short-run Fluctuations of the Chinese Economy.

supply of labor for economic growth. However, labor supply in China is reaching a turning point.[1] The population growth rate has been declining since 2010, and the size of the working-age population will peak in 2015. As a result, negative effects of labor scarcity on economic development will gradually emerge. This change in supply side is one of the factors responsible for the rise in inflation rate in 2011.

The dependency ratio has also reached a turning point, it bottomed out in 2010. The rise in the dependency ratio will decrease the investment growth rate and increase the consumption share. It is therefore inevitable that the economic growth pattern of China will change.

---

[1] United Nations Population Information Network, http://www.un.org/popin/

Besides, the one-child policy which has lowered the growth rate of the labor force, the children who were born in the 1980s and 1990s have an aversion to becoming blue-collar workers. The "social fever" for college education has interacted with the "ivory-tower" education system to create an excess supply of college graduates. As a result, blue-collar worker shortages and college graduate unemployment coexist. This decline in labor supply and structural mismatch in skills are constraining China's long-term economic growth.

1.2. Changes in capital accumulation

Another important determinant of long-run economic growth is capital factor input. Figure 2 shows that both government and corporate savings rate began a sustained rise around year 2000, while household savings rate has declined to some extent. In 2007, the government savings rate was almost 10%, the corporate savings rate, 20% and the household savings rate, 20%. The rise in the government savings rate and the corporate savings rate are responsible for the rapid increase in the aggregate savings rate in China.

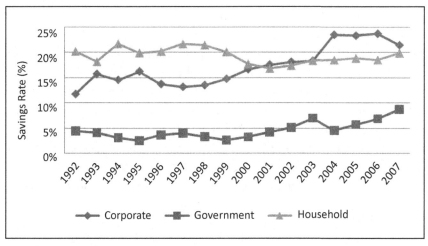

Source: *China Statistical Yearbook.*

Figure 2. Savings Rate by Different Sectors.

Table 1. Savings Rate by Different Sectors (An International Comparison).
(Share of the Sector's Saving in GDP, %)

	China	U.S.	France	Japan	South Korea	India
National Savings Rate	52.3	14.3	20.7	25.5	31	28.3
1. Household Savings Rate	22.5	4.8	10.8	8.2	4.5	22
2. Corporate Savings Rate	21.6	10.3	9.5	19.4	14.8	4.8
3. Government Savings Rate	8.2	−0.9	0.3	−2.2	11.7	1.5
The Gap between Savings Rate in China and Other Countries		38	31.6	26.8	21.3	24
1. Household Savings Rate		17.7	11.7	14.3	18	0.5
2. Corporate Savings Rate		11.3	12.1	2.2	6.8	16.8
3. Government Savings Rate		9.1	7.9	10.4	−3.5	6.7

Note: 1. Data for China is from *China Statistical Yearbook 2010*;
2. Data for other countries is from Louis Kuijs (2005).
3. Data for China is for year 2008, while data for other countries is 2002.

Table 1 compares China's savings rate behavior with those of U.S., France, Japan, South Korea, and India. (The first four foreign countries are OECD countries.) The household savings rate in China is much higher than the household savings rates in the OECD countries: 20% versus 5–10%. However, the difference with India is not very significant.[2] Obviously, the relatively higher household savings rates in China and India are results of institutions and their stages of economic development. In short, with the development of the Chinese economy, the household savings rate in China will decline gradually.

The corporate savings rate in China is significantly higher than those in the U.S., France, and India, but its difference with Japan and South Korea is much smaller. What is worth mentioning here is that though China's corporate savings rate is higher than many other countries, its share of corporate savings in total national savings is not among the highest. For example, corporate savings in the U.S. and Japan constitutes the most important component of national savings, amounting to about 85%.

---

[2] World Bank Database, http://data.worldbank.org.cn/

Corporate savings in China are high for two reasons. First, labor compensation is extremely low in China, enabling firms to accumulate more. Second, after the 1994 tax reform, state-owned enterprises (SOEs) did not turn in their profits to the government for a long period of time. Even though they turn in dividends now, the dividend share in total profit is still very low. For example, in 2010, SOEs paid only 44 billion RMB to the government out of 1987.06 billion RMB in profit, i.e., only 2.2% of the total profit.[3] The dividend payout ratio of listed firms and private firms in China is also lower than the average level in other countries. Except for a few financial firms and listed firms, the profits of state-owned enterprises are almost never distributed as dividends, especially for those firms with monopolistic powers. Profits are the most important financial sources of reinvestment for non-state-owned firms because they have great difficulties in getting loans from banks. Our expectation is that the further marketization of the Chinese economy (especially the normalization of the labor market, capital market and resource market) will cause the corporate savings rate to decline.

Table 1 shows that the government savings rate in China is lower than that of only South Korea. This is because economic development in China is mostly directed by the government, which is also the case in South Korea (He and Cao, 2005). However, this policy regime is not sustainable because government-directed investments are low in efficiency. The inevitable decline of the government's role in economic development implies future decreases in government investment expenditures.

Table 2 shows that the GDP shares of expenditures on education and on healthcare are both relatively low in China, even when compared with India. Currently, government consumption expenditures are about 11% of total GDP. We expect this share to be raised by 10 percentage points in the future to bring it to around 21%. Using data for 2008, this means that government consumption expenditures should be raised to 2.1 trillion RMB, which would decrease the government savings rate to around 1.6%, which is similar to the government savings rate in India. However, because the Chinese government controls substantial

---

[3] Data from the Ministry of Finance of the People's Republic of China, http://www.mof.gov.cn/

Table 2. Shares of Government Expenditures on Education and
Healthcare in Government Expenditures. (Share in GDP, %)

Country	Education	Healthcare
Australia	4.8	6.4
Japan	3.7	6.4
South Korea	4.6	2.8
New Zealand	6.9	6.3
China	2.9	1.1
India	3.3	1.2

Note: Data for countries except China are for year 2004,
from Zhang (2006); Data for China is for 2009.

resources, we expect the savings rate of the Chinese government to drop
only to around 5%, which is 3 percentage point lower than the government savings rate in 2008.

To sum up, in the long run, the savings rates of households, corporations and government will all decrease with the transition to a complete market economy. The national savings rate will decline from 52.3%
in 2008 to about 28.6–34% in the future. As the potential for capital
accumulation in China falls, there will be a decrease in the potential
economic growth rate.

1.3. Changes in Total Factor Productivity (TFP) growth

Using 1990 as the base year, we calculated the TFP growth rate in China,
which is shown in Figure 3.[4] TFP growth in China has been positive
except in 1989 and 1990, when fiscal policy was tightened to fight
against inflation. Figure 3 shows three periods of rapid TFP growth in
China since 1978, (a) the beginning of the reform in 1978 and the full
implementation of the contract responsibility system in rural areas in
1982, (b) the beginning of the 1990s, after Deng's southern tour speeches
which unleashed a wave of market-oriented institutional reforms, (c) the

---

[4] Capital stock data from 1978 through 1998 are extracted from Zhang and Shi (2003),
while those from 1999 through 2009 are estimated based on these historical data and the
amount of each year's fixed capital investment.

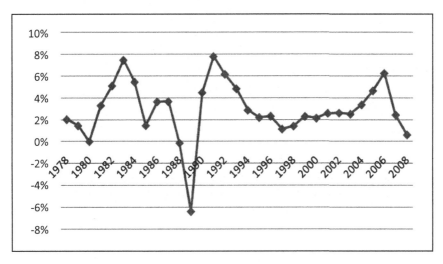

Figure 3. TFP Growth in China.

acceleration of the globalization process after China's entry into WTO in 2001.

Tables 3 and 4 show that 1978 (the year that the process of reform and opening up was started) was a turning point in TFP growth. The average annual TFP growth rate was low and volatile in 1953–1976, e.g., 1.5% in 1953–1959 and −15.2% in 1960–1962. In 1979–2002, however, the average annual growth rate was 2.9% and accounted for 29.3% of the GDP growth rate. Clearly, economic reform is the key reason explaining why China has experienced persistent positive TFP growth and thus output growth over the past thirty years.

Table 5 shows that in 2007–2008 China reached the development stage that Korea reached in 1987–1988 and Japan in 1968–1969, a GDP per capita of about US$5,000 (measured in terms of purchasing-power parity). According to Table 6, the TFP growth rate in Korea and Japan slowed down after 1987–1988 and 1968–1969 respectively, with the slow-down much more pronounced for Japan. These two experiences suggest that the TFP rate in China will decline in the future.

However, we argue that China's regional economic disparity may prevent the TFP growth in China from falling as much as Japan. Compared with the more developed eastern area, China's middle and

Table 3. Pre-Reform TFP Growth and Its Contribution to Output.

	1953–1959	1960–1962	1963–1970	1971–1976
TFP Growth Rate	1.5%	−15.2%	4.2%	−1.3%
Output Growth Rate	10.8%	−11.9%	9.9%	4.6%
TFP Growth as % of output growth	13.6%	−127.7%	42.5%	−27.8%

Source: Zhang and Shi (2003).

Table 4. Post-Reform TFP Growth and Its Contribution to Output.

	1979–1989	1990–1999	2000–2009	1979–2009
TFP Growth Rate	3.0%	2.7%	2.9%	2.9%
Output Growth Rate	9.6%	10.0%	10.3%	9.9%
TFP Growth as part of output growth	31.8%	27%	28.2%	29.3%

Table 5. A Comparison of China, Korean and Japan (World Dollar).

	China		Korean		Japan	
Year	2007	2008	1987	1988	1968	1969
Per Capita GDP	4761	5568	4951	5655	4590	5250

Source: World Bank

Table 6. Japan and Korean TFP Growth Rate around Its Transitional Period.

Time Period	Japan (%)	Time Period	Korean (%)
1960–1965	1.478	1981–1985	1.003
1965–1970	1.946	1986–1990	1.020
1970–1973	0.686	1991–1995	0.996
1973–1975	1.481	1996–1998	0.958
1980–1985	0.469	1999–2005	1.026

Source: Japanese data from Jorgenson (1992); Korean TFP data from Zhang (2010).

western areas are much less developed, and thus may enjoy strong technological catching-up effects in the near future. Furthermore, with the implementation of China's 12th five-year plan, there is increasing investments in high-tech industries and R&D. Taking these into consideration, we believe the TFP growth rate in China will be about 1.5% to 2% in 2012. Further decline of TFP growth rate in the long run is inevitable if the institutional transition of China is not carried out successfully.

1.4. Rising environmental cost

The issues of resource constraint and environmental cost must be considered in Chinese economic growth. China imported 235 million tons of crude oil in 2010, making China the second largest crude oil importer in the world after the U.S. (456 million tons). The energy consumption per unit of GDP in China is not only higher than in developed countries, but also higher than in India and Russia.[5] Increasing the efficiency of energy consumption and developing energy saving technology will be key to the sustainable long run economic growth in China.

China's sulfur dioxide emission reached 22 million tons in 2009 and it spent 452 billion yuan on waste gas management and relevant expenditures, accounting for 1.49% of GDP.[6] Environmental cost will have a negative impact on the economic growth rate in the long run.

2. Short-Run Fluctuations of the Chinese Economy

To analyze the short-run fluctuations of the Chinese economy in the recent period, we analyze the government policy from four perspectives:

1. lag effect of the four-trillion-yuan economic stimulus plan;
2. credit constraints and financial disintermediation from the excessive contractionary monetary policy;
3. forthcoming changes in the leadership of the central government and the local governments;
4. price control on real estate market.

---

[5]*BP Energy Outlook*, 2030, www.bp.com/statisticalreview
[6] *China's Environmental Statistics*, 2010.

2.1. The four-trillion-yuan fiscal stimulus plan

In order to fight against the global financial crisis, the Chinese State Council issued the four-trillion-yuan stimulus plan in November 2008. Taking into account the stimulus spending of local governments, the total stimulus package led to a total investment of over 24 trillion yuan. This huge amount of stimulus has revived the economy, but at a high cost.

First, the fiscal stimulus reinforced the unbalanced investment structure. A large proportion of the fund from the stimulus plan was spent on transportation infrastructure. In the first three quarters of 2009, infrastructure investment has increased by 52.6% compared to the year before, e.g., investment in railroad construction increased 87.5%.[7] As most stimulus funds were channeled though bank loans, this has increased the credit risk of the banking system.

Second, the fiscal stimulus has crowded out private investment because the large government borrowing has increased interest rate.

Third, the fiscal stimulus has increased the inflation rate, especially real estate prices in big cities.

Figure 4 below shows the effect of the government stimulus plan on CPI and PPI. The lag effects of fiscal policy will continue to influence current economic growth negatively in 2012.

2.2. The recent contractionary monetary policy

The bank deposit interest rate was lowered four times in 2008, causing it to decline from 4.14% at the beginning of the year to 2.75% at the end of the year. Bank reserve requirement rate was also lowered three times from 17.5% on September 15, 2008 to 15.5% on December 22, 2008. However, with the emergence of inflation pressures, monetary policy began to contract in 2009. Since the end of 2008, the base rate for bank deposit has increased 5 times; it reached 3.5% on July 7, 2011. Meanwhile, reserve requirement rate was raised 12 times, and it reached a historical high of 21.50%. The current high rate of reserve

---

[7] *China Statistical Yearbook*, 2010.

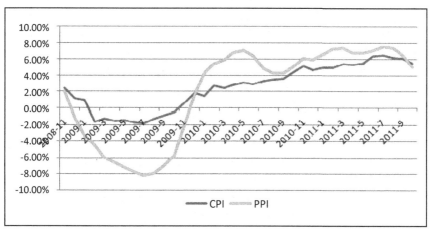

Source: CEIC.

Figure 4. Chinese Monthly CPI and PPI Growth since November 2008.

requirement creates a great burden to society by disrupting the normal liquidity needs of the economy. As a result, the interest rates have increased, and financial disintermediation and usurious loans have become widespread.

Banks have experienced deposit outflows, e.g., 16 publicly listed banks had a total deposit of 54.79 trillion in 2011:Q3, compared with 54.89 trillion in 2011:Q2. In December 2011, deposits declined more precipitously. In the first ten days of the month, total deposits of the four big commercial banks decreased by 400 billion, while the amount of new loans issued was only 30 billion.

The control on real estate prices has constrained macroeconomic policies greatly. Right now, the central government is still determined to maintain control over real estate prices in the face of lag effects from the 2008 four-trillion-yuan stimulus plan and loose monetary expansion policy. Cautious monetary policy will continue in the short run. With the deterioration of economic performance, monetary policy is likely to reverse. However, the low quality of the local government debts and the stronger regulation of the banking system will weaken the effects of the forthcoming loose monetary policies. It is hence very likely that the growth rate of Chinese economy will be low in 2012.

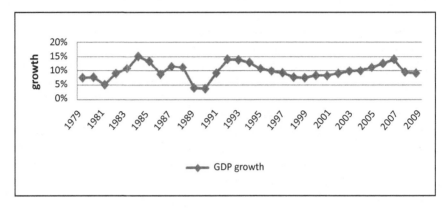

Figure 5. GDP Growth in China.

2.3. The impact of administrative changes

There will be a change in the administrative leadership of China at the end of 2012. Figure 5 shows that in the post-1978 period, there has always been a rapid economic growth in China after each government administrative change. The economy grew rapidly after the administrative changes in 1987, 1992 and 2002. The exception was in 1997 when credit was tightened to fight the Asia financial crisis. This political-cycle-type of phenomenon is made possible because the public sector controls a large part of China's economic resources.

The expansionary effects of the personnel changes in the leadership of the central government on the economy are channeled through changes in monetary and fiscal policies, and the expansionary effects of the personnel changes in the leadership of the local governments are generally channeled through new investment incentives. This five-year cycle in the change in administrative leadership is not a sustainable impetus for economic growth since it could drive the economy to a boom only temporarily.

2.4. The impact of real estate regulations

Under the pressure of the housing bubble, the Chinese central government has been implementing a comprehensive set of real estate regulations. Although the regulations have successfully stopped house prices from rising, they are also impacting investors' confidence negatively. Meanwhile, given the bearish stock market, buying real estate is actually the only way for private savings to gain a high profit. If this investment channel continues to be blocked by strict regulations, it will be more difficult to transfer potential investment into industrial capital, thus impeding the economic growth in China. The fact is that housing regulation influences not only the real estate market and related industries, but also financial efficiency and thus the whole economy.

2.5. What is the likely macroeconomic situation in 2012?

In 2012, the decline of overseas market demand is a foregone conclusion. The export value in January totals $150 billion, 0.5% lower than the value of the previous year, and close to the level at the end of 2008. Meanwhile, the increase in domestic demand is also limited due to the low household income. Therefore, the combination of low overseas demand and low domestic demand suggests that consumption is not likely to have a large contribution to the economic growth in 2012.

The present situation (in April 2012) suggests that Chinese economic growth has lost its momentum. The Chinese government may hence loosen its fiscal policy. However, government investments are of low quality and low-efficiency, and may not facilitate sustainable economic growth. So, we think that the effect of fiscal policies is likely to be limited, and may even reinforce the existing unbalanced structure of the Chinese economy. The Chinese government may also loosen its monetary policy. However, we also think that the effect of monetary policy on economic growth may also be limited because of low investor confidence, and the over-indebtedness of the local governments.

Under the background of international economic instability, EU debt crisis and weak recovery of the U.S. economy, the fragile investment confidence caused by the rigid housing regulations are inducing a wave of capital outflow from China, which amounted to US$26 billion in the first three quarters of 2011. Capital outflow will also be a big challenge for the Chinese economy in 2012.

3. The Major Reforms Needed in the Future

The above analysis suggests that the Chinese economy is under double pressure of long-run slowdown and short-run inefficiency. We believe that only by deepening marketization reforms China could achieve sustained, healthy development in the future. More specifically, China must continue to enhance the rural-to-urban movement of the population, promote the process of capitalization (especially the capitalization of rural land), remove the interest rate control in the financial market, and more importantly, make the government more service-oriented.

3.1. Reforms in the labor market

According to the Sixth Nationwide Population Census, more than 260 million people have been living in a place different from where their Hukou (official residence) is registered, among which 220 were rural migrant workers. This number is 110 million, or 81.03% larger than in 2000. In the current institutional and economic context, these rural migrants cannot become legitimate permanent urban residents and receive the higher level of social services provided to the official urban population. As a result, although 666 million people are living in Chinese urban areas, we cannot say there are 666 million urban residents in China, because about a quarter of them are floating population with rural Hukou.

Figure 6 shows that the proportion of migrant population in urban population has been increasing substantially after 2005, while the proportion of newly increased urban population (people who had been able to convert from rural Hukou to urban Hukou) in migrant population has been decreasing. In short, the speed of urbanization lags behind the speed of migration. And the process of urbanization can be accelerated only after substantial reforms in the provision of social security and public services to urban residents. China needs to deepen the reform in the labor market, and the increased population agglomeration in the metropolis areas will enhance domestic demand.

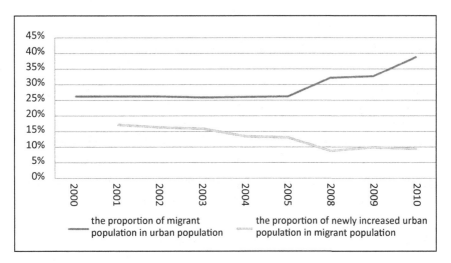

Figure 6. Migration and Urbanization in China.

3.2. Reforms in the land market

In China, urban land is state-owned, while rural land is collectively-owned. The conversion of rural to urban land must go through a process of government land acquisition. The capital gains from land conversion provide a big temptation for land grabs by the local governments. According to the Chinese Academy of Social Sciences, 65% of the 187,000 incidents of public unrest are caused by land disputes. This suggests that the basis of fiscal revenue for the local government should be changed from land sales to a property tax system.

In all, reforms are needed in the rural area to capitalize the land of farmers by giving farmers full property rights to the land and establishing a unified land market. This land capitalization is the equivalent of an efficient liquidity injection and it may act as the starting engine for the next round of Chinese economic growth. Rural land reform has many other positive impacts on the nation's economic development, including increasing rural population's income and helping the migrants to become permanent urban residents.

3.3. Reforms in the financial market

The present system of controlled interest rates has caused the coexistence of overinvestment in the public sector and thus underinvestment in the private sector. This misallocation of capital resources blocks the innovation and entrepreneurial activity of the economy.

The rural land reform combined with the marketization of interest rate can provide a great impetus for China's financial development. Channeled by the free interest rate as the price signal, the liquidity brought about by rural land reform will flow to the areas with the highest efficiency and thus promotes economic development. Meanwhile, the mortgage backed security created by the privatization of rural land will also guarantee the stability of the financial system.

3.4. Transformation of the governmental function

Several problems arise from the current role of the government in the Chinese economy. First, while output competition between local governments highly promotes economic growth, it also brings serious problem, including local protectionism, market segmentation, and duplication of infrastructure. Second, urban housing construction motivated by the fiscal revenue from land sale has resulted in excessive industrial construction. Third, local government debt problems are becoming a potential threat to the economy. According to the China International Capital Corporation, of the 10.7 trillion RMB local government debt, the government has repayment obligations for 6.7 trillion, which accounts for 63% of the local fiscal income. If we take into consideration the contingent liabilities, this proportion will amount to 85%. As local government relies much on the land sale income, decreasing housing price will reduce their repayment ability.

The government must change its role from implementing economic construction to providing basic service and public goods, such as the institutional guarantees, legal system, and social securities. To achieve such a goal, the performance evaluation and incentive system of the local officials should also be changed.

4. Conclusion

Although the economic growth rate in China is still relatively high in 2011, serious potential hazards lie in the economy and they are major challenges to continued high growth. In this situation, both the long-run and short-run factors should be given enough attention in macroeconomic management.

From the perspective of long-run factors, the growth rates of labor, capital and TFP are all on a downward trend; and environmental costs are increasing. In short, the overall Chinese economy is likely to slow down. From the perspective of short-run factors, as overseas demand decreases because of the recession in developed economies, and as domestic demand grows slower because of stagnant household income, the major impetus for economic growth has to come from public policies. However, because of the negative effects of controlled interest rate and financial disintermediation, there is not much room for fiscal and monetary expansion in 2012. The change in key administrative personnel at the end of 2012 can be an impetus for economic growth in the short run, but its long-run effect is under uncertainty.

In conclusion, under the complex and uncertain international environment, the macro policies in China should focus on the functional transformation of the government, as well as on further market-oriented reforms, especially reforms in the land, credit and labor markets. The resulting sound market system will lay the foundation for sustained and healthy economic development in China.

References

Bai, Chong-En, Hsieh, Chang-Tai and Qian, Yingyi, 2006. The Return to Capital in China. Brookings Papers on Economic Activity, 2.

Brealey, R., Hodges, S. and Capron, D., 1976. The Return on Alternative Sources of Finance. *Review of Economics and Statistics*, 58(4): 469–477.

Baumol, W., Heim, P., Malkiel, B. and Quandt, R., 1970. Earnings Retention, New Capital and the Growth of the Firm. *Review of Economics and Statistics*, 52(4): 345–355.

Caves, D.W., Christensen, L.R. and Diewart, W.E., 1982. The Economic Theory of Index Numbers and Measurement of Input, Output and Productivity. *Econometrica*, 50.

Fagerberg J., 2000. Technological Progress, Structural Change and Productivity Growth: A Comparative Study[J]. *Structural Change and Economic Dynamics*, 11.

Friend, I. and Husic, F., 1973. Efficiency of Corporate Investment. *Review of Economics and Statistics*, 55(1): 122–127.

Gugler, K., Mueller, D. and Yurtoglu, B., 2003. The Impact of Corporate Governance on Investment Returns in Developed and Developing Countries. *The Economic Journal*, 113: 511–539.

Gong, B.H. and Sickles, R.C., 1992. Finite Sample Evidence on the Performance of Stochastic Frontiers and Data Envelopment Analysis Using Panel Data. *Journal of Econometrics*, 51.

Hildreth, C. and Houck, J.P., 1968. Some Estimators for a Model with Random Coefficients. *Journal of American Statistical Association*, 63.

He, Xinhua and Yongfu, Cao, 2005, Jiexi Zhongguo Gaochuxu (Explaining the High Savings Rate in China). *Statistical Studies of the World Economy (Shijie Jingji Tongji Yanjiu)*, Vol. 2.

Jorgenson, Muroda, 1992. Productivity and International Competitiveness in Japan and the U.S. 1960–1985[M]. *International Productivity and Competitiveness*, 735–890

Mueller, D. and Reardon, E., 1993. Rates of Return on Corporate Investment. *Southern Economic Journal*, 60(2): 430–453.

Mueller, D. and Yurtoglu, B., 2000. Country Legal Environments and Corporate Investment Performance. *German Economic Review*, 1(2): 187–220.

OECD, 2005. *Economic Survey: China*. 2005/13-September.

Solow, R.M., 1957. Technical Change and the Aggregate Production Function. *Review of Economic and Statistics*, 39(3): 312–320.

Singh, L., 2004. Technological Progress, Structural Change and Productivity Growth in Manufacturing Sector of South Korea. The Institute of World Economy, Seoul National University.

Wurgler, J., 2005. Financial Markets and the Allocation of Capital. *Journal of Financial Economics*, 58(1–2): 187–214.

Young, Alwyn, 2003. Gold into Base Metals: Productivity Growth in the People's Republic of China during the Reform Period. *Journal of Political Economy*, 111(6).

Zhang, Jun and Shi Shaohua, 2003. The Total Factor Productivity Changes in Chinese Economy: 1952–1998 [J]. *World Economic Papers*, 2: 17–24.

Zhang, Xionghui, 2010. A Research of the Contribution of Technology Progress and Technological Efficiency to Economic Growth. Shandong University, PhD dissertation.

PART III

Institutional Reforms for Middle-term Growth:
Upgrading the Hardware and Software

Reforming China's Public Pension System: Coping Effectively with Aging, Urbanization and Globalization

Jin Feng and Lixin He

1. Introduction

China will be facing a dwindling labor force and a rapidly aging population structure by the end of this decade. These new circumstances will bring great challenges to the social welfare system in China, especially for the pension system, which relies on population growth and economic growth for its sustainable functioning. Furthermore, the institutional arrangement of the pension system has powerful impact on economic growth and national competitiveness.

The reform of China's pension system will involve actions on many fronts, including increasing the retirement age, improving labor productivity, expanding the pool of people who pay in, and raising the rate of return in the investments of the pension fund. Furthermore, it is necessary to take into account not only population aging, but also the opportunities that come with urbanization and the requirements addressed by economic globalization. Besides, the sustainable functioning of the pension system relies on institutional reform to incentivize employers and employees to participate. As a policy decision, it is necessary to maintain a wide-coverage, low-level public pension system. Recent economic recession and the enormous social welfare burden that underlie the European debt crisis is a warning call for China to look at the establishment of a social welfare system from a new angle.

2. The Basics of the Current Pension System

The establishment of China's pension system has gone through four phases.[1] The first phase began when "Labor Insurance" was introduced in 1951 as an unfunded employer-sponsored pension program that covered the employees of state-owned enterprises (SOEs) and collectively owned enterprises. There was also a separate pension system for public (civil service) employees — Public Employee Pension (PEP) — but the rural population did not have any formal old age social security.

The second phase extended from the mid-1980s to early 1990s. With marketization of the economy and reform of SOEs, the enterprise-based pension system hindered fair competition and the mobility of labor. Pooling of pension at the municipal level or county level was introduced but the system remained a pay-as-you-go (PAYG) system financed by enterprises.

The third phase was from early 1990s to 2000. China adopted a 3-pillar pension system for urban employees in 1997 to deal with the aging of the population and the pension burden of the SOEs. The new system was called Basic Old Age Insurance system (BOAI). The first pillar is a PAYG system, financed by employers. The second pillar is a mandatory funded system, financed by both employers and employees. The third pillar is a voluntary retirement savings.

The fourth phase began in 2000 and is characterized by the expansion of the coverage of pension system to non-SOE forms. Participants in the BOAI system went from 45% of total urban employees in 2000 to 56% in 2010 (see Figure 1). To achieve universal coverage, the New Rural Pension Scheme (NRPS) was established in 2009 to cover rural residents, and the Urban Residents Pension Scheme (URPS) was established in 2011 to cover urban non-employed residents. For rural migrant workers, the Social Insurance Law was enacted in 2010, and it specifies that rural migrant workers are entitled to the same treatment given to urban workers.[2]

---

[1] For an introduction to the development of Chinese pension system, please refer to Barr and Diamond (2010), He (2008), and Zhang (2007).

[2] The Ministry of Labor and Social Security (MOLSS) proposed in 2009 a special pension scheme for rural migrant workers with low premiums; employers pay 12% and employees

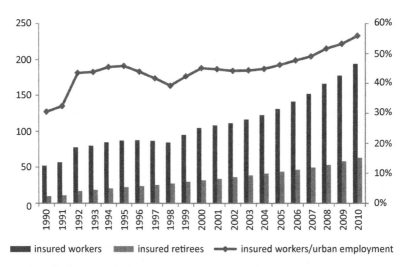

Source: China Statistics Yearbooks.

Figure 1. Employees/Retirees in Basic Old Age Insurance System, 1990–2010 (millions).

BOAI has the widest coverage of the four pension schemes — BOAI, PEP, URPS and NRPS — and now also covers all the employees in the urban private sector. At the end of 2010, BOAI covered 257 million people (194 million employees and 63 million retirees), with 32.84 million being rural migrant workers. In 2010, the revenue of BOAI fund was 1.34 trillion and the expenditure was 1.06 trillion (see Figure 2). The main reason why the contributions into BOAI is still greater than the benefits paid out is because of the steady expansion of coverage, i.e., the expansion made the increase in participants exceeds the increase in retirees. Furthermore, BOAI also receives government subsidies, which totaled 196.5 billion in 2010, representing more than a 30 fold increase over a little more than a decade. If the government subsidies are discounted, then the BOAI funds in 14 provinces (including Shanghai, Jiangsu, Hubei and Hunan) are in a deficit. In this case, BOAI would

pay 4.8%; all contributions go to individual accounts; and after retirement, the balance of individual account is used to pay pension. But the scheme was not put into practice.

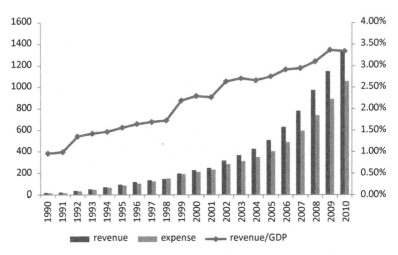

Source: China Statistics Yearbooks.

Figure 2. Revenue and Expenditure in Basic Old Age Insurance System, 1990–2010 (billions).

have reported a total deficit, possibly, as large as 67.9 billion in 2010, instead of the surplus.

In 2009, the pilot NRPS started in 27 provinces, autonomous regions and four municipalities. By the end of 2010, NRPS covered 102.77 million rural people with 28.63 million among them receiving pension payments. NRPS fund revenue totaled 45.3 billion, of which 22.5 billion was premiums paid by participants, and NRPS expenditure was 20 billion.

The revenue of all the four pension funds mentioned above accounted for 3.5% of GDP. Table 1 summarizes the key features of the four pension schemes. The first part of BOAI is a compulsory defined benefit scheme, with employers obligated to pay 20% of employees' wage bill as contribution. Employees with 15 years or above history of contribution are entitled to the pension benefits. The replacement ratio (pension benefit as a percentage of wage before retirement) is determined by the number of years of contribution. For example, a retiree after 35 years of contribution will have a pension replacement ratio of 35%. The second part of BOAI is the individual account, with individual contribution 8% of his wage. The average replacement ratio of first and second pillars taken together is 58.5%.

Table 1. Key Features of the Different Pension Schemes.

Categories	Basic Old Age Insurance system (BOAI)	Public Employee Pension (PEP)	Urban Residents Pension Scheme (URPS)	New Rural Pension Scheme (NRPS)
Year of Establishment	1951: Current Practices Finalized in: 1997	1953: Current Practices Finalized in: 1978	2011	2009
Participants	Urban employees in enterprises	Urban employees in public sectors	Urban non-employed 16 years or above	Rural residents 16 years or above
Contribution	**Social pooling:** 20% of payroll (depending on locality) **Individual accounts:** 8% of individual wage	No contribution required	**Individual accounts:** Individual contribution + government subsidy	**Individual accounts:** Individual contribution + government subsidy
Benefit	**Social pooling:** Minimum 15 years of contribution. 1 percent accrual rate 1%; 35% based on 35 years of contribution **Individual accounts:** Individual account Pension. Total replacement ratio of pension from social pooling and individual account: 58.5%	Average Replacement ratio: 70–90%	Basic Pension + Individual account Pension	Basic Pension + Individual account Pension
Mandatory or not	Yes	Yes	No	No

Sources: Collected from Relevant State Council Documents by authors.

NRPS and URPS are voluntary schemes with government subsidies. Individual contributions and government subsidies are all put into individual accounts. And the amount of contribution is determined by local economic conditions with regional variance and urban-rural variance. Participants with 15 years (or more) history of contribution are entitled to receive 55 RMB in basic pension upon 60 years old. The basic pension is provided entirely by the central government in the middle and western provinces. In the eastern provinces, the central government and the local government each pays half of basic pension. Local governments can raise basic pension benefit according to situations on the ground, and are responsible for the outstanding financial needs. On average nationwide, the replacement ratio for rural per capita net income is about 20%.

3. The Problem Posed by an Aging Society

The ratio of retirees against worker has risen from 18.6% in 1990 to 32.5% in 2010, i.e., a change from 5.4 workers supporting a retiree to 3 workers supporting a retiree. This is the result of shifts in the age distribution of the Chinese population. From 1950 to 2010, the number of people over 60 increased 3 fold to 165 million, it rose from 7.5% of the total population to 12.3%. The proportion of 65-year-olds and above has risen from 4.5% to 8.2%. The proportion of people in the 15–59 age group has risen 58.3% in 1950 to 68.2% in 2010; and the proportion in the 15–64 age group has risen from 61.3%% to 72.4%% (see Figure 3). The rise in the population shares of both the aged group and of the working age group reflected the rapid decline in China's fertility rate which lowered the population share of the 0–14 age group from 34.2% to 19.5%.

The outcome is that while the old-age dependent ratio (elderly/ working age) has risen over time, the total dependent ratio ([elderly + young]/working age) has decreased since mid-1950s, giving rise to an era of population dividends.[3] The ratio of 65-year-olds or above against the 15–64 population has risen from 7% to 11% in 2010.

---

[3] Source: Population Division of the Department of Economic and Social Affairs of the United Nations Secretariat, World Population Prospects: The 2010 Revision, http://esa. un.org/unpd/wpp/index.htm.

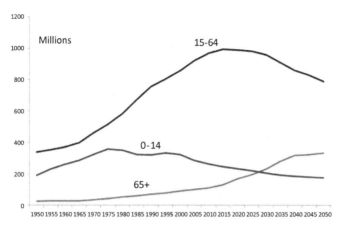

Sources: United Nations World Population Prospects: The 2010 Revision (middle variance); Actual numbers of contributors and retirees are from *China Labor Statistics Yearbooks*.

Figure 3. Age-specific Population Change.

The total fertility rate (TFR) in China is around 1.6, which is lower than the replacement rate of 2.1. While there is uncertainty regarding the future trend of TFR, international experience suggests that it is unlikely that TFR would rise even if the one-child policy is scrapped. Economies with similar language and cultural traditions to China, like Hong Kong, Singapore, and Taiwan, have experienced sharp declines in TFR. TFR dropped from over 5 to below 2 in Taiwan in the 1950s, in South Korea in late 1950s, and in Hong Kong in the early 1960s. The speed of TFR decline in these three economies exceeded that in Western Europe when its demographic transition occurred.

It is unavoidable that China's dependency rate on pension would rise. Figure 4 shows that the ratio of the number of 65-year-old or above to the number of 15–64 would rise from 11.3% in 2010 to 24% in 2030; and the ratio of the number of 60-year-old or above to the number of working age would jump from 18% to 40%. Because BOAI covers less than 60% of the urban employed, the dependency ratio in the pension system is bigger than that of the total population (Figure 4). In regions where population aging is most advanced, the regional BOAI funds are running deficits, with government subsidies keeping these pensions afloat. This is

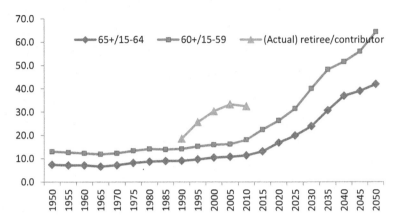

Sources: United Nations World Population Prospects: The 2010 Revision (middle variance); Actual numbers of contributors and retirees are from *China Labor Statistics Yearbooks*.

Figure 4. Old Age Dependent Ratio of Population and of BOAI System.

an important reason why government subsidies to the pension system have risen from RMB 5 billion in 1997 to RMB 196.5 billion in 2010.

4. The Incentive Problem in Basic Old Age Insurance

The evasion of social insurance contribution is a universal phenomenon. In the 1990s, 50–60% firms in Latin America evaded their social security obligations (Gillion et al., 2000). According to Nyland, et al. (2006), the Bureau of Labor and Social Security in Shanghai audited about 6000 firms during 2001 to 2004. In 2001, 71% firms paid less than the prescribed social insurance, and 81.8% firms paid less than that prescribed in 2002.

The contribution rate in China is higher than most countries. Total social insurance contribution rate for employers is 29–37% (BOAI: 20–22%; Health insurance: 6–12%; Unemployment insurance: 2%; Injury insurance: 0.5%; Maternity insurance: 0.5%); and employee contributes 12%, of his own wage (BOAI: 8%; Health insurance: 2%; Unemployment insurance: 2%), with lower bound of 60% of average wage and higher bound of 3 times average wage. Employers can cheat by not registering employees as formal ones at local government bureaus; hiring employees as temporary employees or family members; postponing social insurance contribution payment; and, reducing reported nominal wage to reduce contribution.

Some employees are also not willing to join the insurance programs. The low-income group faces unstable employment and hence faces high uncertainty about its eligibility for future benefits. Young people have high demand for current consumption, and the high contribution rate reduces their consumption. So there is an incentive for collusion between the employers and the employees to default on pension contributions.

Finally, local governments do not punish default on contribution payments with the severity that is needed to deter cheating. Local governments normally focus on targets related to economic growth and adopt preferential policies to reduce employers' tax and contribution burden. Therefore it is understandable that they are lax in enforcing contribution requirements.

With deepening economic globalization, low-cost labor is becoming more and more essential in competitiveness for Chinese products. Enterprises and local governments in regions with high export dependence lack incentives to promote social insurance. Table 2 compares the social insurance and old age insurance revenue and expenditure in different regions. In the 2008–2010 period, Shanghai, Beijing, Tianjin, Xinjiang, Qinghai and Ningxia have social insurance expenditures approaching or exceeding 4.5% of GDP; while Jiangsu, Zhejiang, Fujian, Anhui, Shandong, Guangdong and Guangxi have social insurance expenditures lower than 2.8% of GDP. The actual contribution rate of BOAI in Guangdong, Jiangsu, Zhejiang, Fujian and Beijing is lower than the national average. For example, Guangdong's average contribution per participant accounts for only 10% of average wage.[4]

Feng et al. (2010) show that, after regional social and economic factors have been controlled, a province's dependence on foreign trade (trade/GDP) corresponds negatively with its size of social insurance and

---

[4] Legally-binding contribution rate varies regionally. In Shanghai BOAI contribution rate is 30%, employer and individual contribution combined. It is 11% in Guangzhou, 16% in Donguan, 18% in Shenzhen, Zhuhai and Huizhou, 26% in Fujian, and 28% for most regions nationwide.

Table 2. China: Regional Differences in Pension (Mean, 2008–2010).

Region	Social Insurance Expenditure/GDP (%)	Social Insurance Revenue/ GDP (%)	BOAI Expenditure/GDP (%)	BOAI Revenue/ GDP (%)	BOAI Benefit/ Average Wage (%)	BOAI Contribution/Average Wage (%)
Nationwide	3.26	4.30	2.37	3.06	23.41	49.83
Beijing	5.39	6.85	3.41	4.41	13.62	37.15
Tianjin	4.32	4.91	3.03	3.37	21.49	37.63
Hebei	2.88	3.69	2.19	2.72	25.67	58.88
Shanxi	3.76	5.64	2.88	4.35	27.55	56.82
Inner Mongolia	2.39	3.16	1.82	2.32	24.63	51.69
Liaoning	5.20	6.32	4.08	4.76	24.17	46.15
Jilin	3.52	4.52	2.82	3.45	25.72	45.60
Heilongjiang	5.52	6.76	4.40	5.11	31.89	49.78
Shanghai	6.95	7.53	4.84	5.12	21.13	33.56
Jiangsu	2.67	3.71	1.84	2.54	17.19	44.24
Zhejiang	2.43	3.54	1.55	2.26	11.13	48.07
An'Hui	3.00	3.98	2.23	2.90	22.65	47.16
Fujian	1.97	2.49	1.33	1.53	13.85	53.97
Jiangxi	2.58	3.34	2.05	2.49	18.06	48.26
Shandong	2.44	3.19	1.82	2.35	20.53	65.39
Henan	2.27	2.80	1.77	2.10	20.53	52.02
Hubei	3.35	4.27	2.65	3.28	23.14	48.10
Hunan	3.05	3.95	2.31	2.94	23.07	46.21
Guangdong	2.07	3.41	1.34	2.31	10.24	48.88
Guangxi	2.44	3.86	1.82	2.89	29.09	46.16
Hainan	4.50	5.83	3.51	4.22	22.82	54.02
Chongqing	4.26	5.53	3.41	4.27	27.90	43.60
Sichuan	4.34	6.12	3.33	4.63	30.22	45.33
Guizhou	3.21	4.45	2.29	3.11	26.02	52.34
Yunnan	3.24	4.30	2.01	2.64	29.78	53.82
Shanxi	3.30	4.14	2.52	2.95	24.25	52.88
Gansu	4.13	5.43	3.03	3.91	31.97	60.08
Qinghai	4.91	6.35	3.30	4.08	26.74	58.35
Ningxia	3.95	5.84	2.92	4.37	25.53	53.37
Xinjiang	5.29	7.25	3.56	5.02	31.83	55.39

Source: Social insurance revenue and expenditure are from *China Labor Statistics Yearbooks* (2009–2011), GDP from *China Statistics Yearbooks* (2009–2011).

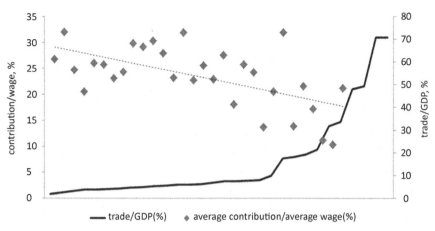

Note: The horizontal axis represents provinces, from the lowest to the highest dependence on foreign trade.

Figure 5. Relationship between BOAI Contribution and Dependence of Foreign Trade (2008–2010, 30 Provinces).

old age insurance (Figure 5). Eastern provinces have high foreign trade dependence, averaging 81%, which is 2.12 times higher than the national average and 5.7 times higher than middle and western provinces. Ceteris paribus, the dependence on foreign trade renders the BOAI expenditure/ GDP ratio to be 12% lower than the national average and 50% lower than the ratios of the middle and western provinces

5. The Problem of Low Investment Return on Pension Funds

By the end of 2010, BOAI had a surplus of 1.54 trillion, and that of NRPS and enterprise annuity was 42.3 billion and 208.9 billion respectively.[5] The National Social Security Fund (NSSF) was established in 2000 as a strategic reserve fund to cope with future pension needs. Its financing mainly comes from government treasure. SOEs are required to send 10% of their IPO revenue to NSSF. In 2010, the National Social Security Fund

---

[5] Human Resource and Social Security Statistics Report, 2010.

(NSSF) had an amount of 780.9 billion.[6] The total amount of money in pension funds stood at 2.87 trillion in 2010.

China's regulation on the investment of pension fund is stricter than that for NSSF. Pension fund investment is confined to government bonds and bank deposit, while NSSF can be invested in a variety of channels, including bank deposit (not lower than 10%), government bonds (not lower than 50%), corporate bonds (not higher than 10%), financial bonds (not higher than 10%), securitization products (not higher than 40%) and stocks (not higher than 40%). Some NSSF money is even invested in foreign venture capital. BOAI received a nominal annual return of less than 2% in 2009 when CPI inflation was 2.2%. In contrast, NSSF received an annual investment return of 9.17% in 2004–2010.

According to current rates of investment return of BOAI fund, if no external funding is secured, then expected pension benefits cannot materialize. Table 3 lays out the analytics of how the rate of return on the BOAI portfolio is related to the total replacement ratio received. In principle, the investment return rate should keep up with average wage growth rate in order to achieve the expected replacement ratio. In the recent period, the real wage has been rising 6% annually. By regulation,

Table 3. Individual account Investment Return's Effect on Pension Benefits.

Years of Contribution	Investment Return (r) and Wage growth rate (g)	Replacement Ratio (social pooling)	Replacement Ratio (individual account)	Overall Replacement Ratio
30	$r = g + 4\%$	30%	37.3%	67.3%
30	$r = g$	30%	20.7%	50.7%
30	$r = g - 2\%$	30%	15.9%	45.9%
30	$r = g - 4\%$	30%	12.5%	42.5%

Note: The real average wage is assumed to grow 6% annually. The return rate on the social pooling component is assumed to be the wage growth rate.
Replacement ratio of social pooling = monthly pension from pooling account/monthly wage before retirement. Replacement ratio of individual account = monthly pension from individual account/monthly wage before retirement.

---

[6] National Social Security Fund Annual Report, 2010.

a person who earns an average wage and has contributed for 30 years can expect to get a 30% replacement ratio from social pooling component of BOAI. In the individual account component of BOAI, if the investment return rate that is 4 percentage points higher than wage growth rate, then this second BOAI component will add an additional 37.4 percentage points to the replacement ratio, thus yielding a total replacement ratio of 67.3%. If the investment rate equals the growth rate of the wages, then the total replacement ratio will be 50.7%, which is less than the officially expected replacement ratio of 58.5%.

With the cumulative increases in URPS fund and NRPS fund, the issue of fund investment will become more prominent. If the investment return in these schemes is lower than expected, future financial balance of the schemes will be put under great pressure. And the pension system will be far less attractive.

6. The Problem of Inequality in Pension Benefit

There are significant disparities among pension benefits from different schemes. In particular, public employees, including civil servants are entitled to pension benefits far higher than that for enterprises employees, on average 1.45–1.83 times higher, with a replacement ratio 1.5 times higher. Since the reforms of BOAI in the mid-1990s, the gap has persisted. In the past decade, the replacement ratio of enterprise employees and that of public employees are generally decreasing, but the replacement ratio of BOAI has been consistently lower (Figure 6). Public employees have an average pension replacement ratio of 65–67%, while that for enterprise employees stands at 47%.

The gap has existed for two main reasons. First, the replacement ratio for PEP is 20% higher than BOAI. Second, PEP is calculated according to the individual's wage just before retirement, while the basic wage used in BOAI combines the national average wage and individual's wage during the entire working life of the person. The PEP wage is much higher than the BOAI wage in normal cases. This is a big change from the period before the pension reform in the middle of 1990s when retirees from the civil service and the enterprises got roughly the same pension benefits.

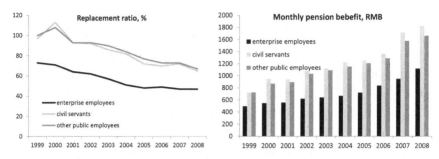

Note: Replacement Ratio = Retiree Monthly Pension Payment/Monthly Wage.
Sources: Labor and Social Security Yearbooks, 2009; China Statistics Yearbooks, 2000–2009.

Figure 6. Pension Benefit for Enterprise Employees and Public Employees.

There is a serious issue of equity here about the public sector retirees receiving higher pension benefits than enterprise retirees, employment opportunities in the public sector are not open to all and the labor market is not competitive, wildly different pension benefits depending on employment sectors raised equity issue. In 2008, the State Council carried out trial reform of PEP in Guangdong, Shanxi, Zhejiang, Shanghai and Chongqing, where public sectors with profit targets would see their employees covered by the BOAI system. However, this reform has stalled.

7. Pension Reform 1: Raise Labor Participation Rate

The size of the labor force is also influenced by labor participation rate. Population aging has, no doubt, helped cause China's labor participation rate to decline. The male labor participation rate has declined from 88.53% in 1952 to 84.36% in 1999; and the female labor participation rate from 76% to 71%. Since 2000, decreases in labor participation rate are more pronounced. In 2005, this figure stood at 62.5%. The fifth national census in 2000 showed that the highest labor participation rate is in the 29–45 age group, 97% for male and 87% for female. Labor participation rates decline significantly for men after 60 and for women after 55.

Table 4 shows that the labor participation rates for those above 50 years old are lower in China than in most OECD countries. The labor

Table 4. Age-Specific Labor Participation Rate.

	50–54	55–59	60–64	65+
China	76.9	65.7	49.3	19.8
Among Chinese:				
Males	88.8	78.1	59.5	27.5
Females	64.9	52.8	38.6	12.8
Urban:	59.3	43.1	25.3	8.9
Rural	88.7	81.1	65.9	27.6
Chinese Hong Kong	65.2	47.8	28.1	6.9
Chinese Taipei	62.1	44.0	30.9	7.4
France	78.8	54.6	14.4	1.1
Japan	80.6	73.9	52.6	19.4
Korea	72.6	63.2	54.5	30.3
Sweden	84.3	79.5	59.6	10.1
England	79.9	69.0	43.2	6.8
U.S.	79.9	69.0	53.2	6.8
OECD Average	77.9	69.8	51.0	14.9

Source: 1% sample census in China, 2005.
Labor Participation Rate = (employed + job seekers)/population.
Statistics of other countries come from Herd et al. (2010).

participation rate for the 50–54 age group in China is 76.9% compared to 80.6% in Japan, 84.3% in Sweden, and the OECD average of 77.9% lower than most countries. In the urban areas of China, the participation rate of the 50–54 group is lower than 60%, nearly 20 percentage points lower than in OECD countries. Old women registered an even lower labor participation rate, with this figure for 55–59 group at around 50% and less than 40% for the 60–64 age group. This phenomenon has to do with China's low retirement age: males at 60 and females at 55.

Postponing the retirement age is a very effective way to address the burden that comes with rising old age dependency ratio. In China, it is not rare for retirees with pension benefits to be employed again. And, since according to the "Labor Law," retirees are no longer obligated to contribute in pension system, employing retirees who have pension benefits is less costly for employers. Furthermore, postponing the retirement age of people with higher human capital enlarges the knowledge base. Since October 2010, Shanghai has put in place a flexible retirement system, personnel with skills in demand can postpone retirement.[7]

One concern about postponing the retirement age is whether this would cause the unemployment rate of young people to rise. Theoretically, a higher labor participation for old people will not necessarily result in a lower employment rate for young people. First, the changes in the labor participation rate for the old and the young are subject to the same macroeconomic forces, and hence the two rates may rise or drop simultaneously. Second, the labor productivity of young people is higher than that of old people and in a competitive labor market, enterprises are more likely to hire young employees. Third, old people's wage income usually exceed their pension benefits and therefore when their consumption demands rise and stimulate economic growth, more employment opportunities will be opened up.

Empirical studies in different countries have proved that the participation rates of the young and the old are not a zero-sum phenomenon. In France, Belgium and Italy, 60% of men in the 55–65 age group drop out of the labor force, but in Japan the ratio is only 20% and in America it stands at 40%. Meanwhile, the unemployment rates for 20–24 year-olds in these countries are not much different (Gruber et al., 2009). Empirical evidence from a number of developed countries over a 10-year period shows no systematic relationship encouraging early retirement and lowering unemployment; and there is no reason to think the basic insights are different in developing countries (Lim et al., 2011).

8. Pension Reform 2: Improve Labor Productivity

The key to reforming pension system lies in improving labor productivity. When productivity is rising, the wealth created by younger generation can support a larger group of old people. With growing output, the PAYG system remains in balance without the need for either a reduction in pensions or an increase in contributions. Increased output is possibly

---

[7] Shanghai's local policies stipulate that the retirement age for men can be up to 65 and for women 60.

the best solution for funded schemes, since it will help to control inflation in goods market and deflation in assets market (Barr, 2000).

Table 5 reports the World Bank's estimates of the growth in China's labor productivity in the next two decades. While China's labor productivity growth rate will drop along with the GDP growth rate, it will still remain at a high level, e.g., 5.5% annually from 2026 to 2030 (Table 5). This will increase the amount of effective labor and offset the negative influence of population aging.

Table 5. Projected Labor Productivity Growth (1995–2030).

	1995–2010	2011–2015	2016–2020	2021–2025	2026–2030
GDP annual growth (%)	9.9	8.6	7.0	5.9	5.0
Labor growth (%)	0.9	0.3	−0.2	−0.2	−0.4
Labor productivity growth (%)	8.9	8.3	7.1	6.2	5.5
Share of employment in agriculture (%)	38.1	30.0	23.7	18.2	12.5
Share of employment in service (%)	34.1	42.0	47.6	52.9	59.0

Source: The World Bank, DRC, 2012, *China 2030: Building a Modern, Harmonious, and Creative High-income Society.*

It should be pointed out that future productivity increase is dependent on some crucial factors: firstly, it is dependent on the quality of the labor force. The educational level of China's labor force has been rising. The average education received by workers as of the 1964 census was only 2.34 years, while the figure climbed to 8.48 years in 2004. The number of enrollment in high education per ten thousand population climbed from 45.7 in 1995 to 218.8 in 2010. Faced with population aging, expanding investment in human capital is a necessary strategy. Secondly, it is dependent on economic restructuring. Labor productivity in agricultural sector is lower and there is huge room for rural laborers to shift to non-agricultural sectors, so that the proportion of people working in agriculture will drop and that in service sectors will rise greatly. Therefore, policies that facilitate the mobility of labor is a crucial part of ensuring rising labor productivity.

9. Pension Reform 3: Accelerate the Urbanization Process

China's main pension system BOAI covers less than 60% of its urban employed population, leaving vast numbers of rural migrant workers uncovered. The number of migrant workers covered by BOAI totaled 32.84 million in 2010, accounting for only 21% of all migrant workers in urban areas. In 2009, migrant worker in Shanghai had a social insurance participation rate of 18.7% (Yuan and Chen, 2010).[8] With the process of urbanization going further, more rural residents will take up jobs in non-agricultural sectors. Protecting the rights of rural migrant workers and incorporating them into the social insurance system is a basic necessity for achieving social justice. However, more than 200 million migrant workers working in non-agricultural sectors do not have urban residential permits (urban Hukou) and therefore do not have equal treatment in social welfare services. The urbanization rate as measured by Hukou holders is only about 33% in 2011. Breaking up the Hukou barrier and enabling all urban workers to the same public services and social welfare is a basic part of urbanization itself.

Incorporating rural migrant workers into urban pension system can increase the number of contributors and thus, with the number of retirees constant, the worker/retiree ratio of urban pension system can be improved for a long time. This would mean solvency for some urban pension funds. Consider the case of Shanghai, the city with the most acute aging problem in China. Shanghai has had pension fund deficits since the beginning of this century. In 2010, the migrant population in Shanghai exceeded 8 million, and most of them are at working age. Since 2003, the annual increase of migrant workers has been above 2 million. Meanwhile, the human capital of migrant workers has been converging to that of the local working age people. And the residential rate of migrant workers is getting higher along with their education level. For example, migrant workers holding college or higher degrees have a 25.1% probability of staying in Shanghai for 15 years. Clearly, the higher the

---

[8] There was a specific social insurance for migrant workers in Shanghai. The contribution rates in this scheme were lower than those in urban social insurance. This specific scheme is under transition to the urban social insurance in order to unify social insurance programs to workers of different identity.

residential rate, the higher probability of incorporating them into the BOAI system. Suppose the annual increase of migrant workers go 2.5 million in 2010 to 1.3 million in 2025, and suppose that the age structure of migrant workers remains unchanged, but their education level keeps increasing, then simulations show that if participation rate of migrant workers in social insurance can increase linearly up to 50% or beyond, the deficit in the BOAI system of Shanghai can be brought under control (Yuan and Chen, 2010).

Urbanization is also conducive to a higher level of rural pension benefit. The main incentive for participation in NRPS is lies in the government subsidy. Currently, benefit and subsidy in NRPS are both low. Urbanization would reduce the absolute number of old rural residents, and hence a higher government subsidy per person will be achieved. Feng and Guo (2011) shows that if the urbanization rate reaches 70% in 2050, the number of rural residents above the age of 60 would be 120 million, which is about 28.5% of total rural population. The financing challenges that come with the aging of rural population can be offset by urbanization and increases in government revenue. And it will be feasible to raise the replacement ratio in NRPS to 30% while keeping central government subsidy level below 4.5%.

10. Pension Reform 4: Reduce the Contribution Rates Moderately

In the age of globalization, a high level of social welfare is a serious challenge to competitiveness, especially for developing countries that still rely on cheap labor as their competitive edge. Therefore economic globalization calls for controlling welfare benefits (Garrett, 2001; Garrett and Mitchell, 2001). Numerous research indicate that global competition has put downward pressure on welfare benefits, namely the Race to Bottom effect (Mishra, 1999; Huber, 2001; Rudra, 2002; Yoon, 2009). In China's integration into the world economy, its competitiveness rests in large part on low-cost labor. A large size of social insurance is not only unrealistic, but also costly in operation. Employers and even local governments would have an incentive to evade contributions.

Table 6 shows that China's contribution rate is among the highest in the world, even higher than Sweden, the U.S. and France. China enacted

Table 6. Comparison of Contribution and Benefit of Pension System.

Country or Region	Contribution Rate	Replacement Ratio
Sweden	18.5%, employer: 11.5%, employee: 7%	70.9%
Germany	Lower than 20%	55.1%
U.S.	12.4%, employer: 6.2%, employee: 6.2%	68%–90%
France	18%, employer: 10.8%, employee: 7.2%	50%
China's BOAI	28%, employer: 20%, employee: 8%	58.5%

the "Social Insurance Law" in 2010 to help enforce the regulations requiring employers to pay contributions for their employees. But at a more fundamental level, the creation of incentives for compliance by employers and employees is more vital.[9] According to experts from World Labor Organization, Bailey and Turner (2001), the reduction of contribution rates is the most effective way to solve poor compliance in contributions to social insurance.

How to ensure the solvency of the pension fund when the contribution rate is reduced? There are some possibilities from an optimistic view. First, low contributions would attract more enterprises and individuals to participate in the system. And the expansion of coverage would improve the cash flow of the pension funds and help maintain balance for some time. Second, low contribution rate should translate into lower benefits. As stated above, postponing retirement age is an overwhelming trend, which would go a long way towards reducing the financial burden on pension funds.

On the basis of a low-level social welfare system, employers can decide whether to provide additional old age security, including enterprise annuities, to meet the demand for higher social security. Employers of high value added products place more emphasis on productivity, and providing higher social security would contribute to higher productivity.

---

[9] The case in Shanghai shows that lower contribution rate improves the compliance with social insurance. Shanghai has a lower social insurance for enterprises located in suburb district, which called township social insurance. Using this exogenous difference in contribution rate caused by policy, study finds that generally, a lower contribution rate can cause more compliance (Feng and Zhang, 2012).

11. Pension Reform 5: Promote Equity in the Pension System

Equity in pension system does not mean equal benefits, rather, equal opportunity is the most fundamental objective. It is worth noting that higher pension benefits for public employees is the common policy of many countries to prevent corruption by the knowledge of getting handsome pension benefits after retirement. If the labor market is perfect, and individuals can have free choice of employment sectors, then there is no inequity problem. However, for employees in enterprise who joined the labor force before the reform when choice was limited, the legacy cost of the reform should not be their responsibility. There should be special funds compensating their losses in pension benefits. In the long term, an equal pension system relies on the elimination of unfairness in labor markets.

It is also a common practice to have different social security systems for rural and urban regions. For example, Germany and France are early European examples of setting up special rural social security systems. Belgium's social insurance regarding the self-employed is different from other employees. It is common for government to subsidize the under-privileged. Because of their low income, even a low contribution could be a hurdle for them to get social insurance. So the equity between rural and urban system does not mean uniformity in policies, but it means that basic requirement can be met equally.

Meanwhile, equity also means that the structure of the system should not compromise low-income earners' interests. For example, migrant workers face two major difficulties in joining the social insurance pool. First, it is difficult for them to afford contribution. Migrant workers generally get meager pay and the enterprises that employ them are not able to afford contributions either. Second, it is difficult for them to transfer their contribution when moving from one city to another. Regulations now stipulate that dropping out of coverage means only partial refund of contributions, turning pension contribution into a hidden tax burden. Research done in Yangtze River regions show that migrant workers, because of their low income level, are more inclined to join a low level social insurance so that present consumption needs can be met (Yuan et al., 2009).

12. Pension Reform 6: Improve the Governance of Public Pension Funds

The low investment return of pension funds in BOAI system has raised concerns among policy makers in recent years. In early 2012, Guangdong Province entrusted the management of its 100 billion pension revenue to the NSSF because, as explained earlier, NSSF has broader channels for investment and has achieved annual return rates more than 9% in 2001–2010, much higher than inflation rate. But it should be noted that NSSF invests nearly 20% of the fund in the Chinese stock market and therefore the fluctuations in investment returns relate to the overall changes in the stock market. For example, in 2008, the rate of investment return of NSSF was −6.79%, while the inflation rate of that year was 5.9%. Moreover, as measured by capital market efficiency, China's capital market is an inefficient market, which manifests itself in wild fluctuations in prices. In short, trusting NSSF with the management of pension insurance fund involves unclear risks and uncertainties in returns.

A critical institutional arrangement impacting investment performance and determining the success of management of pension funds is the governance structure of a pension fund. In the broadest sense, governance refers to the "processes and structures used to direct and manage the affairs of the pension plan, in accordance with the best interests of the plan participants" (Palacios, 2002). The board of directors is essentially the only available control mechanism in public pensions, and so the creation of a board that has the appropriate incentives to be an effective monitor and manager of a fund is an essential issue in governance.

A government organization is not necessary a good manager, since the targets of government might be different from those of participants. A fund manager from government sectors may take into consideration not only the investment return but also the politics of the country. Iglesias and Palacios (2000) and Kaufmann et al. (2002) have shown that investment performance of asset allocation decisions based on broad socio-political considerations are consistently lower than the interest rate paid by banks to individual savings accounts in those same countries.

13. Conclusion

Reforms in public pension system in China in the past thirty years have followed the guiding principles of reducing benefits, strengthening the link between contributions and benefits and expanding coverage. As more and more people are covered by one type of pension scheme or another, a number of problems and foreseeable challenges have come to the fore, such as an aging population, high contribution rate, disparity in benefits and low investment return on pension funds. Hence, there have been many studies that focused on the reform of China's pension system.

Barr and Diamond (2010) have proposed a nationwide system of tax-financed (non-contributory) pensions, awarded on the basis of age and residence to everyone. Fiscal sustainability is achieved by balancing the level of benefit and the earliest eligibility age. Sin (2005) has focused on parametric reforms, for example, increasing the retirement age, and accumulating an adequate contingency reserve to absorb economic and demographic shocks in the short and medium terms.

It should be noted that reforming the pension system relies on comprehensive social and economic reforms. The ability of an aging society to afford its elderly people is dependent on productivity increases. Therefore, the fundamental solution to solving the aging problem lies with increasing human capital investment; changing economic growth patterns, e.g., transferring labor from low-productivity sectors to higher productivity sectors; and increasing effective labor supply. As for fairness and equality in pension benefits, a pension system should be judged by whether it gives individuals a free choice. For a compulsory pension system, there must be built-in incentives to raise returns on investment. Using the capital market to increase returns on pension funds is a necessity. A sound capital market can yield higher returns on pension funds, but pension funds should not be put into the capital market for the sake of improving capital market. The intrinsic problems in China's capital market will become worse if pension funds are channeled into it. Pension fund investment should also not be confined to domestic capital markets. The key is to have sound governance for public pension funds.

References

Barr, N., 2000. Reforming Pensions: Myths, Truths, and Policy Choices. IMF Working Paper, WP/00/139.

Barr, N. and P. Diamond, 2010. Pension Reform in China: Issues, Options and Recommendations.

Bailey, C. and J. Turner, 2001. Strategies to Reduce Contribution Evasion in Social Security Financing. *World Development*, 29: 385–393.

Feng, J., X. Zhang and T. Zhang, 2010. Will Globalization Degrade Social Insurance? A Study Based on Chinese Cross-Provincial Differences. *Journal of World Economy* (in Chinese) 11: 37–53.

Feng, J. and Y. Guo, 2011. A Study on Government Subsidy on New Rural Pension Scheme. *Chongqing Social Sciences* (in Chinese), 7: 50–58.

Feng, J. and S. Zhang, 2012. The Effect of Contribution Rate of Social Insurance on Firm's Compliance: A Study Based on the Policy of Shanghai. *Journal of Shanghai Economic Study* (in Chinese), 3: 47–55.

Garrett, G., 1998. Global Markets and National Politics: Collision Course or Virtuous Circle. *International Organization*, 52(4): 787–824.

Garrett, G. and D. Mitchell, 2001. Globalization, Government Spending and Taxation in OECD. *European Journal of Political Research*, 39: 145–177.

Gillion, C., J. Turner, C. Bailey and D. Latulippe, 2000. Social Security Pensions: Development and Reform. *International Labor Organization*, pp. 27–100.

Gruber, J., K. Milligan and D. Wise, 2009. Social Security Programs and Retirement Around the World: The Relationship to Youth Employment Introduction and Summary. NBER Working paper No. 14647.

He, L.X., 2008. The Public Pension System Reform in China: An Institutional and Empirical Analysis of the Economic System Transition Period. University of Tokyo Press.

Herd, R., Yu-Wei Hu and V. Koen, 2010. Providing Greater Old-Age Security in China. ECO/WKP 6 (www.oecd.org/eco/surveys/china).

Huber, E., 2001. *Development and Crisis of the Welfare State*. Chicago, IL: University of Chicago.

Iglesias, A. and R.J. Palacios, 2000. Managing Public Pension Reserves (Part 1). The World Bank.

Kaufman, D., A. Kraay and P. Zoido-Lobaton, 1999. Governance Matters. Working paper, The World Bank.

Mishra, R., 1999. *Globalization and the Welfare State*. Northampton, MA: Edward Elgar.

Nyland, C., R. Smyth and C. Zhu, 2006. What Determines the Extent to Which Employers Will Comply with Their Social Security Obligations? Evidence from Chinese Firm-level Data. *Social Policy & Administration*, 40(2): 196–214.

Palacios, R., 2002. Managing Public Pension Reserves Part Two: Lessons from Five Recent OECD Initiatives. The World Bank.

Rudra, N., 2002. Globalization and the Decline of the Welfare State in Less-Developed Countries. *International Organization*, 56(2): 411–445.

Sin, Y., 2005. China: Pension Liabilities and Reform Options for Old Age Insurance. The World Bank Working Paper, No. 2005-1.

Wang, Y., D. Xu, Wang Z. and F. Zhai, 2000. Implicit Pension Debt, Transition Cost, Options and Impact of China's Pension Reform — A Computable General Equilibrium Analysis. World Bank, Policy Research Working Paper.

World Bank, DRC of China, 2012. China 2030: Building a Modern, Harmonious, and Creative High-income Society.

Yuan, Z. and Q. Chen, 2010. A Simulation and Proposal of Incorporating Migrant Workers into Shanghai's Urban Old-age Insurance System. *Demographics and Economy* (in Chinese), 6: 40–46.

Yuan, Z., Z. Li and J. Feng, 2009. Pension Benefit in Urbanization. *Journal of Nankai Economic Study*, 4: 3–14.

Zhang, W., 2007. Further Reform of China's Pension System: A Realistic Alternative Option to Fully Funded Individual Accounts. *Asian Economic Papers*, 6: 112–135.

Unraveling the Gridlock on Fiscal Reform in China: Government, Market and Central-local Relations[*]

Yan Zhang

1. Introduction

For a country with vast territories, a huge population and enormous regional differences, maintaining stability and dynamism in the overall economy is a challenge that has plagued China for thousands of years. A decentralized central-local governance structure is hence a necessity in China. The allocation of fiscal power and the corresponding demarcation of government power is an important element of the central-local government relationship in China. The local economic development incentive that originated with fiscal decentralization has been credited as the main impetus for economic growth in the past 30-odd years. The fiscal contract system reform in the 1980s opened the door to overall macro economic reform. Since the tax reform and tax-sharing reform carried out in 1994, the fiscal relationship between central and local governments has not been changed much. But with the decline in the share of local government revenue and the widening of the provincial gap between revenue and expenditure, along with the funding pressures brought by economic restructuring, there have been more and more calls for reforms in central-local fiscal relations. Is it conceivable that a restructuring in central-local fiscal relation could stimulate a successful

[*] We are grateful to the Humanities and Social Science Research Foundation (08JJD790151) and the National Philosophy Social Science Big Project Foundation (11&ZD003) for their support. The research for this paper was undertaken as part of the *Government and Market: Self-regulation and National Governance* Research Series of the third phase of Pushing Forward Social Studies Program of the 985 Project at Fudan University. We thank the Fudan Database and Yang Yanmin for assistance.

economic transition for the next 5 to 10 years, and, therefore, maintain social harmony?

There are several fundamental issues in central-local fiscal relation in China that need to be resolved. The heavy reliance of the local governments on land sales to finance their operations has often put them at odds with the macroeconomic adjustments and economic reforms proposed by the central government. Competition among the regions has intensified local protectionism; the basic public services bearing are provided inadequately; and the uneven development among the regions is not addressed. These issues are all connected to the allocation of revenue resources and expenditure obligations between the central and local governments. Clearly defining the relationship between the government and the market, improving local governments' revenue-collecting capacity, and demarcating the respective expenditure responsibilities of the central government and the local governments will improve greatly the equality and efficiency of the central-local fiscal arrangements. The strengthening of public supervision of government actions is also fundamental to solving the gridlock facing the central and local governments.

2. Rapidly Rising Fiscal Revenue and the Room for Tax Relief

China's consolidated budgetary fiscal revenue in 2011 was 10.4 trillion yuan (an increase of 24.8 percent from the previous year), and amounted to 25.7 percent of GDP. Local fiscal revenue and expenditure in 31 provinces, autonomous regions and municipalities (excluding Hong Kong, Macau and Taiwan) was 5.24 trillion yuan and 10.89 trillion yuan, accounting for 50.5 percent and 84.8 percent of the national levels respectively. Tax rebate and transfer from central to local governments totaled 3.99 trillion yuan (an increase of 23.4 percent over 2010), and represented 36.6 percent of the local government's fiscal expenditure.

On the revenue side, national fiscal revenue stands at a high level and is expanding very fast; and the bulk of the increase in fiscal revenue is held at the central government level while local governments, especially those in under-developed regions, face stringent budgetary constraints. Figures 1 and 2 show the increase in national fiscal revenue from 1978 to 2010. In the period 2000–2010, the annual growth rate of

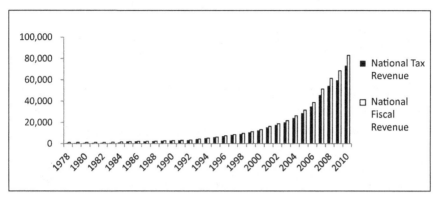

Source: *China Statistics Annals 2011.*

Figure 1. Increases in National Fiscal Revenue and Tax Revenue (1978–2010).

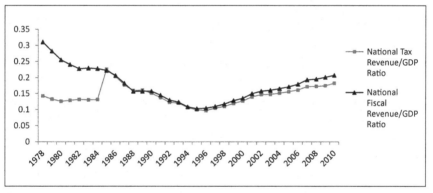

Source: *China Statistics Annals 2011.*

Figure 2. China Fiscal Revenue and Tax Revenue: Ratio to GDP (1978–2010).

budgetary fiscal revenue was 20 percent, with tax revenue increasing at an annual rate of 19.2 percent, representing 1.3 times the growth of GDP. The budgetary fiscal revenue in 2009 accounted for 20.1 percent of GDP, and total revenue, including both budgetary and extra-budgetary revenue, stood at 22 percent of GDP.[1]

---

[1] Judged by IMF standards, full-spectrum government revenue exceeds 13 trillion yuan, accounting for 34 percent of GDP (*Frontier Study on Chinese Economy*, 2011).

If China's rapid economic growth qualifies as a "miracle," then the growth of fiscal revenue at a pace two to three times as fast as GDP growth is a "miracle plus." This "miracle plus" phenomenon has sparked debates as to what underlies this rapid increase in revenue and whether the overall tax burden is too heavy. After adjusting for inflation, structural differences in GDP, and the progressivity in tax rate, the vast scope of China's tax with fewer and fewer loopholes has been found to be an important contributing factor to the rapidly rising tax revenue (Gao, 2006). The increases in tax enforcement efficiency have been influenced by the rapid growth in expenditure and by new fiscal incentives (Lv and Fan, 2006). The tax burden varies across regions, with that in the western and under-developed regions at relatively high levels (Ma and Yu, 2003), an outcome that is related to fiscal incentive and tax base constraints — an issue that we will discuss later.

The relatively high tax burden naturally creates negative incentives for businesses and individuals, and this high tax burden should be recognized as a signal of space for restructuring the tax system. Research indicates that, prior to 2002, China's property tax categories and income taxes have not played a role in redistributing income (Li and Geng, 2005; Liu and Ma, 2002), using macro-economic statistics from 1985 to 1999, found that the taxes on capital and labor reduced total factor productivity growth, while the taxes on consumption raised investment rate without impacting labor supply but impacting positively on total factor productivity. They have therefore proposed reducing taxes on capital and labor and increasing taxes on consumption to meet revenue need; and advised against a fast shift to a tax system that is mainly based on the income tax.

At the policy level, the corporate income tax for foreign-owned enterprises and domestic enterprises were integrated in 2007 to provide a more level playing field for domestic businesses; and the re-orientation of the value added tax from production to consumption in 2009 has reduced redundant taxation.[2] The experiments on the transformation of

---

[2] Productive value added tax does not allow the cost used to purchase the fixed assets (including yearly depreciation) to be deducted from the sales of commodities and services, while the consumptive value added tax allows the cost used to purchase material and fixed assets in the current period to be deducted.

business tax into value added tax and the elimination of some administrative fees have indicated that these changes would create a positive incentive for tax-paying bodies.

3. Low Local Revenue, High Central-local Transfer Payments

Against the background of rapidly rising fiscal revenue, local governments are complaining that the increasing pool of fiscal revenue has not been distributed reasonably. Figure 3 shows the ratio of local revenue and expenditure against the national total from 1978 to 2010. The share of local fiscal revenue has stayed low since 1994. It went from 71.9 percent in 1992 to 44.3 percent in 1994, to 51.1 percent in 1997, and then to 50.8 percent in 2011.

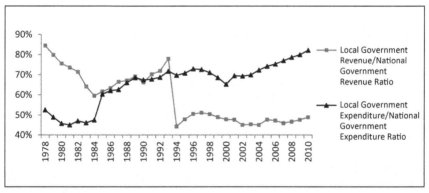

Source: *China Statistics Annals 2011.*

Figure 3. The Percentage of Local Fiscal Revenue and Spending to National Fiscal Revenue and Spending (1978–2010).

The share of local expenditure to national expenditure has been increasing since 1984, albeit erratically. It went from less than 50 percent in 1984 to 70.8 percent in 1995, to 65.3 percent in 2000, and to 82.2 percent in 2010. The result is that the amount of central-to-local transfers has been increasing since 1994.

Figure 4 breaks down the central-to-local fiscal transfers going to the eastern, interior and western regions. The fiscal transfers going to

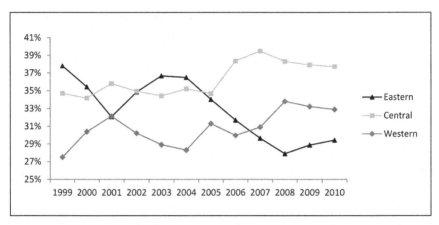

Note: Eastern regions include Beijing, Tianjin, Hebei, Liaoning, Shanghai, Jiangsu, Zhejiang, Fujian, Shandong, Guangdong, Guangxi, Hainan; Interior regions include Shanxi, Inner Mongolia, Jilin, Heilongjiang, An'Hui, Jiangxi, Henan, Hubei, Hunan; Western regions include Chongqing, Sichuan, Guizhou, Yunnan, Tibet, Shanxi, Gansu, Qinghai, Ningxia, Xinjiang.
Source: China Fiscal Statistics Annals.

Figure 4. Share of Net Transfer Payments from Central Government to Eastern, Interior and Western Regions (1999–2010).

the central and western regions have increased since 2002 when the Western Region Development Program was started. The share of central-local transfers received by the eastern region, central region and western region was, respectively, 29.4%, 37.7% and 32.9% in 2010.

The central-local tax rebate policies that were enacted in 1994 ensured that developed regions got more non-corresponding transfer payments, which led to the result that at least before 2002, transfer payments widened regional income differences (Raiser, 1998; Ma and Yu, 2003). Tsui (2005) found that differences in non-agricultural taxes were the main cause of fiscal inequality, with income tax accounting for 21 percent of the fiscal inequality and tax rebate and transfers for 20 percent of fiscal inequality. On the whole, the current transfer payment system in China needs improvement.

The tax-sharing reform in 1994 divided taxes into central taxes, local taxes and central-local shared taxes. The value added tax is a central-local shared tax, with 75 percent of tax revenue from domestic VAT going to the central government and the remaining going to local governments; and all import VAT revenue goes to the central govern-ment. Business tax is a local tax with all revenue going to local govern-ment except those taxes paid by the Railway Bureau. Before 2002, personal income tax was a local tax. After the 2002 income tax sharing reform, its revenue was split evenly between central and local govern-ments. After 2003, its revenue was split by 60/40 between the central and local government. Corporate income tax was originally paid according to the locale of the businesses. After 2002, it was shared by the central

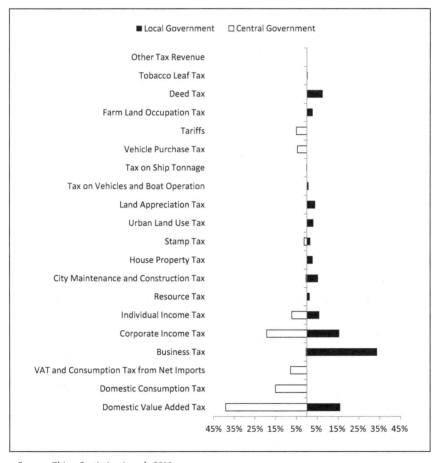

Source: *China Statistics Annals 2010.*

Figure 5. Categories and Ratio of Central-local Tax Revenue.

and local government like personal income tax. Thus, all local taxes are small taxes and their revenues lack stability. The outcome is that the local governments' dependence on land sales for revenue was deepened. Figure 5 reports the categories of tax revenue for the central and local government, and the share of each type of tax in total tax revenue in 2010.

The 1994 tax-sharing reform eliminated the "enrich the local business and enriching the local people" incentive to the local governments (that was introduced by the fiscal contract system practiced in the 1980s). It now motivated the local officials to step up tax-collecting efforts and raise the share of central government taxes in order to be evaluated favorably by the performance criterion set by the central government. Chen et al. (2002) concluded that tax-collecting efforts were over-stimulated, turning tax-collecting practices into "grabbing hands." Wang and Gong (2009) found a tendency by local governments to expand non-tax revenue.

4. Huge Local Expenditures, Low Spending Efficiency, and Low Priority for Education

The tax-sharing reform in 1994 did not change the spending obligations of central and local governments. The spending obligations of local governments were essentially the same as in the 1980s. However, the fiscal situation of 1980s featured strong local fiscal power and weak central fiscal power and the local government took over many obligations of the central government. In 2011, the budgetary government expenditure accounted for 31.8 percent of national GDP figures, of which 85 percent was local expenditure. In 2004, capital construction was 12 percent of fiscal expenditure and the share for expenditure on science, education and culture was 18.1 percent.[3]

A low ratio of public services expenditure is the main inadequacy in fiscal expenditure in China. For example, the Education Reform and Development Guidelines of 1993 proposed that educational spending

---

[3] The ratio has risen to 25.9 percent in 2011, showing that the spending composition of government is transitioning toward public services for improving people's livelihood.

should account for 4 percent of GDP in 2000. National fiscal expenditure in education rose to above 3 percent of GDP for the first time in 2001 and increased slowly to reach 3.7 percent in 2010. Compared with world average education spending, educational spending in China is inadequate. This is unfortunate because Guo and Jia (2009) have found that increasing elementary education spending would contribute to the accumulation of non-skilled labor capital and higher success at the higher education level, thereby contributing to overall human capital accumulation and economic growth. It is also unfortunate that educational resources have been distributed unevenly between regions and between rural and urban areas. Chen, Zhang and Yang (2010) found that educational spending difference was the most determining factor of income gap between rural and urban areas.

The central government has handed over too much of the responsibility on education to the local governments. Educational inequality is a serious problem: 85 percent of provincial educational spending was funded by the provinces themselves, while 85 percent of sub-provincial educational spending was funded at municipality and county level. The bulk of fiscal expenditure on compulsory education was still in the hands of government below the provincial level.

Zhang, Li and Xia (2010) have shown that the decentralization in fiscal spending on education has no significant impact on overall local education, but has significant negative impact on educational output in rural areas and positive impact on urban educational output. As poorly-educated parents are more likely to have poorly-educated children, the gap in educational quality between regions and between urban and rural areas would persist and therefore is detrimental to balanced development. So fiscal power on education should be further centralized in accordance with the amendments articles to the laws on compulsory education. Moreover, the central government should further invest in education in rural areas because the marginal output of educational investment in rural areas is far higher than in urban areas.

Fu and Zhang (2007) found that the competition among local governments for foreign direct investment has exacerbated the tendency to over-emphasize capital construction and de-emphasize human capital investment and public services. They also found that the strategies of invigorating the country through science and education and through the Western Development Program strategies has not helped to raise investment in education. Inadequate provision of public service in China is tightly associated with its political and fiscal incentive towards local governments. We will discuss this channel more in Section 6.

5. The Risks of Hidden Local Debt

In response to the 2008 global financial crisis, the Chinese central government put forth 10 measures to boost domestic demand. The plan amounted to 4 trillion yuan, with central government increasing investment by 1.18 trillion yuan, and the local government investing the rest. The central government helped the local governments get the funds by allowing the issuance of policy loans, local corporate bonds, and issuing local government bonds through the central fiscal authorities. The upshot was that the capital-raising vehicles of local governments exploded in number. According to the *Banking Regulatory Commission*, 8,221 investment platform companies were set up by the end of June, 2009. Of them 4,907 were investment companies at county levels. The *2010 China Regional Financial Report* shows that by the end of 2010, China had more than 10 thousand capital-raising platforms owned by local government, an increase of 25 percent from 2008 levels. The *Auditing Report on Local Governments* shows that only 54 county governments did not incur any debt, and the total debt of local governments in China was 10.72 trillion yuan. Of the total, the local governments were responsible for repaying 6.71 trillion, a ratio of 62.6 percent; the ratio of debts with obligations under the bond account was 21.8 percent; and other debts with possible bailout obligations were 15.6 percent. The ratio of direct debt to local fiscal revenue was 52.25 percent.[4]

---

[4] In 2010, the ratio between central and local financial debt (RMB 17.45 trillion) and GDP is 43.8%, which does not exceed the international warning line of 60%. Among them, 78 municipal governments and 99 county-level governments have responsibility for paying debts which are more than 100% of their local GDP.

Because local government debt has many forms and lack supervision, official statistics may understate the true scale of debts.[5] In fact, although local governments were banned from issuing bonds before 2009, local governments have a great incentive to do so. This is especially serious in county and village-level government. As early as 1999, statistics based on survey in Hunan showed that 88.2 percent of village and county-level governments had debt, with each indebted rural county averaging 3.63 million yuan in debt. The most debt-ridden county was 51.11 million in debt, the equal of more than a decade's fiscal revenue. Some counties and villages had even used up their 2003 budget ahead of time in 1999 (Yao and Yang, 2003).

The emergence of local government debt trouble is unavoidable because China has not solved the problem of establishing the banking system's independence from the local governments. In the early 1990s, the fiscal and central banking reform had severed the horizontal link between local governments and banks and therefore prevented debt monetization. But the expansion of local debt has given rise to the effective monetization of local fiscal deficits because bad debt incurred by local governments will be paid by central government through state credit. Therefore, it is usual for banks and local government to form investment vehicles to borrow. Moreover, without democratic decision-making and supervision, the local governments tend to pursue short-term gains at the expense of future solvency. This pursuit of better short-term performance has worsened the explosion of local debt.

The development of local capital-raising platforms and the rise in bad debts from the 4 trillion fiscal stimulus policy was an act of the central government handing over its macro-regulation responsibilities to the local and even county governments. The outcome of macroeconomic

---

[5] Moody's International Rating Company estimated that China's local debt was underestimated 3.5 trillion by using central bank statistics and statistics from the auditing bureau. It thought that the underestimated debts ran a higher risk of default. A recent message is that the China Banking Regulatory Commission could have wrongly rated 1.8 trillion yuan worth of loans raised by agencies and companies of the local governments as sound loans. And some banks have falsely classified government subsidies as project cash flows. Source: http://finance.eastmoney.com/news/1345,20120326198099639.html

regulation functions being performed at the micro-level is that the 3-trillion-yuan local investment target turned into a 10-trillion-yuan local investment phenomenon, threatening the stability of the banking system and the overall economy. Because of differences in capital-raising capacities among regions, the 4-trillion stimulus project widened the developmental gaps between regions.

According to statistics released by the auditing bureau, 4 trillion worth of local debt (37.8 percent of total) will become due in China from 2011 to 2013. At a time when fiscal revenue growth is slowing, land sales revenue is dropping and the returns on infrastructure are stagnant, the repayment of debts is a big challenge for the local governments. Currently the central government has adopted rollover operations to help local governments tide over the first debt payment peak period. In October 2011, the State Council approved local debt-issuing power for Shanghai, Zhejiang, Guangdong and Shenzhen, and this is a significant step towards regulating local government debts. Judging from the initial bond-selling situations, banks were the major buyers. The important point to make is that the expansion of local debts is directly related to the central-local fiscal decentralization structure and the urge to boost the economy on local governments' side. Reforming central-local fiscal relations and enhancing transparency in local budgetary processes are fundamental to solving local debt problems.

6. Four Landmines Created by the Interaction between Vertical Political Management and Decentralized Economic Management

In comparing China and Russia's decentralization performance, Blanchard and Shleifer (2001) found that political differences made up an important dimension. As two great countries with backgrounds steeped in planned economy traditions, China and Russia adopted different styles of supervision of public officials. Russian local officials can defy federal government orders, while central government orders held absolute sway for local officials in China. The official appointment and dismissal systems, the performance evaluation system, the retirement system, tenure system, and local posting system have been important mechanisms with which the Communist Party of China (CPC) controls its own cadres. The short supply of promotion opportunities created positive competition among government officials of the same ranks to meet the social-economic goals laid out by the central government. Of course, the political background and connections of officials could also be important factors in influencing promotion decisions (Tao et al., 2010).

Such a vertical governance structure, however, is highly reliant on the highest-level government being correct in its policy choices and in its implementation protocol. Otherwise the error would be magnified at each level of implementation.[6] Furthermore, while the vertical political management system and the decentralized economic system have interacted to generate the sizzling growth of the Chinese economy, this same interaction has also laid four landmines on the path of current as well as future economic restructuring and sustainable development.

The first landmine is that the emphasis on the growth rate of local GDP in the performance evaluation system has distorted the actions of local governments and local officials. In order to develop local economies and thereby get higher performance rankings, local governments would likely resort to protect obsolete industries, restrict market access, and even turn a blind eye to some illegal activities and undertake needless beautification projects (facelift projects). This behavior has negative consequences for long-term economic growth both regionally and nationally.

The second landmine lies in the necessity that a local government has to rely on local businesses to develop the local economy. The interests of local businesses can run counter to the short-to-medium term objectives of central governments while according well with the medium-to-long term goals of local governments. These local governments are likely to carry on local policies that are opposed to the short-term central government policies, especially in resisting contractionary macroeconomic policies. The regional competition in GDP maximization would

---

[6] The four trillion economic stimulus plan in China which led to risks of local government debts is a striking negative example.

thus result in a higher frequency and bigger magnitudes of national economic fluctuations.

Another scenario is that the multiple goals of the governments can be competing goals, e.g., economic growth can be incompatible with social justice, income equality and environmental protection in the short run. In such situations, the local governments are likely to lean towards policies that yield immediate and more measurable results, while acting half-heartedly on the other goals.

The third landmine from the interaction between a vertical political structure and a decentralized economic structure is the creation of an innate desire by the local government to intervene in the economy. The political structure is high duplicative, with myriad of government agencies and ministries running down from the central to various local levels, and it is in the self-interest of the various government agencies to prevent the reduction of government power. So, in order to realize regional development goals, a local government has the incentive to use its own manpower (rather than delegate the task to the private sector) in order to get a bigger budget and translate that into measurable governance results. Therefore, a local government is always unwilling to cut jobs for civil servants. Meanwhile, facing economic competition, local governments who are used to planned economic systems are inclined to use government investment to promote regional development. Some under-developed regions have even resorted to raising taxes to get more financing. All of these actions are harmful for private-sector development.

The fourth landmine is the uneven provision of public services by the local government. Since local governments are focused on short-term economic goals, the project that cannot yield quick economic returns are likely to be neglected. The declining share of government spending on agriculture, science, education and culture stands testimony to this point. Fu and Zhang (2007) have shown that it was exactly the fierce competition between local governments that has exacerbated the negligent attitude local governments held towards human capital investment and public services. The local governments are biased toward infrastructure investment that could quickly boost GDP figures and increase employment. The distorted composition of public services is not only reflected in the structural makeup of government spending, but also in the differences in regional and urban-rural spending on the same items. Because infrastructure investment brings bigger economic returns in developed areas and urban areas, public services also widen regional differences and the urban-rural gap.

In brief, the centralization of revenue and decentralization of expenditure from the tax-sharing reform in 1994 has institutionalized imbalances in power that have led to mounting local public debts, distorted revenue and expenditure structure, the overreach of local governments and poor public services. Zhang and Gong (2005) have found that the positive effects of fiscal decentralization in middle and western regions are relatively small, especially in middle regions. The fiscal decentralization practiced in China, in fact, widens regional gaps and provides inadequate public services; and the social instability and wide regional differences are posing significant threats to the stable development of the Chinese economy.

7. Three Landmines from Government-Dominated Urbanization

In 2011, China's urbanization rate exceeded 50 percent, a full 20 percent up from the 1990 level. At least in the previous period, the local-government-dominated urbanization has brought about win-win situations. For local governments, urbanization brought both budgetary and extra-budgetary revenue as well as new urban development and industrial upgrading, which would translate into higher economic growth and better ranking in performance evaluations. For local residents, government-dominated urbanization quickened the process of urbanization, raised living standards, income and improved living conditions. For businesses, urbanization improved infrastructure and increased returns on investment on the margins. But government-dominated urbanization also lays landmines in the path of China's economic growth.

The first landmine is the creation of the property bubble. It must be pointed out that land sales also increase revenue from the local land appreciation tax, urban maintenance tax, urban land use tax, stamp tax, property tax and land transfer fee. Indirectly, the development of relevant industries and the overall economic growth increase business tax and income tax revenues. In 2010, the tax revenue of local governments relating to the property market totaled 826.61 billion yuan, accounting for 25.28% of local tax revenue. From 2001 to 2010, China's land transfer fees increased 24 times, reaching 2.9 trillion in 2010.

Land sales tie together the financial interests of the local government, the property sector and the local financial institutions. The selling of land at high prices has caused China's property market to go through several bouts of price hikes and affected people's livelihood very negatively. After several rounds of fruitless macroeconomic regulation, the central government has imposed stringent restriction policies on sales. The smaller amount of land sales and lower land prices have meant lower revenue for the local government, which means that they have less ability to service the bank loans that were taken out for property development. And the drop in the prices of houses threatens the solvency of many local financial institutions further because investors now have the incentive to default on loans that exceed the value of the property.

The second landmine is the unintentional neglect of industrial development. Because land sales yield immediate economic returns, local government can easily get addicted to land sales and reduce its attention on the growth of the industrial and service sectors. Urban renewal, building new urban districts and turning rural residents into non-rural residents can boost economic development and improve people's livelihood in the short term but, without the sustaining force of real economies, the newly urbanized population would face a lack of employment opportunities, thus hindering further urbanization and economic growth. Furthermore, when urbanization proceeds too fast in an area, the rise in land prices and housing prices would stifle innovations in economic development (*Frontier Study on the Chinese Economy*, 2011). It is therefore important to assure that the government-dominated urbanization would be built on job-creating industrial development.

The third landmine in government-dominated urbanization is that the errors in urbanization strategies carried by local governments could exacerbate interpersonal, interregional and urban-rural income gaps. Inadequate compensation in land appropriation and insufficient job opportunities in the new city will harm the farmers' interests. And urban development will push up the cost of living, including housing prices, thus making poor people and those without properties much poorer in relative terms. These two groups of people had the costs of government-dominated urbanization thrust upon them involuntarily. Finally, Roberts et al. (2012) have shown that returns obtained through infrastructure such as roads are reaped more by rich regions; and so, if there are barriers to population flows, then the outcome is widened regional income gaps.

In short, relying on land sales for local fiscal revenue is not sustainable and can easily distract the government from industrial development, push up property prices, and worsen regional developmental gaps in the long run. The local government must therefore reduce their intervention in urbanization.

8. Reform Measure 1: Demarcate Clearly the Fiscal Spending Obligations of the Central Government and the Local Governments

The spending obligations of the government at the different levels must be sharply demarcated in order to achieve efficiency and fairness. First, the central government should take charge and strengthen vertical control over macroeconomic regulation, judiciary affairs, supervision over the safety and quality of food, consumer and medical products. Second, in matters that bear on the urban-rural gap, intervention and management from the central government should be reinforced, e.g., it is advisable that the central government takes over from provincial governments, the role of coordinating compulsory education in rural areas. Third, power to decide on all other matters should be delegated to the local governments, and it is important that this delegation of power does not stop at the provincial level. The prefecture, county, village, and town governments must also be empowered to decide on expenditure so that the efficiency of fiscal expenditures below the provincial level can be raised.

9. Reform Measure 2: Demarcate Clearly the Revenue-collection Power of the Central Government and the Local Governments

First, at the present moment, the tax system in China mainly consist of turnover taxes, the share of direct taxes should be increased so that taxes on transactions and incomes become two equal pillars of the state revenue system. Even if the overall tax system is not going to shift to an income-tax-focused system, individual information should be better collected to pave the way for transitioning from taxing personal incomes to taxing household incomes.

Second, the value added tax should be extended to service sectors in order to promote the development of service sectors and industrial restructuring.

Third, the types of taxes that experience strong fluctuations in receipt or that are subject to the strong influences of external factors should be designated as central taxes. The types of taxes that are stable in receipt or that have low degrees of exposure to external influences (e.g., property tax for example) should be local taxes.

Fourth, there should be an increase in the local government's autonomy to adjust the tax code and to use tax policies to intervene in the economy.

Fifth, because transfer payments are, in general, problematic on account of efficiency and fairness, local governments should be allowed to levy locale-specific taxes to reduce reliance on land sales and to promote economic development.

Sixth, giving more funds in the form of transfer payments to the backward regions and backward rural areas, is important, but efficiency and fairness should be closely monitored.

10. Reform Measure 3: Implement Democratic Supervision in a Timely Manner

The democratic practices carried out in China's rural areas (Martinez-Bravo et al., 2011) have shown that direct election of village officials has:

- made officials more responsive to the calls for spending in accordance with villagers' needs,

- changed the previous top-down obedience structure, and
- maintained political stability.

Increasing political participation can also:

- reduce the bias for urban development, and
- narrow the urban-rural gap.

In short, widening political participation has played a positive role in fostering responsive governance and enhancing social harmony.

The likelihood of different levels of governments being hijacked by special interest groups is connected with the degree of organized popular participation in government decision-making process (Bardhan and Mookerjee, 2000). Though rural residents account for around 60 percent of China's population, rural residents' rate of organized political participation is low both at the national level and the county level, while the rate for urban residents in local decision-making is higher than in national decision-making. So enhancing political participation of rural residents will reduce the likelihood of local governments being hijacked by urban interest groups and, hence, contribute to the narrowing of the urban-rural gap.

References

Bardhan, P. and Mookerjee, D., 2000. Capture and Governance at Local and National Levels. *American Economic Review*, 90(2): 135–139.

Blanchard, Oliver and Shleifer, Andrei, 2001. Federalism with and without Political Centralization: China versus Russia. *IMF Staff Papers*, 48(4): 171–179.

Chen, Binkai, Zhang, Pengfei and Yang, Rudai, 2010. Government Education Input, Human Capital Investment, and the Gap between Urban and Rural Incomes in China. *Management World*, Issue 1: 36–43.

Chen, Kang, Hillman, A.L. and Gu, Qingyang, 2002. Fiscal Recentralization and Behavioral Change of Local Governments. *China Economic Quarterly*, Issue 4: 111–130.

Fu, Yong and Zhang, Yan, 2007. Chinese-Style Decentralization and Fiscal Expenditure Structure Deflection: The Cost of Growth over Competition. *Management World*, Issue 3: 4–12.

Gao, Peiyong, 2006. Riddle of the Sustained and Rapid Tax Increase in China. *Economic Research Journal*, Issue 12: 13–23.

Guo, Qingwang and Jia, Junxue, 2009. Public Education Policy, Economic Growth and Human Capital Premium. *Economic Research Journal*, Issue 10: 22–35.

Li, Shaorong and Geng, Ying, 2005. The Effects of Tax Revenue Structure on Economic Growth and Income Distribution. *Economic Research Journal*, Issue 5: 118–126.

Liu, Rongcang and Ma, Shuanyou, 2002. On Taxation and Economic Growth — The Effects of Taxation Imposed on Labor, Capital and Consumption. *Social Sciences in China*, Issue 1: 67–76.

Lv, Bingyang and Fan, Yong, 2006. The Progress and Characters among Provinces of Tax Collection and Administration Efficiency after the Tax Revenue Sharing System. *The Journal of World Economy*, Issue 10: 69–77.

Ma, Shuanyou and Yu, Hongxia, 2003. A Case Study of Local Tax and Regional Economic Growth. *Management World*, Issue 3: 36–43.

Martinez-Bravo, Monica, Gerard Padró i Miquel, Nancy Qian and Yang, Yao, 2011. Do Local Elections in Non-Democracies Increase Accountability? Evidence from Rural China. NBER Working Paper 2011, 16948, http://www.nber.org/papers/w16948.

Qiao, Baoyun, Martinez-Vazquez, Jorge and Xu, Yongsheng, 2008. The Tradeoff Between Growth and Equity in Decentralization Policy: China's Experience. *Journal of Development Economics*, 86(1): 112–128.

Raiser, M., 1998. Subsidising Inequality: Economic Reforms, Fiscal Transfers and Convergence Across Chinese Provinces. *Journal of Development Studies*, 34(3): 1–26.

Research Group on China's Economic Growth, 2011. Urbanization, Fiscal Expansion and Economic Growth. *Economic Research Journal*, Issue 11: 4–20.

Roberts, M., Deichmann, U., Fingleton, B. and Shi, T., 2012. Evaluating China's Road to Prosperity: A New Economic Geography Approach. *Regional Science and Urban Economics*, 42(4): 580–594.

Tao, Ran, Su, F.B., Lu, X. and Zhu, Y.M., 2010. Can Economic Growth Bring About Promotion? — Logical Challenge and Provincial Empirical Reassessment of Promotion Tournament Theory. *Management World*, Issue 12: 13–26.

Tsui, K.Y., 2005. Local Tax System, Intergovernmental Transfers and China's Local Fiscal Disparities. *Journal of Comparative Economics*, 33(1): 173–196.

Wang, Zhigang and Gong, Liutang, 2009. Fiscal Decentralization and Non-tax Income of Local Governments: Based on Provincial Fiscal Statistics. *World Economic Papers*, Issue 5: 17–38.

Yao, Yang and Lei, Yang, 2003. System Supply Imbalance and China State Finance. *Strategy and Management*, Issue 3: 27–33.

Zhang, Yan and Gong, Liutang, 2005. The Tax-sharing Reform, Fiscal Decentralization, and Economic Growth in China. *China Economic Quarterly*, Issue 4: 75–108.

Zhang, Yan, Li, Yinglei and Xia, Jijun, 2010. How to Achieve Decentralization in Compulsory Education? — Economic Analysis from Level-to-Level Administration to Unified Planning at Provincial Level. Working Paper, Fudan University.

China's Financial Sector Development: Understanding the Past and Shaping the Future

Liqing Zhang and Xiaofen Tan

1. Introduction

Before 1978, China adopted a highly centralized planned economic system, with a very undeveloped and depressed national banking sector. Specifically, the quantity of production and sales were totally subject to the government's arrangements, and the national bank was more or less a "cashier" rather than an active financial institution that intermediates between the savers and investors. In order to identify correctly China's reform agenda for the financial sector going forward, it is relevant to understand China's experience with financial sector reform over the past 30 years. Roughly speaking, the process of China's financial sector reform can be divided into three stages: the early stage of financial development (1979–1993), the deepening of financial reform (1994–2002), and the adjustment of the financial sector to globalization (2003–present).

2. 1979–1993: The Early Stage of Financial Development

2.1. The establishment of the basic framework of the central bank system and the commercial bank system

On December 1, 1948, the People's Bank of China (PBC) was established as a comprehensive national bank in charge of the currency issuance and credit management. For decades, PBC not only played a role of monetary authorities, but also performed functions of a commercial bank, providing deposit and lending. Since all these commercial banking business were strictly in line with the national economic plan, PBC actually served as the "accountant and cashier" for the Ministry of Finance and the State Planning Commission. In 1984, PBC was transformed into a central bank by transferring its commercial banking business to the Industrial and Commercial Bank of China. The tasks of the restructured PBC were to supervise the financial industry, and to carry out macroeconomic management through two policy instruments: the discount rate on purchasing loans from the commercial banks, and the credit quota that every financial institution is subject to.

The Agricultural Bank of China (ABC) and the Bank of China (BOC) became independent of PBC in 1979; the China Construction Bank (CCB) was made independent in 1983; and the Industrial and Commercial Bank of China (ICBC) became independent in 1984. To complement these four specialized banks, 11 joint-stock banks (such as Bank of Communications, CITIC Industrial Bank, and China Merchants Bank) were established.

2.2. The beginning of the capital market, non-bank financial institutions and financial globalization

China resumed issuing the treasury bonds in 1981; and implemented a pilot program for the transaction of treasury bonds in 61 cities in 1988 to lay the foundation for the development of a secondary market for the treasury bonds. In 1984, commercial banks started to issue financial bonds to fund construction projects. The Shanghai Stock Exchange and Shenzhen Stock Exchange were founded respectively in 1990 and 1991, and the State Council established China Securities Regulatory Commission (CSRC) in 1992 to supervise the securities market. (CSRC lifted the issuance quota on the listing of firms in 2000.)

Various kinds of insurance companies began to spring up from 1985. The American International Assurance Co. Ltd. set up its first China-based branch in Shanghai in 1992, marking the arrival of foreign insurance companies. In 1979, the Bank of China set up a trust consulting department, and the China International Trust and Investment Corporation was founded. In 1981, China Leasing Company was established; and, in 1987, Dongfeng Automobile Finance Company, the first internal finance company of a large enterprise, was set up.

In 1979, the Japan Export-Import Bank established its first representative office in Shanghai, and, in 1981, branches of foreign financial institutions were allowed to operate in the four cities known as the Special Economic Zones (Shenzhen, Zhuhai, Xiamen, and Shantou). In 1991, China introduced special shares (B-shares) that were sold only to foreign individuals and corporate institutes. In 1993, a group of domestic enterprises was listed in the Hong Kong stock market.

3. 1994–2002: The Deepening of Financial Reform

In 1996, PBC established a national unified interbank market; and introduced the treasury bond repurchase system to enable open market operations. In 1998, PBC set up nine trans-provincial branches as well as business management departments in Beijing and Chongqing. The central bank had gradually shifted its major operation tools from direct control through loan quotas to base money management through monetary policy tools used in the developed market economies. PBC also handed over its supervision of securities institutions and insurance companies to new regulatory bodies.

The four major state-owned commercial banks (the Big Four of ABC, BOC, CCB, and ICBC) were not really commercial banks because they also engaged in policy-directed lending. In 1995, their policy-directed lending functions were taken over by three new policy banks: China Development Bank, Export-Import Bank of China and Agricultural Development Bank of China. The four wholly state-owned banks also began re-structuring to strengthen their competitiveness by using asset-liability ratio management, building up loan loss reserves, writing off bad loans, and improving internal management and risk control. In 1999, the non-performing loans of the Big Four were moved to four asset management companies.

The multiple exchange rate system was unified in January 1994 and later that year, branches of foreign financial institutions were allowed in 11 inland central cities. In December 1996, some foreign financial institutions were allowed to conduct RMB-denominated business in Pudong, Shanghai for foreign-funded enterprises and foreign individuals. In 1999, foreign banks were allowed to set up branches in all central cities in China; thereby expanding further the RMB business scope of foreign banks in Shanghai and Shenzhen and in the national interbank funding market. When China entered the WTO in 2001, the opening-up of its financial sector received a boost.

4. 2003-to-Present: Financial Reforms in a More Integrated World

In 2003, the China Banking Regulatory Commission was founded to take over the regulatory function of the PBC over the banking institutions. The separate business regulatory system not only made the financial regulation more professional but also freed the PBC from possible conflict between the dual role of monetary policy and regulatory policy.

After the completion of the recapitalization of the Big Four banks (a process that began in 2003), they have been successfully listed on the stock market (with the state maintaining a dominant controlling share in each), and their governance structure has been improved with the presence of foreign and domestic strategic investors. Three steps have been taken to promote financial innovation in the state commercial banks:

1. Some commercial banks (such as ICBC, CCB, and Bank of Communications) were given permission to set up fund management corporations;
2. Non-financial corporate debt financing tools (such as subordinated bonds of commercial banks, hybrid capital bonds, short-term financing bills, and small to medium-sized enterprise commercial notes) and financial derivatives (such as securities lending, forward rate agreement, and RMB interest rate swap) were launched, and;
3. The working of the commodity futures market was further standardized, and the trading of stock index futures was launched.

On July 21, 2005, China announced that the value of the renminbi would be based on market supply and demand with reference to a basket of currencies. The varieties of financial products in China's foreign exchange market have become increasingly abundant because the restrictions on capital account transactions have been lifted gradually. Greater access to China's financial market has been granted to foreign financial institutions by implementing the QFII (Qualified Foreign Institutional Investor) facility, and allowing foreign institutional investors to issue RMB bonds in the domestic financial market. The minimum share-holding period for overseas shareholders has been shortened from at least 10 years to at least 5 years. In June 2007, the QDII (Qualified Domestic Institutional Investor) facility, which enabled domestic institutions to invest in foreign securities market, was implemented, marking a major step forward for the Chinese securities industry to be more involved in overseas market.

Progress has also been made to allow the appearance of truly privatized domestic financial institutions. In March 2007, China's first village bank — Huimin Village Bank in Yilong County, Sichuan went into operation. On February 29, 2012, Wenzhou's first private capital management company, the Xintong Private Capital Management Company Ltd. of Ouhai District, was approved on a trial basis.

Table 1 shows the state of China's financial sector in 2009 after 30 years of financial reform. China's financial sector has evolved from the sole domination of the People's Bank of China as a regulator and an operator to a more diversified financial institution system. There are now state-owned commercial banks, joint-stock commercial banks, private banks, foreign banks and various non-bank financial institutions such as securities traders, securities companies, insurance companies, trust companies, and rural and urban credit cooperatives.

5. Financial Stock Indicators

The M2/GDP ratio is often adopted to measure the degree of financial deepening in a certain country. This indicator focuses on the extent of monetization of the economy. Generally speaking, the higher the ratio, the better monetized the economy, and the more advanced the financial industry. The M2/GDP ratio in China has grown from 32% in 1978 to 181% in 2011. Table 2 reports that China's ratio of 181% in 2011 is unusually high as the ratio for the USA is 71%, Japan 170%, South

Table 1. The Financial Institution System of China at the end of 2009.

	No. of Institutions	Market Share of Its Assets (%)
Policy banks and China Development Bank	**3**	8.8
Policy banks	(2)	–
China Development Bank	(1)	–
Commercial banks	**238**	77.1
Major commercial banks	(17)	(65.9)
Large commercial banks	(5)	(50.9)
Joint-stock commercial banks	(12)	(15.0)
Urban commercial banks	(143)	(7.2)
Rural commercial banks[1]	(43)	(2.4)
Foreign-funded banks (locally registered)	(35)	(1.7)
Urban credit cooperatives	**11**	0.0
Rural cooperative financial organizations	3,295	11.0
Rural credit cooperatives	(3,056)	(7.0)
Rural cooperative banks	(196)	(1.6)
Rural commercial banks	(43)	(2.4)
Postal Savings Bank of China	**1**	3.4
New rural financial institutions	**172**	–
Village banks	(148)	–
Microfinance firms	(8)	–
Rural mutual cooperatives	(16)	–
Non-bank financial institutions[2]	180	2.0
Asset management companies in the banking industry	(4)	–
Trust companies	(58)	–
Finance companies of enterprise groups	(91)	–
Foreign funded finance companies (locally registered)	(2)	–
Financial lease companies	(12)	–
Currency brokerage companies	(3)	–
Auto finance companies	(10)	–

Note: (1) Due to the double counting of the rural commercial banks under the items *commercial banks* and *rural cooperative financial organizations*, the market shares of the assets held by all Chinese financial institutions add up to 102.3%. (2) Due to the separately regulation among banking, securities and insurance, the numbers of non-bank financial institutions here do not cover the securities company and insurance company.
Source: China Banking Regulatory Commission (CBRC) 2009, Annual Report.

Table 2. International Comparison of the M2/GDP Ratio (%).

Year	China	Japan	South Korea	India	USA	Australia	South Africa	Brazil
2000	135.68	122.44	64.14	52.28	60.53	65.73	52.27	24.06
2001	144.36	125.82	70.78	55.15	64.89	66.89	52.98	24.70
2002	153.75	131.41	72.08	58.82	68.21	68.68	55.41	26.90
2003	162.88	134.88	74	60.24	67.19	70.13	60.45	24.29
2004	158.94	136.41	70.89	61.56	64.56	74.01	62.48	25.42
2005	163.20	139.16	79.23	69.73	61.66	80.27	61.32	27.13
2006	163.07	139.81	82.32	71.80	61.31	89.72	65.45	27.92
2007	161.66	140.29	85.67	75.77	62.01	94.92	69.26	29.36
2008	151.31	146.62	93.77	82.84	64.68	98.32	69.02	35.39
2009	177.83	160.18	117.32	91.38	70.50	103.35	66.23	36.04
2010	180.90	160.92	121.03	95.43	69.39	103.84	63.02	36.14
2011	180.68	170.05	126.47	92.72	71.26	103.95	60.64	39.03

Source: Based on data collected from *International Financial Statistics Yearbook*.

Korea 126%, Australia 104%, Brazil 39%, India 93% and South Africa 61%. China has clearly experienced a great monetization of its economy and significant deepening of its financial market.

It would be wrong, however, to think (from the cross-country comparison in Table 2) that the degree of financial deepening in China is higher than, or, at least, equivalent to that in the developed countries like the USA. The main reason behind the high M2/GDP ratio is that China's underdeveloped capital market has only a very limited variety of investment products. For any country that is growing, the wealth accumulated by its citizens will escalate. The wealth is usually in the form of highly liquid financial assets like deposits, fairly liquid assets like stocks and bonds, and illiquid real assets like properties. When the capital market is underdeveloped, enterprises rely mainly on bank loans to raise funds, resulting in a flood of broad money that causes increasing M2/GDP ratio.

Or, to put it differently, because of the limited scale of capital markets like the bond market and the stock market, the Chinese people cannot invest their accumulated wealth into assets such as corporate bonds and stocks. As a result, they can only hold the bulk of their wealth in the form of bank deposits, which naturally results in the high growth of M2.

The key to interpreting the unusually high M2/GDP ratio in China is to consider M2 as an investment instrument for citizens and enterprises rather than as a medium of exchange. In economies in which funds are raised mainly through bank loans, like China and Japan, the M2/GDP ratio tends to be on the high side. In economies with developed stock markets, like the USA and Europe, the M2/GDP ratio tends to be on the low side. If the total of financial assets that American households possess is used to compare with the nominal GDP, the U.S. ratio would be over 300% which is much higher than China's M2/GDP ratio. If the financial assets that U.S. enterprises possess are also taken into account, the U.S. ratio will be even higher. In other words, the primary reason why M2 is on the high side in China is that the underdevelopment of China's capital market does not give the people sufficient investment instruments.

6. The Financial Flow Indicators

The total social financing refers to the total amount of funds that the real economy receives from the financial system in a year. Table 3 shows that the funds in China come in forms like loans in local and foreign currencies, entrusted loans, trust loans, bank acceptance bills, corporate bonds, stocks of non-financial enterprises, insurance claims, and the property investments of insurance companies. The total social financing has been expanding rapidly, from 2 trillion yuan in 2002 to 14.3 trillion yuan in 2010, which is an annual growth rate of 27.8%.

Table 4 shows that the total social financing has been rendering significantly more support to the economy over time. The ratio of total social financing to GDP is 35.9% in 2010, which is 19.2 percentage points higher than that in 2002.

7. The Structure of External Financing for the Non-financial Sectors

The record of financial sector development in the major developed countries shows that the structure of external financing for the non-

Table 3. Total Social Financing (Unit: billion yuan).

Year	New RMB Loans	New Foreign Currency Loans	New Entrusted Loans	New Trust Loans	New Bank Accepted Bills	Corporate Bond Financing	Equity Financing for Non-Financial Enterprises	Insurance Claims	Property Investments by Insurance Companies	Others	Total
2002	1800	72.4	17.6	–	-68.5	31.3	58.7	41.1	–	–	1952.6
2003	2770	229.1	61.6	–	201.8	54.7	54.7	51.3	–	–	3423.2
2004	2260	137.7	318.4	–	-28.7	51.6	66	60.2	–	–	2865.2
2005	2350	105.9	97.3	–	2.9	200.4	34.3	71.6	–	–	2862.4
2006	3180	100.3	188.5	84.2	152.4	84.2	136.3	84.2	–	–	4010.1
2007	3630	290.2	337.5	171.7	669.2	230.9	479.7	106.6	5.9	–	5921.7
2008	4910	61.8	425.8	315.9	109.9	556.2	336.5	151.1	6.9	–	6874
2009	9590	929.4	675.9	436.5	464.7	1295.6	450.6	169	14.1	70.4	14096.3
2010	7950	414.7	1129.6	386.1	2330.7	1201.1	586.2	185.9	14.3	100.1	14298.6

Source: People's Bank of China, CEIC.

Table 4. Total Social Financing and GDP.

Year	Total Social Financing (Billion Yuan)	GDP (Billion Yuan)	Total Social Financing/ GDP (%)
2002	1953	12048	16.2
2003	3423	13664	25.1
2004	2865	16080	17.8
2005	2862	18713	15.3
2006	4010	22224	18.0
2007	5922	26581	22.3
2008	6874	31404	21.9
2009	14096	34090	41.4
2010	14297	39798	35.9

Source: Bank of China, CEIC.

financial sectors (i.e., households, enterprises, and governments) is always closely linked to the level of economic development. Specifically, as the economy grows, the structure of external financing shifts steadily from indirect financing instruments (such as bank loans) toward direct financing instruments (such as bonds and equity). The present ratio of direct financing to indirect financing in the developed countries is around 7:3.

Table 5 reports the composition of external financing instruments used by the non-financial sector in the 2001–2010 period. The data suggest that although the stock and bond markets have been increasingly used to raise funds as shown in Table 3, the fact is that bank loans still play the dominant role in the financial system. In the period of 2001–2010, bank loans had always been responsible for more than 75% of the external financing of the non-financial sectors. The external financing ratio of stock and corporate bonds never exceeded 20%. If the national debt is excluded, then the bank loans will account for an even higher share of the external financing of enterprises. China's experience is obviously different from those of the developed economies, which had led Ronald McKinnon and Edward Shaw to identify financial development with the diversification of financial tools. We interpret the

Table 5. The Share of External Financing Sources for Non-financial Sectors in China (%).

Year	Bank Loan	Stock	Government Bond	Corporate Bond
2001	75.9	7.0	15.7	0.9
2002	80.2	4.0	14.4	1.4
2003	85.1	3.9	10.0	1.0
2004	87.9	5.2	10.8	1.1
2005	78.1	6.0	9.5	6.4
2006	82.0	5.6	6.7	5.7
2007	78.7	13.1	3.6	4.6
2008	82.4	5.8	1.7	10.1
2009	81.2	3.0	6.3	9.5
2010	75.2	5.5	8.8	10.5

Note: Non-financial sectors include households, enterprises, and public sectors. The flotation of financial institutions is not included in the stock. The corporate bond is comprised of corporate credit, short-term financing bill, medium-term note and company credit.
Source: People's Bank of China, *China's Monetary Policy Report*.

non-diversification of financing tools in China to be the result of continued significant financial repression in China.

8. Five Main Flaws in China's Financial System

First, China's financial system is marked by an excessive degree of monopoly power held by the state-controlled financial institutions. The "big four" state-owned commercial banks hold more than 70% market share of the whole banking sector, whereas over 20 equity banks (led by Ping An Bank) hold 23% share, other medium-sized and small banks hold 5–6% share and foreign banks hold 2% share. The U.S. has more than 8000 banks, and the top ten U.S. banks hold only 30% of the financial sector's overall capital. Owing to regulations that enable the big interest rate gap between deposit and loan, China's banking financial institutions can earn large amount of profits. In 2011, China Commercial Bank made 1.04 trillion yuan in net profits, with over 70% of it coming from the interest rate margin between deposits and loans.

Second, a comparison with the developed countries makes clear that China's bond market still has ample room for making progress:

- the investor structure is far from reasonable as evidenced by the commercial banks taking up more than 50% in China's government bond;
- because of the insufficient supply of fixed-income products and inadequate liquidity, the government bond yield curve does not display the usual shape and thus cannot be used as market benchmark; and
- in developed countries such as U.S. and Europe, the over-the-counter market has close connection with the trading floor through various infrastructures. The lack of financial infrastructure in China's over-the-counter market is causing market inefficiency.

Third, there is the increasing probability that the shadow banking system could destabilize the economy in the future. The shadow banking system refers to non-bank financial institutions like mortgage companies, hedge fund, and structured investment vehicles (especially the off-balance ones). These non-bank financial institutions offer many of the services of commercial banks but are not subject to prudential supervision regulations. The shadow banking system in China emerged in response to the administrative regulation of interest rate and to avoid supervision. According to Nomura Securities' estimation, the total loans from China's shadow banking system have reached 8.5 trillion yuan.

The rapid development of shadow banking system has undermined the stability of banking systems, and weakened macroeconomic control. Firstly, many banks buy financial products packaged by trust companies to get higher returns. The trust companies would then reinvest these capitals in high-risk fields (such as shares and real estate), hence linking the solvency of the banks to these speculative assets. Secondly, the shadow banking system reduces the effectiveness of monetary policy by boosting financial disintermediation. In recent years, China's financial system was abundant with liquidity even though the growth of base money was not higher than the average level — an outcome of the boost to the velocity of currency circulation from the large credit growth in the shadow banking system.

Fourth, the interest rate is still too tightly regulated. The tight control of the interest rates has blocked the diversification of credit market instruments and encouraged the bank to depend on the large spread between the loan rate and the deposit rate.

Fifth, the exchange rate regime still lacks flexibility. This is true even after the daily floating band for the exchange rate of RMB against U.S. dollar has been changed on April 16, 2012 from 0.5% to 1.0%. The exchange rate inflexibility has reduced the independence of monetary policy and become one of the main sources of external imbalance.

9. Six Action Items for the Financial Reform Agenda

First, the entry barriers into the financial industry should be lowered further. It is important to permit the establishment of more private banks and private financial institutions (non-state funded financial institutions). The more diversified and decentralized the financial industry, the more competitive and efficient the financial industry, and the better the financial services that the consumers would receive. The barriers to the introduction of new financial products and the issuance of new shares and bonds should be lowered as well, provided that there is adequate prudential supervision.

Second, interest rates should continue to be liberalized by removing gradually the ceiling on the deposit rate, accelerating the deregulation of the loan interest rate, abolishing the restrictions on the urban and rural lending rates in the near future; and simplifying the restrictions on the foreign currency deposit rate. In order to cope with these changes, the financial institutions should be encouraged to strengthen their pricing and risk management ability. The liberalization of interest rate may cause more competition in the financial sector, which could cause excessive risk-taking, and, therefore, it is very important to accelerate the establishment of deposit insurance system and to strengthen the system of financial supervision and regulation.

Third, the development of the bond market must be sped up to reduce the dominance of the state commercial banks. It is necessary to push for a wide variety of fixed income products like treasury inflation-protected securities (TIPS), high yield bonds, and credit derivatives. It is important to strengthen the market infrastructure by creating independent and well-run rating agencies, trading companies, auditing agencies, and registration and custody institutions.

Fourth, PBC should reduce its intervention in the foreign exchange market. Because capital mobility is going to rise in the future, China should enlarge the flexibility of its exchange rate regime in order to maintain the independence of its monetary policy and avoid significant external imbalance. China should enlarge the exchange rate floating band step by step and eventually achieve *pure* floating. China should also encourage the introduction of derivatives to enable hedging by market participants. The central bank should make more use of the interest rate policies, reserve requirements and taxation to control the flow of speculative capital.

Fifth, the independence of the central bank should be strengthened by having the People's Bank of China be directly responsible to the National People's Congress, rather than to the State Council.

Sixth, the prudential supervision and regulation of the financial system should be improved by:

- creating a set of comprehensive index for analyzing the macroeconomic and financial risks; paying special attention to the systemically important financial institutions in order to avoid the situation of "too big to fall";
- establishing a countercyclical regulation system on bank credit, and intensifying focus on liquidity, leverage ratio, and deposit reserve ratio;
- promoting cooperation among various regulation departments to achieve harmony between macro-prudent management and micro-prudent supervision. Specifically, it is urgent to push for the collaboration among the three regulators of the financial system (China Banking Regulatory Commission, China Securities Regulatory Commission, and China Insurance Regulatory Commission) because bureaucracies naturally create "silo-ization" of the areas they are in charge of.

On Regional and Inter-household Inequality in China[*]

Guanghua Wan, Jingjing Ye and Juzhong Zhuang

1. Introduction

"Let some people get rich first" was the famous saying of Deng Xiaoping, when China began to unshackle its economy in the late 1970s. Over the past 30 years, the dramatic economic growth transformed China from a centrally planned low-income country to a middle-income market economy. However, the rise in living standards came along with the widening gaps between the rich and the poor, rural versus urban people, and inland versus coastal areas. To illustrate, in 2010, the average urban resident earned 3.2 times as much as the average rural resident. The per capita income in Shanghai is 5.8 times that in Guizhou province. In addition, disparity also exists within provinces and among urban or rural dwellers. For example, the richest 20% of urban households receive 42% of total urban income, whereas the poorest 20% receive only 6.5%.[1]

In response, the central government has launched large-scale interventions. The campaign of "western development" launched in 1999 targets the east-central-west divide, and the movement of "constructing new socialist countryside" initiated in 2005 aims to bridge the urban-rural gap. This is followed by the declaration, in October 2006, of "building a harmonious society" which represents a comprehensive

[*]This work is part of the project entitled "Urbanization with Efficiency and Equity in China" funded by the National Natural Science Foundation of China through grant 71133004. Yunnan provincial government provided support through its "100 Top Scientists Program" (Bairen Jihua).
[1] http://www.economist.com/node/639652

attack on inequality. Recent government policy measures to encourage rural-urban migration, increase funding for education and health services for the poor, and rebalance the economy away from investment and exports toward domestic consumption and public services should all help reduce social disparities. The importance and urgency of the inequality problem in contemporary China have attracted considerable research interests and a sizable literature has emerged (Wan, 1998, 2004, 2007; Wan and Zhou, 2005; Chen, Wan and Lu, 2010).

This paper provides a comprehensive account of the inequality issue in China, and highlights three important observations. First, inequality is widespread, rising and threatening China's future. Second, urban-rural segregation is the most important driving force behind the fast rising income disparity. Third and finally, among the policy options, China must reform the stringent household registration system; ensure equal entitlement of and access to basic services across spatial boundaries; develop complete financial market especially for rural entrepreneurs, and assist industrial transfer from coastal to inland areas.

2. The Profile of Income Inequality in China

In its pre-reform period, China can be characterized as a society with equality of poverty — a largely egalitarian society with very low per capita income. This egalitarian system offered little incentive for working hard or smart. In late 1978, China began economic reforms by introducing the rural household production responsibility system. Under this system, arable land was decollectivized and allocated to individual households on the basis of household size and household labor force. Any produce over and above the state procurement and collective retention was kept by the individual households. This reform, coupled with rises in grain procurement prices in subsequent years, helped enhance farming productivity and raise rural income. Meanwhile, due to fairly equal allocation of land among laborers and households, the income gains were shared rather equally. In other words, China's economic growth in the early 1980s was pro-rural and largely inclusive. As a consequence, overall income inequality in China declined during this period since the urban-rural gap comprises a large proportion of China's total inequality (Wan, 2007). This decline in turn helped reinforce the impact of growth on poverty reduction. It can be said that without the narrowing gap and declining inequality, the remarkable large-scale poverty reduction in China could not have been achieved.

By the mid- or late 1980s, rising rural income induced demand for industrial goods then stimulated development of non-agricultural sectors. Meanwhile, the impact of the rural household production responsibility system had leveled off[2] and the reform emphasis was shifted to the urban areas. More importantly, the openness policy instituted since the mid-1980s, favoring the east region, has enabled the coastal areas to grow faster. These have caused a growing regional inequality and widening urban-rural gap. At the individual level, the dramatic socio-economic transformations, particularly the privatization move, have produced opportunities for some to get rich while others were left behind. Thus, income inequality has risen at a fast pace and along all dimensions. Today, China's income inequality is as severe as, or even higher than, some Latin American countries.

Aside from income inequality, the inequality of educational outcomes and of assets has also risen (Lee, 2008; Li, Wei and Ding, 2005). On the one hand, the urban bias in terms of access to higher education, medical care and other public services has become worse over time. On the other hand, China's uniquely decentralized fiscal system has aggravated spatial inequality in non-income variables. Under this system, local governments rely primarily on local tax collection to fund basic social services including education and primary healthcare. Consequently, poor localities have not been able to afford these services, and poor households have not been able to pay for the high cost of basic education and healthcare.

It is commonly accepted that there exists a general increasing trend in inequality in China although the trend and variations around the trend could differ depending on the variable (GDP, income or consumption) or the dimension of inequality (regional, inter-person or urban-rural disparity) under consideration. It is important to point out that the

---

[2] By the end of 1986, all households in rural China adopted the production responsibility system.

inter-person inequality encompasses regional and urban-rural gaps as its components and governments may prioritize any component in designing and implementing policy measures during a particular period of time. Thus, it is appropriate to start with the construction of an inequality profile at the individual or household level and then move to its regional or urban-rural component.

Unfortunately, individual income data from China are not often available or accessible. Even at the household level, accessibility is a major obstacle. The China Household Income Project Survey (CHIPS) data represent the most widely-used source for inequality analysis. But it only covers 1988, 1995, 2002 and 2007, and the 2007 wave is not yet released to the public. One way to circumvent the data problem is to generate synthetic samples using grouped observations (Shorrocks and Wan, 2009). Figure 1 plots the kernel probability density estimates of per capita income. It clearly shows the changes in the distribution of real income in China during 1990–2008. As the mean of the distribution

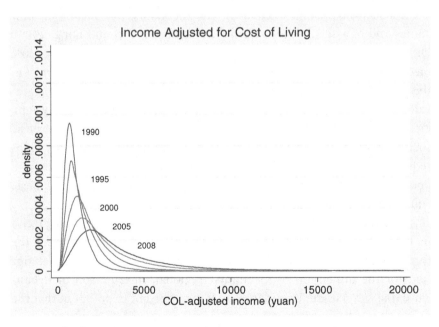

Sources: Authors' estimate

Figure 1. Distribution of Income Adjusted for COL (Cost Of Living) in China.

shifts to higher levels, income distribution became more and more dispersed over time, suggesting rising inequality.

Using summary measures of the Gini coefficient and the Theil index, inter-household income inequality is computed and reported in Table 1. When nominal income data were used, the Gini coefficient was 0.346 in 1990 and 0.459 in 2008. After adjusting for variations in the price levels across provinces, the Gini coefficient became 0.298 in 1990, and increased to 0.392 in 2008. Clearly, not allowing for spatial price differences overestimates the Gini coefficients by about 15–20%, a finding discovered by Wan (1998) more than 12 years ago.

Table 1. Inter-household Income Inequality in China.

Year	Theil Index		Gini Coefficient	
	Nominal	Adjusted	Nominal	Adjusted
1990	0.197	0.144	0.346	0.298
1995	0.266	0.173	0.399	0.325
2000	0.290	0.192	0.414	0.341
2005	0.372	0.256	0.460	0.387
2008	0.369	0.265	0.458	0.392

Adjusted = deflation by spatial cost of living
Source: Lin et al. (2010).

Figure 2 plots the estimates of Gini and Theil indices corresponding to the adjusted data, both curves exhibiting the same trend. This is not surprising as Shorrocks and Wan (2005) found that different inequality measures are highly correlated. The almost linearly rising trend does not conform to our discussion in the Introduction of this paper. This is because Figure 2 does not cover the earlier period due to the incompleteness of grouped data in earlier years. To supplement Figure 2, we obtained the Gini estimates from the World Income Inequality Database and plot them in Figure 3. Not unexpected, the two sets of estimates are inconsistent. Generally speaking, the estimates in Figure 3 are larger, possibly due to the use of unadjusted data. However, the unadjusted estimates presented in Table 1 seem to match Figure 3 for the overlapping years.

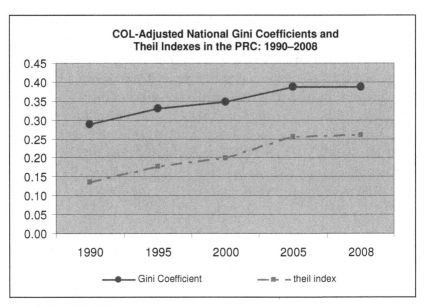

Source: Authors' calculation.

Figure 2. Inter-household Inequality in China.

In the absence of better alternatives, we discount the Figure 3 estimates by 15% and combine Figures 2 and 3 to form the time profile of
inter-household income inequality in China. The resultant Figure 4
shows that income inequality declined from the onset of economic
reform till mid-1980s and since then has been on the rise. Over a short
duration of just over 30 years, inequality as indicated by the Gini index
grew by 50% from 25.4% to 38.8%.

Figure 5 plots the rural-urban income ratio for provinces whose
data are available. Consistent with Figure 4, the ratio declined from 1978
to 1985 but has generally risen since 1985. The correlation between the
overall inequality and the urban-rural ratio is quite visible. In particular,
the ratio was low for 1983 and 1984, forcefully demonstrating the impact
of government support in terms of grain price rise on rural income in
the early years of China's reform. The declines in the urban-rural income
ratio after mid-1990s can be attributed to the introduction of the so-
called "provincial governor grain bag responsibility system." Despite
these policy shocks, the urban-rural income ratio maintained a generally

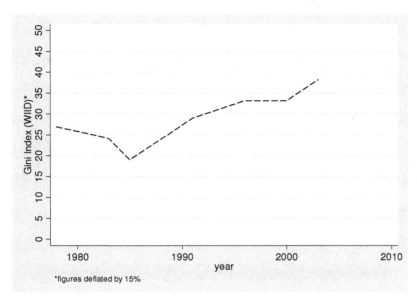

Source: WIID database.

Figure 3. Inequality in China (from WIDER).

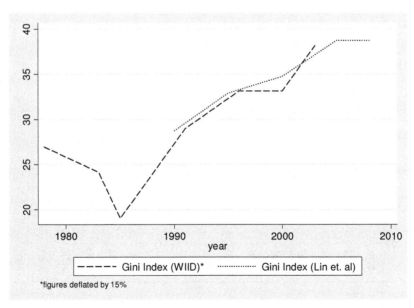

Source: WIDER (undated) and Lin et al. (2010).

Figure 4. Inter-household Income Inequality in China (1978–2008).

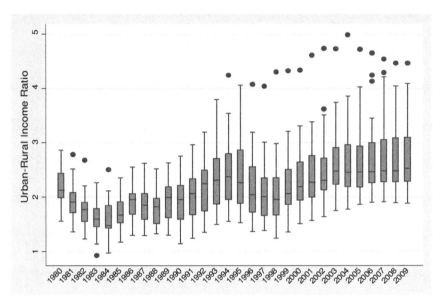

Source: Authors' estimates.

Figure 5. Urban-Rural Income Ratio, China (1980–2009).

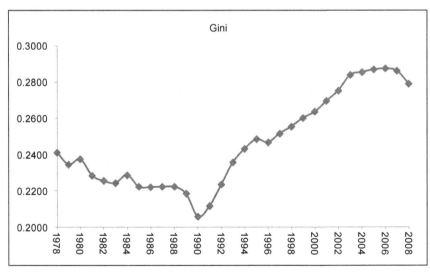

Source: Wan (2011).

Figure 6. Regional Inequality in China.

increasing trend until the very present. At the aggregate national level, the overall urban-rural income ratio almost doubled from 1.9:1 in 1985 to 3.3:1 in 2009.

What about regional inequality? Taking each province as a unit of analysis and using per capita GDP as the proxy of income, inter-province or regional inequality is plotted in Figure 6 below. The figure shows that regional inequality broadly follows the trend of the overall inequality (and the urban-rural income ratio) although the early decline lasted till 1990 instead of mid-1980s. An interesting finding from Figure 6 is the stabilization of regional inequality since 2003 and the most recent dip. It would be interesting to explore if these signal the beginning of the end of rising inequality trend and the start of the second half of the Kuznets curve, as already speculated by some in China. We will discuss this issue in Section 4.

3. The Consequences of Rising Income Inequality

Having documented the rising trend of inequality in China in Section 2, it is natural to ask why this matters. After all, China began its miracle growth by breaking the so-called iron rice bowl, or in the words of Deng Xiaoping, letting some get rich first. Clearly, Deng Xiaoping viewed inequality as an impetus to ignite growth and anticipated some increases in inequality. However, the pace of such increase was probably not anticipated. Although the rising growth tide has lifted boats for almost all, China has become one of the most unequal societies in less than 25 years.

For many years now, inequality has been ranked among the top three most concerned socio-economic problems in China. The ranking largely reflects the serious impacts or consequences of the rising inequality, as briefly discussed below.

First, the most publicized impact of rising inequality is on social cohesion and political stability. For thousands of years in China's history, the authority has frequently encountered unrests arising from unequal distributions and relied on border prosperity to enhance national sovereignty. Conversely, around 75% of China's minorities live in the poor western areas which are home to only 22% of the national population. Thus, high regional inequality threatens China's unity or sovereignty and may cause ethnic tensions. This must be one of the major considerations underlying the western development campaign. On the other hand, repeated reports of conflicts between property developers and dispossessed farmers, and between factory employers and their migrant workers reflect the uneasiness and anger of the deprived. In a recent study, Wang, Chen and Lu (2009) find that migrants are becoming increasingly unsatisfactory with local governments. This lack of confidence and trust is likely to breed crimes against urban residents and the public, even render government policies ineffective.

Second, rising inequality means those in the bottom of the society cannot afford investment, being financial or human capital. Traditionally, gaining entry into universities represents a major avenue for many poor households to step out of poverty. Prohibited fees for entering quality schools, plus intensifying competition for entrance into senior high schools and colleges, now prevent many poor households from educating their children properly. This is detrimental not only to poverty reduction but also to national prosperity as education and human capital formation are known to have spillover effects.

Third, and related to the second impact, rising inequality is found to adversely affect economic growth in China. Apart from inability of the poor to invest, high inequality exerts pressure for redistribution which may distort incentive mechanisms in the economy and comes with considerable transaction cost. High levels of inequality may also diminish growth when the wealthy can manage to tilt policies and environment in their favor. To analyze the impact of growth on inequality and vice versa, Wan, Lu and Chen (2006) introduce the polynomial inverse-lag model in a system of equations framework, enabling simultaneous identification and measurement of these impacts, under any time horizon: short-run, medium-run, or long-run. They find that inequality is harmful to growth no matter what time horizon is considered and that the growth-inequality relationship is non-linear.

Fourth, it is well-known that rising inequality hinders poverty reduction. On the one hand, the impact of growth on poverty reduction is smaller when inequality is high even in the absence of worsening distribution. On the other hand, rising inequality offsets poverty-reducing impacts of growth. Relying on the popular Foster-Greer-Thorbecke measures, Zhang and Wan (2008) decompose poverty and its changes under different datasets and alternative assumptions about poverty lines and equivalence scales. The analyses show that both income growth and favorable distributional changes can explain China's remarkable achievement in combating poverty in rural areas in the first half of the 1990s. However, in the second half of the 1990s, both rural and urban China suffered from rapidly rising inequality and stagnant income growth, leading to a slowdown in poverty reduction, and even to a reversal in the poverty trend. In a separate paper, Wan (2008a) demonstrates that redistribution is more important than growth as a policy instrument in combating poverty.

Fifth, while rising inequality may lead to increases in savings rate, this is precisely what China does not want as the country has been fighting for expansion of domestic consumption since the late 1990s. High inequality dampens private demand simply because the relatively rich are not consuming while the poor cannot afford basic consumption. In this context, the enlarging rural-urban gaps is the most significant culprit as, on average, rural residents only earn less than one-third of what urban residents earn. The average income of Shanghai is more than ten times higher than the rural average of Guizhou or Gansu. Worse still, only a little more than one-third of China's population can be classified as being urban. The absolute majority of China's consumers are rural. Even including the 200 million migrants, China's urbanization rate in 2009 was under 47%. It must be pointed out that these migrants face various kinds of discrimination. They earn much less than those who have urban Hukou and their marginal prosperity to consume is lower. As is known, those who do not have urban Hukou receive nil or little social protection. Thus, they are more risk-averse and tend to save more out of the already low income for the "rainy" days, especially for the vulnerable and disadvantaged. All these are related to urban-rural disparity and are detrimental to domestic demand. A recent study by Chen, Lu and Zhong (2010) finds that migrant workers would spend 22% more if they obtain urban status, holding everything else the same.

Finally, the adverse impacts of rising inequality in China are not only internal. It has contributed to the trade imbalance, generating pressures on China's exports and having caused many trade-related disputes.

Moreover, as noted by Milanovic (2005), inequality trends and patterns in China determine, to a large extent, the profile and changes of the global counterparts.

4. What Caused the Rise in China's Income Inequality?

The rising inequality and its adverse impacts presented above appeal for appropriate interventions. However, effective interventions must be based on a good understanding of the causes underlying the rising inequality in China. It is worth noting that there are economists who speculate that inequality in China has reached its peak. This speculation relies either on the plots of provincial inequality against income levels or the Kuznets hypothesis.

Figure 7 does appear to suggest an inverted U pattern, with a turning point around 5000 RMB which China has reached already. However, this plot is deceptive because the data points supporting the declining segment of the curve are all from rather affluent provinces,

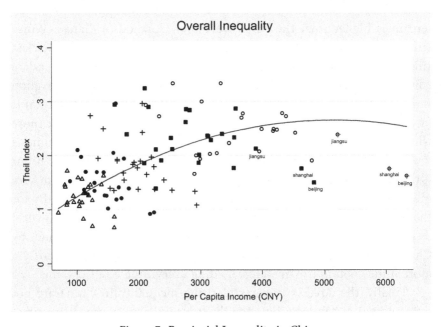

Figure 7. Provincial Inequality in China.

particularly Beijing and Shanghai where urban-rural gaps are small. Does that mean as income grows, urban-rural gaps will decline? The answer is no. Urban-rural gaps have been on the rise since mid-1980s. The small gaps in Beijing and Shanghai are due to their special autonomous city status which cannot be replicated elsewhere. Taking away the four observations, the fitted line will become a straight line, implying further worsening of inequality.

4.1. The Kuznets hypothesis: Inevitable cost of growth?

As Lewis (1954) pointed out, growth does not take place everywhere and not everyone is positioned to gain from growth at the same rate. Thus, initial growth may inherently be accompanied by rising inequality. Kuznets (1955) offered anecdotal evidence and discussed in details why the growth-inequality relationship may exhibit an inverted U-pattern. This is commonly referred to as the Kuznets hypothesis or Kuznets curve. The implication of this hypothesis is rather profound. If accepted, rising inequality constitutes an indispensable part of the growth process and policy interventions are deemed unnecessary and ineffective.

There were declines in regional inequality in recent years too. Do these signal the beginning of the second half of Kuznets curve? Not necessarily so. First of all, inequality declined in the early reform period which was not sustained. Second, very dynamic transformations have taking place in the Chinese economy, particularly for the more advanced regions which are undergoing upgrading and moving into the service sector. At the same time, industrial transfer has begun within China, driven by fast rising labor cost and improved infrastructure. During this process, the usual adjustment cost is most likely to be occurring thus growth in the coastal region suffers while technology upgrading takes place. Meanwhile, these regions are coming to a bottleneck of development: they are supposed to move from industry-centric to service-centric but the stringent household registration system deters urbanization thus service development which is supposed to replace manufacturing as the engine of growth is adversely affected. Nonetheless, reforms of the household registration system are forthcoming. Once implemented, the

Table 2. Rural and Urban Income Inequality in China, 1990–2008.

Year	Theil Index		Gini Coefficient	
	Rural	Urban	Rural	Urban
Nominal Income				
1990	0.159	0.082	0.306	0.220
1995	0.186	0.118	0.329	0.266
2000	0.195	0.145	0.341	0.297
2005	0.205	0.203	0.345	0.345
2008	0.200	0.202	0.339	0.343
COL-Adjusted Real Income				
1990	0.138	0.067	0.288	0.201
1995	0.152	0.088	0.301	0.232
2000	0.170	0.115	0.319	0.267
2005	0.180	0.173	0.326	0.322
2008	0.183	0.179	0.327	0.325

Source: Lin et al. (2010).

coastal areas may spring ahead again. In that case, regional inequality may resume its rising trend.

Moreover, the applicability of the Kuznets hypothesis in China is questionable because it relies on a key assumption that population flow from low-inequality sector into high-inequality sector. In China, however, the inequality in the urban sector has been low relative to the rural counterpart (Table 2) although urban inequality has been rising, approaching the level of rural inequality. Clearly, the theory or mechanism underlying the Kuznets hypothesis contradicts realities and cannot explain rising inequality in China. In what follows, we will outline and discuss several major contributors to China's inequality.

4.2. Location

One of the most important contributors to inequality in China must be location, reflecting differences in endowments of untradeable resource including localized culture and human capital. This is particularly true because the rigid household registration system (Hukou) impedes labor mobility. The impact of Hukou is best reflected by the consistently growing urban-rural gap (cf. Figure 5). According to Wan (2007), up to 70% of regional inequality is attributable to this gap, and all increases in the regional inequality in recent years are completely accounted for by this expanding gap. As far as the inter-household inequality is concerned, this percentage is as high as 28% in 1995 and grew to more than 30% in 2002 (Sicular et al., 2007). It is worth noting that the high contribution of urban-rural gap to total inequality is not unique in China. After reviewing international evidence, Shorrocks and Wan (2005) report that this contribution ranges from less than 20% in Greece to 26–30% in the Philippines. In fact, earlier findings are surprisingly consistent with our recent estimates presented in Figure 8 below, which confirms the growing prominence of urban-rural gap in composing total inter-person inequality.

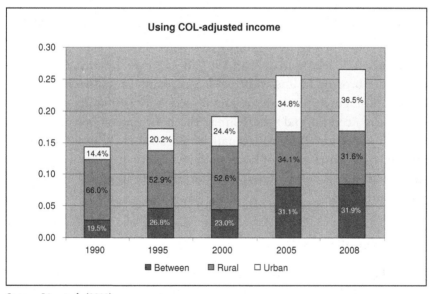

Source: Lin et al. (2010).

Figure 8. Composition of Inter-household Inequality in China.

What about the contribution of location to regional inequality? According to Wan, Lu and Chen (2007), the contribution of East-Central-West gaps in composing regional inequality has been declining, from a

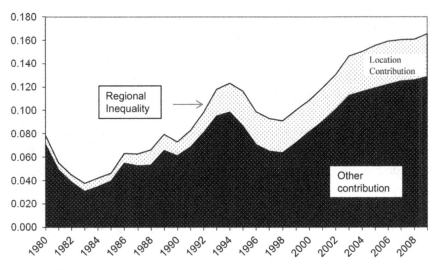

Source: Authors' estimate.

Figure 9. Contribution of Location to Regional Inequality in China, 1980–2009.

contribution of less than 18% in 1987 to just over 15% in 2001. These results are broadly in line with the decomposition results shown below (Figure 9). Figure 9 indicates regional inequality is dominated by gaps within east, central and west China. The between-component (largely indicating location impacts) is small. Based on these findings, it can be inferred that contribution of location to inequality in China will become smaller as infrastructure develops, labor mobility improves and urbanization proceeds.

4.3. Decentralized fiscal policy

China has one of the most decentralized fiscal systems in the world, more decentralized than OECD countries and middle-income countries, particularly on the spending side. More than half of all expenditure takes place at the sub-provincial level. In part, the sheer size of the country explains this degree of decentralization, but the structure of government and some unusual expenditure assignments also give rise to the unequally increasing government transfer (Gao, 2008). Functions such as social security, justice, and even the production of national statistics are largely decentralized in China, whereas they are central functions in most other countries.

Thus, fiscal disparities emerged. The richest province has more than 8 times the level of per capita public spending than the poorest province. In the U.S., the poorest state has about 65 percent of the revenue of the average state, and in Germany, any state falling below 95 percent of the average level gets subsidized through the *Finanzausgleich* (and any receiving more than 110 percent gets taxed). In Brazil, the richest state has 2.3 times the revenues per capita of the poorest state (Dollar and Hofman, 2008). Consequently, the fiscal disparities among subnational governments are larger in China than in most OECD countries.

Inequalities in spending are even larger at the sub-provincial level. The richest county, the level that is most important for service delivery, has about 48 times the level of per capita spending of the poorest county (Dollar and Hofman, 2008). These disparities in aggregate spending levels also show up in functional categories such as health and education where variation among counties and among provinces is large. These differences in public spending translate into differences in social outcomes. Up through 1990, there were only modest differences across provinces in infant survival rate, but by 2000 there had emerged a very sharp difference, closely related to the province's per capita GDP. So too with the high-school enrollment rate: there used to be small differences across provinces. By 2003, high-school enrollment was nearing 100% in the wealthier provinces while still less than 40% in poor provinces.

There is some redistribution within China's fiscal system, but not enough. Poor areas have very little tax collection and hence cannot fund decent basic education and healthcare. Some of their population will relocate over time. But for reasons of both national efficiency and equity, it would make sense for the state to ensure that everyone has good basic education and healthcare, so that when people move they come with a solid foundation of human capital.

China's highly decentralized fiscal system results in local government in many locations not having adequate resources to fund basic social services. As a consequence, households are left to fend for themselves to a remarkable extent. The average hospital visit in China is paid 60% out-of-pocket by the patient, compared to 25% in Mexico, 10% in

Turkey, and lower amounts in most developed countries. Poor households either forego treatment or face devastating financial consequences. In the 2003 National Health Survey, 30% of poor households identified a large healthcare expenditure as the reason that they were in poverty.

The situation in education is similar. In a survey of 3,037 villages in 2004, average primary school fees were 260 yuan and average middle-school fees, 442 yuan. A family living right at the dollar-a-day poverty line would have about 888 yuan total resources for a child for a year; sending a child to middle-school would take half of that. Not surprisingly, then, enrollment rates are relatively low in poor areas and for poor families.

4.4. Institutional factors

Inequality may have been exacerbated rather than mitigated by a number of policy features. Restrictions on rural-urban migration have limited opportunities for the relatively poor rural population. The inability to sell or mortgage rural land has further reduced opportunities. In the absence of the Hukou system, rural-urban gap could be reduced considerably and the inter-province disparity would be smaller too. The Hukou not only impedes labor mobility and institutionalizes urban bias; it interacts with other policy factors in raising inequality. Under the current system, migrants have little chance to gain employment in monopoly industries which usually pay well. Inter-province relocations, even for urban residents, are not barrier-free.

Apart from the open door policy which favored the coast, emerging monopoly and policy biases towards state owned enterprises all contribute to sector segregation, which is found to contribute more and more to total inequality in China (Chen, Wan and Lu, 2010).

4.5. Trade and globalization

It is well-known that China's phenomenal growth owes a great deal to trade and FDI (both reflecting globalization). Equally well-known is the fact that coastal area in China gained much more than the inland area from the export-led growth strategy. It is thus not surprising to see a significant role of trade and globalization in driving inequality in China. According to Wan, Lu and Chen (2007), trade accounts for 12% of regional inequality in the late 1980s and grew to more than 14% in early 2000s. The contribution of FDI also rose, from 5% to almost 7% during 1987–2001. Adding these two together, globalization contributes more than 20% to the total regional inequality in China since 1999, overtaking capital as the sole most important driver of inequality.

4.6. Education

At the household or individual level, education and skills are the major means for earning income thus differences in the endowment of schooling and returns to education must help explain income inequality. Using enrollment data, Lee (2008) finds deteriorating educational inequality across provinces and the deterioration becomes worse at higher levels of the education ladder. Meanwhile, returns to education are found to be on the rise in China, further aggravating the inequality impacts of the educational endowments. Based on Sicular et al. (2007), education explains more than 25% of rural-urban gaps. However, the contribution of human capital to regional and inequality only amounts to 5–7% (Wan, Lu and Chen, 2007).

5. Policy Suggestions

The preceding section offers analytical results which can be translated into the following policy suggestions.

5.1. Speed up the urbanization process

Based on the decomposition analysis presented in this paper, the enlarging gap between urban and rural areas and the growing inequality within the urban sector are the major sources of the increases in national inequality. In 1990, the between urban-rural inequality and within-urban inequality accounted for 19.5% and 14.4%, respectively, of the national inequality; in 2008, the contribution rose to 31.9% for the former and 36.5% for the latter. While the within-rural inequality also increased, the extent of the increase was small and, consequently, its contribution to national inequality declined from more than 66.0% in 1990 to about 31.6% in 2008.

Since the urban-rural gap comprises a large component of the regional and household income inequality (see also Wan, 2007) and the contribution is too large to be amenable to fiscal policy intervention or redistribution, the only option left is to support rural-to-urban migration so to allow rural people to share the urban portion of the national cake. In other words, the government must encourage and support rural residents to permanently settle in urban China. Such an option as advocated by Wan (2011) is also essential for transforming China from a manufacturing-led to a service-led economy.

It is worth noting that similar arguments apply for the regional income disparity. In other words, when the coast grows faster, more population will migrate to settle in the coast. Thus, on a per capita basis, the regional gaps can be maintained within certain range. This is where the institutional barrier of Hukou system comes into play.

In this context, abolishing the household registration system is only a necessary but not really sufficient condition for tackling the urban-rural gap. In other words, the expectation that urban-rural gap will automatically disappear after reforming the household registration system is misperceived. This is demonstrated by the persistence of urban-rural disparity in India, Mexico, Philippines and many other countries where labor and population movement is free. What is required is that government initiatives including fiscal policy, taxation policy and other social-economic policies must be geared towards facilitating urban settlement of rural residents.

A common criticism of this proposal is that the urban areas cannot absorb the huge amount of surplus population from rural China, which is in the order of 550 million. In particular, employment and job creation are of concern. However, the simple fact that there already exist 200 million migrant workers in urban China implies that the urban system already supports some 700 million rural residents in terms of employment opportunities and household income. What is needed is physical relocation of the migrant families. Note that permanently settling the 750 million rural population in the cities will double the urban population. This itself would generate a huge amount of jobs, as discussed below.

Is the worst case scenario — all cities doubling their sizes — beyond comprehension? This can be best answered by considering the largest city in China — Shanghai. The 2007 population of Shanghai net of migrants is about 14 million. Under the worst case scenario, simple extrapolation would give rise to 28 million under our proposal. In relative terms, this represents less than 2% of China's population. And voices of 50 million for Shanghai are being aired by leading economists from Shanghai. These economists argue that many big cities in other parts of the world such as Tokyo, London, New York, Sydney and Mexico accommodate 15% or more of their national population, almost eight times the 2% proposed for Shanghai. In fact, the current population of Shanghai including migrants is estimated to have already reached 20 million. Of course, China may encourage faster growth of small and medium sized cities thus their sizes will more than double while large cities such as Shanghai will expand less.

To minimize the social and environmental problems potentially associated with massive migration, a step by step procedure is necessary where migrants with long term jobs or secure housing should be given priorities. Those with better education should also enjoy concessions. In fact, some cities such as Shenzhen have recently adopted a scoring system, with demographic and other characteristics of potential migrants being taken into consideration. This was advocated by Wan (2008a), who suggests that to ease fiscal pressure new migrants may be provided with limited and phasing out access to financial assistance in housing, education, healthcare and other welfare provisions. Community colleges should be set up in the cities to provide training and education to temporary and long-term migrants and their family members.

5.2. Development of financial market and fiscal reform

According to Wan, Lu and Chen (2007), equalization of domestic capital stock on a per capita basis across regions will cut regional inequality by 20%. To narrow down gaps in capital possession, it is necessary though difficult to break the vicious circle existing in capital formation. This calls for development of financial market in China, especially in poor rural areas. Policy support for investment in the poor regions is needed in terms of tax concession and bank lending. In particular, continued financial reforms are necessary in order to eliminate discriminations against small farmers and rural activities. Certainly, the gradual withdrawal of bank branches from rural China must be stopped or replaced by development (policy) banks. On the other hand, while various government entities and financial institutions are experimenting with micro-credit schemes, such a complementary scheme must be adjusted to cater for capital formation.

Fundamental changes are needed in the collection and allocation of fiscal resources which so far have favored the developed regions. Thus, there is a need to make fiscal spending and redistributions progressive rather than regressive (Gao, 2008). An equalization in fiscal support would lead to an almost 15% drop in regional inequality and a progressive fiscal scheme would result in a much larger impact. All transfers can be conditional, geared towards physical capital formation and education of the young. Especially, public research and development (R&D) investment in agriculture must be increased to improve farming productivity, and special attention must be paid to the quality of schooling in poor areas.

Moreover, it is useful to promote trade and FDI in inland China. Policy biases that helped expand trade and FDI but are gradually being phased out in coastal China should be implemented elsewhere. The phenomenal expansion of modern infrastructure in inland China does lay the foundation for trade growth and attracting FDI. However, the complementary "soft environment" is yet to be created, where policy initiatives are crucial.

Successfully addressing the three issues discussed above will cut regional inequality by more than 50% (Wan, Lu and Chen, 2007).

5.3. Removal of Hukou and introduction of social protection

Needless to say, the Hukou system must be reformed which may take some time. It would be a gradual process simply due to the sheer size of rural population and its close connection with social welfare payout and

China's fiscal capacity. In the last few years, various localized initiatives have been put in place to integrate the urban and rural sectors. However, these are limited to residents within the same municipality or province and often only apply to those rural households who lost their land for city development. These farmers are often given urban Hukou but they usually do not enjoy all the benefits associated with urban Hukou.

Reforming the Hukou system is necessary but not sufficient to address the issue of industrial segregation. One possibility is to implement anti-monopoly law by breaking down the state-owned giants. An alternative is to introduce public-private-partnerships in these giants. Further opening up of the economy in the service sector is also expected to help reduce monopoly profit thus reduce inter-industry disparities.

More than ensuring a minimum living standard for all, a well-functioning social protection system helps the poor and the vulnerable to invest in human and possibly physical capital, which is essential for improving income distribution in the long run. This will become increasingly important as aging and migration gains momentum in China.

While social protection in terms of pension, healthcare and unemployment benefits are more advanced in the urban areas, the rural sector is significantly lagging behind, not only in terms of breath and depth of coverage, but also in terms of level of benefits. These differences are becoming a hurdle to urbanization and must be addressed. Similar differences also exist between provinces which may adversely affect labor mobility across provincial borders.

One of the most serious problems lies in the non-portability of the various benefits. Overcoming this problem appeals for a nation-wide social welfare system where individuals can have access irrespective of their location of residence and household registration status. While still a long way to go as far as social protection is concerned, it is important for China not to develop into a welfare state. The lessons of overshooting experienced by Canada and Australia ought to be borne in mind.

5.4. Promoting the service sector

It is accepted that job creation will help moderate income inequality as the poor and vulnerable usually possess labor as the only resource, while the rich have capital and other resources. To enhance job creation, China must maintain growth but more importantly must promote the service industry, which is relatively more labor intensive. Needless to say, lifting the share of the service industry in China's national GDP is necessary for China to undertake its structural transformation in the post-crisis era.

At present, the service sector in China contributes about 40% to national GDP and around 35% to total employment. Both are relatively low. If international experience is any guide, China's service sector should account for 50–60% of national GDP and over 60% of total employment. A simple calculation projects 400–456 million jobs in the service sector. The current labor force in the service sector is 240 million, implying a gap of 160–216 million. It must be pointed out that these calculations have not taken into account new jobs to be generated by economic growth, which is expected to remain high and sustainable for the next 20–30 years.

In passing, it is worth noting that heavily investing in farming is unlikely to lead to growth, nor jobs. This is not conducive to narrowing down the urban-rural gap either, which is essentially determined by the productivity differential between farming and non-farming activities. This differential, in turn, is driven by the law of diminishing returns to land or lack of economies of scale in farming, and inelastic demand for farm products. Both are inherent characteristics of farming and are not subject to policy interventions in the long run except by increasing farm size, as evidenced by the declining numbers of farms and increasing farm sizes in Australia, USA, and to some extent Europe.

5.5. Targeting

The decomposition results presented in this paper provide useful insights for targeting when attempting to combating inequality. Although the coastal, central, and western regions all experienced increases in income inequality during 1990–2008, the level of inequality in the coastal region overtook that of the western region in 2008. It is found that during 1990–2008, inequality within the coastal region contributed the most to national inequality, reaching 44.7% of overall inequality in 2008. This calls for attention being paid to coastal region at the macro-level. At the province level, income distribution has always been most unequal in Guangdong, Qinghai, Shaanxi, and Xinjiang. On the other hand, decomposition by province indicates that the biggest contributors to national inequality in 2008 were Guangdong, Jiangsu, Henan, Hunan, Sichuan, and Zhejiang. These provinces deserve further research efforts and must initiate special policy initiatives to address the disparity issues.

6. Concluding Remarks

The dream of Deng Xiaoping to "let some get rich first" has definitely been realized. According to the Hurun Research Institute, in 2010 China had 960,000 millionaires, each with more than 10 million yuan ($1.58 million) in personal wealth, 9.7 percent more millionaires than in 2009. (see www.chinadaily.com.cn/bizchina/2012-02/07/content_14549447.htm). In 2011, the number of billionaire in China (with more than 1 billion US dollars of assets and income) reached 146.

On the other hand, Deng Xiaoping's vision of common prosperity is far from sight. There were still more than 100 million Chinese who merely survived on no more than $1.25 a day (purchasing power parity or PPP-adjusted) in 2008. In the same year, the number of poor living under $2.0 a day (PPP-adjusted) is estimated to be 336 million (Wan and Sebastian, 2011). It is alarming to realize that China went from a well-known egalitarian society to one of the most unequal countries in the world within a short period of three decades.

As noted by Milanovic (2005), China's inequality trends and patterns determine, to a large extent, the global counterparts. On the other hand, as income inequality rises, those at the lower segments of the income ladder cannot afford consumption, rendering investment and export as the main drivers of economic growth. This seriously undermines the sustainability of the Chinese economy. In addition, China's heavy reliance on export represents a major source of global economic imbalance, causing trade frictions with the U.S. and others. Furthermore, high level of inequality means those at the bottom of the society cannot afford investment in financial or human capital. Finally, high inequality has bred and is reinforced by wide-spread corruptions.

The most publicized impact of rising inequality is on social cohesion and political stability. High regional inequality may cause ethnic tensions and threaten China's unity or even sovereignty.

Meanwhile the impact of growth on poverty reduction is smaller when inequality is high even in the absence of worsening distribution. Conversely, rising inequality offsets the poverty-reducing impacts of growth. While rising inequality may lead to increases in savings rate, this is precisely what China does not want as the country has been struggling for expansion of domestic consumption since the late 1990s. High inequality dampens private demand simply because the relatively rich are not consuming while the poor cannot afford basic consumption.

Among the various drivers of inequality, the enlarging rural-urban gap is the most significant and most unjust culprit. Worse still, only one third of China's population can be classified as urban citizens. Even including the reported 200 million rural-to-urban migrants, China's urbanization rate in 2010 was under 50%. It must be pointed out that these migrants face various kinds of discriminations. They earn much less than those who have urban Hukou and they received minimum social protection. In addition to possessing lower marginal prosperity to consume, they are more risk-averse and tend to save more out of the already low income for the "rainy" days. All these contribute to sluggish domestic demand or global imbalance.

Thus, more than anything else, China must eliminate the urban-rural segregation, not just by providing the same Hukou status to everyone. Rural migration must be encouraged and assisted and migrants shall receive extra support at the early stages of resettlement in urban areas. It is important not to introduce any geographic barriers to migration. In other words, there shall be no restrictions or conditions on the origin or destinations of migration. Only by doing so can regional inequality and urban-rural gap be narrowed down and total inequality be significantly contained or even reduced. This policy recommendation of fast urbanization, coupled with social protection, reforms in fiscal policy, and breaking down of monopolistic giants, will help China move towards a harmonious society.

References

Chen Zhao, Guanghua Wan and Ming Lu, 2010. Industrial Segregation: An Increasingly Important Contributor to Urban Inequality in China. *China Social Sciences*, No. 3: 65–76.

Dollar, David and Bert Hofman, 2008. Intergovernmental Fiscal Reforms, Expenditure Assignment, and Governance. In Jiwei Lou and Shuilin Wang (eds.) *Public Finance in China: Reform and Growth for a Harmonious Society*. Washington, D.C.: The World Bank, pp. 223–250.

Gao, Qin, 2008. Social Benefits in Urban China: Determinants and Impact on Income Inequality in 1988 and 2002. In G.H. Wan (ed.), *Understanding Inequality and Poverty in China: Methods and Applications*. Palgrave Mac-Millan, pp. 173–216.

Kuznets, Simon, 1955. Economic Growth and Income Inequality. *American Economic Review*, 45: 1–28.

Lee, Min-Dong Paul, 2008. Widening Gap of Educational Opportunity? A Study of the Changing Patterns of Educational Attainment in China. In G.H. Wan (ed.), *Inequality and Growth in Modern China*. Oxford University Press, pp. 163–184.

Lewis, Arthur, 1954. Economic Development with Unlimited Supplies of Labor. *Manchester School of Economic and Social Studies*, 22: 139–191.

Li Shi, Wei Zhong and Sai Ding, 2005. An Empirical Analysis of Asset Inequality in China. *The Economic Research Journal*, No. 6: 4–15.

Lin Tun, Zhuang Juzhong, Danaris Yarcia and Lin Fen, 2010. Income inequality in the People's Republic of China 1990–2005. In Zhuang, J. (ed.), *Poverty, Inequality, and Inclusive Growth in Asia: Measurement, Policy Issues, and Country Studies*. London: Anthem Press, pp. 119–136.

Milanovic Branko, 2005. Half a World: Regional Inequality in Five Great Federations. *Journal of the Asia and Pacific Economy*, 10(4): 408–445.

Shorrocks, Anthony and Guanghua Wan, 2005, Spatial Decomposition of Inequality. *Journal of Economic Geography*, 5(1): 59–82.

Shorrocks, Anthony and Guanghua Wan, 2009. Ungrouping Income Distributions: Synthesising Samples for Inequality and Poverty Analysis. In Kaushik Basu and Kanbur Ravi (eds.), *Arguments for a Better World: Essays in Honor of Amartya Sen*, Vol II. Oxford University Press, pp. 414–434.

Sicular, Terry, Yue Ximing, Björn Gustafsson and Shi Li, 2007. The Urban-Rural Income Gap and Inequality in China. *Review of Income and Wealth*, 53(1): 93–126.

Wan Guanghua, 1998. Income Inequality in Rural China and Its Changes. *The Economic Research Journal*, No. 5: 36–41.

Wan Guanghua, 2001. Changes in Regional Inequality in Rural China: Decomposing the Gini Index by Income Sources. *Australian Journal of Agricultural and Resource Economics*, 45(3): 361–382.

Wan Guanghua, 2004. Accounting for Income Inequality in Rural China: A Regression Based Approach. *Journal of Comparative Economics*, 32(2): 348–363.

Wan Guanghua, 2007. Understanding Regional Poverty and Inequality Trends in China: Methodological and Empirical Issues. *Review of Income and Wealth*, 53(1): 25–34.

Wan Guanghua, 2008a, ed. *Inequality and Growth in Modern China*. Oxford University Press.

Wan Guanghua, 2008b, ed. *Understanding Inequality and Poverty in China: Methods and Applications*. Palgrave MacMillan.

Wan Guanghua, 2011. Challenges Facing the Chinese Economy: Urbanization as the Silver Bullet. *International Economic Review*, No. 12: 99–111.

Wan Guanghua and Iva Sebastian, 2011. Poverty in Asia and the Pacific: An Update. ADB Economics Working Paper Series, No. 267, Manila, The Philippines.

Wan Guanghua, Lu Ming and Zhao Chen, 2006. The Inequality-Growth Nexus in the ShortRun and Long Run, Empirical Evidence from China. *Journal of Comparative Economics*, No. 34: 654–667.

Wan Guanghua, Lu Ming and Zhao Chen, 2007. Globalization and Regional Inequality in China: Evidence from within China. *Review of Income and Wealth*, 53(1): 35–59.

Wan Guanghua and Zhangyue Zhou, 2005. Income Inequality in Rural China: Regression-based Decomposition Using Household Data. *Review of Development Economics*, 9(1): 107–120.

Wang Hui, Chen Zhao and Ming Lu, 2009. Hukou, Social Segregation and Trust: Evidence from Shanghai. *World Economics Papers*, No. 10: 81–96.

Zhang Yin and Guanghua Wan, 2008. Poverty Reduction in China: Trends and Causes. In Guanghua Wan (ed.), *Inequality and Growth in Modern China*. Oxford University Press, pp. 33–56.

PART IV

Strengthening the Long-term Growth Fundamentals:
Sustaining the Power Supply

Ensuring Efficiency and Equality in China's Urbanization and Regional Development Strategy

Zhao Chen and Ming Lu[*]

1. Importance of Being Urbanized Correctly

There is not a modern country in the world that is not highly urbanized. It is no exaggeration that a sustained increase in the level of urbanization is the prerequisite for China to achieve modernization. China must go beyond merely increasing the urbanization level to formulating an efficient urban system and an efficient urban spatial distribution. The core of an urbanization and regional development strategy that is both efficient and equitable lies in ensuring that the factors of production are freely mobile across the urban-rural divide and across the different regions. This free mobility of production factors will generate a regional economic growth pattern that is driven by mega-cities and city clusters to achieve agglomerated economic development and effective division of labor in regional economies. This growth pattern will be characterized by balanced urban-rural development, and by convergence in per capita income across regions.

Current policies in China restrict the mobility of production factors in multiple ways in order to slow down the process of urbanization, and restrict the population size of big cities. In the "12th Five Year Plan

[*] The authors are grateful for the assistance of the National Social Sciences Foundation Key Project (11AZD084), National Natural Science Foundation Key Project (71133004) and Shanghai "Shu Guang" Project. This article is also a result of the Fudan Lab for China Development Studies and Shanghai Key Subject Construction Program (B101). The authors thank research assistants, Hong Gao and Zhikuo Liu, for their work.

(12-FYP)," the goal is to increase the proportion of urbanized population (the urbanization rate) from 47.5% in 2010 to 51.5% in 2015, an increase of 4 percentage points in five years, which is lower than the 2000–2010 average rate of about 1 percentage point a year. This official target is contrary to the international experience that the urbanization rate normally accelerates when it reaches around 50%! Specifically, the 12-FYP promotes the development of small and mid-sized cities and towns, and restricts the development of mega-cities: "Mega-cities should control their population size, big and mid-sized cities should continue to play an important role in absorbing migrant population. Mid-sized and small cities and small towns need to relax *Hukou*[1] requirements according to actual circumstances."

The growth of towns and cities necessarily mean the reduction of land zoned as rural; and rural land are zoned for either agriculture-use or construction use. (Construction-use land includes rural residential land.) The central government maintains a strict control on the amount of agricultural land in order to ensure adequate land for food production. The conversion of agricultural land into construction-use land is generally a difficult thing to do.

Right now, Chongqing and Chengdu are conducting experiments in land-swap schemes within their municipal boundaries called the "balance between occupation and compensation of agricultural land" scheme. Under this scheme, the amount of agricultural land converted into construction-use land in district A could be increased as long as district B increases agricultural land by an equal amount (i.e., district B reduces the amount of construction-use land by an equal amount). Under this land-swap scheme, the total amount of land for each use is kept the same by consolidating land use in district A and district B. In this process, district B receives an economic compensation from region A.[2]

---

[1] *Hukou* is the household registration system which determines the legal residence of the person, and hence her rights to the social services provided the local government (e.g., access to housing, education and healthcare).

[2] In short, when agricultural land is occupied in the inner suburbs, rural residential land in the outer suburbs are restored to agricultural land and the displaced peasants are allowed to enter the city as urban residents, while also receiving compensation for their displacement.

This "balance between occupation and compensation of agricultural land" scheme is currently only operational only at the municipal level and cannot be employed to ameliorate the inefficiency of construction-use land quota allocation across regions. At the same time, given the insufficient interregional population mobility, the central government supports the development of underdeveloped regions by allocating to them relatively larger construction-use land quotas and fiscal transfer payments.

Three wrong assumptions are behind the policies and institutions that restrict the interregional mobility of production factors, and they are: (1) China's big cities are overly large and are hence marked by inefficiencies; (2) the development of mid-sized and small cities and the development of big cities are two competing urbanization paths; and (3) economic agglomeration in the eastern regions contradict the ideal of balanced regional development. This article will first discuss these three misunderstandings concerning China's urbanization and regional development mode; and then propose an agenda on urbanization and regional development that is efficient and equitable.[3]

2. Are Chinese Cities Too Large?

Modern urban economies are mainly composed of the secondary and tertiary industries and as the economy transitions to the post-industrial phase, the big cities become even more important in the development of services. However, all segments in Chinese society have long held the misconception that the population density in the big cities is too high. The truth however is that, from the international perspective, other than the Chinese mega-cities with 10 million in population, the average Chinese big city still has a lot of room for growth.

First, Henderson and Wang's (2007) study on 142 countries found that there were 94 cities with over 3 million urban population in 2000, and 324 with 1–3 million urban population, and the ratio between the

---

[3] For a comprehensive discussion of the relevant theoretical issues on the adjustment of Chinese urbanization and the urban system, please refer to Lu, Xiang and Chen (2011).

two is at 0.29. When we performed the same calculation on Chinese data, we find the ratio to be 0.12 in 2000, and 0.17 in 2009.

Henderson and Wang (2007) have pointed out that the distribution of Chinese urban population is not concentrated enough. The spatial Gini coefficient for the global urban population was 0.5619. Among the seven countries with the largest population, namely China, India, the U.S., Indonesia, Brazil, Russia and Japan, Japan has the highest Gini coefficient at 0.6579, and China has the lowest spatial Gini coefficient at 0.4234. In addition, according to Fujita et al.'s (2004) calculations, the difference in population size between Chinese cities is far lower than other market economies and is only close to that of Central Asian and other former planned economy countries. In short, Chinese big cities are not large enough and the number of Chinese big cities is inadequate.

Second, with respect to mega-cities, the conclusion that their size has become too big cannot be simply drawn from the total population statistics. Chinese cities are defined according to administrative jurisdiction. Mega-cities (especially, the municipalities with province level status) all have a very large area, and, strictly speaking, are city clusters instead of individual cities. Thus, when making comparisons, distinctions should be made between the core urban district, suburbs and satellite cities. To this end, we regard Beijing, Shanghai and Guangzhou as the core region of the Bohai Rim, Yangtze Delta and Pearl Delta city clusters respectively and compare them with Tokyo and New York.

It could be observed from Table 1 that if Shanghai's, Beijing's and Guangzhou's population density are simply calculated using statistical figures, then the population density of these cities will be significantly lower than that of Tokyo and New York. However, the jurisdiction area of these Chinese cities far exceeds that of Tokyo and New York. Therefore, we specially calculated the population density of the core urban district of these cities using an area comparable to Tokyo and New York. As a result, it was discovered that Beijing and Shanghai's central urban district population density is basically equivalent to that of Tokyo and New York, though Guangzhou's population density is still low. If the Tokyo circle is used as the comparison other, then it would be more or less equivalent to the area of Beijing's jurisdiction, Shanghai plus Suzhou, or Guangzhou plus Foshan. It could be observed that the population density

Table 1. China's Three City Clusters Compared with Tokyo (circle) and New York.

	Tokyo	New York	Tokyo core districts	Tokyo circle	Tokyo circle excluding Tokyo
Population	1298.88	817.51	880.21	3500.00	2201.12
Area	2187.65	783.84	621.98	13400.00	11212.35
Population Density	5937.33	10429.63	14151.69	2611.94	1963.12

	Shanghai	Shanghai's densest district including Pudong	Shanghai's core 12 districts excluding Pudong	Shanghai + Suzhou	Beyond Shanghai's core 12 districts + Suzhou
Population	2302.66	1784.15	1279.42	3239.61	1960.19
Area	6340.50	2065.97	855.56	11219.92	10364.36
Population Density	3631.67	8635.90	14954.18	2887.37	1891.28

	Beijing	Beijing core 6 districts		Beijing	Beyond Beijing core 6 districts
Population	1961.20	1171.60		1961.20	789.60
Area	16410.54	1368.32		16410.54	15042.22
Population Density	1195.09	8562.32		1195.09	524.92

	Guangzhou	Guangzhou 10 districts	Shenzhen	Guangzhou + Foshan	Beyond Guangshou 10 districts + Foshan
Population	1270.08	1107.07	1035.79	1989.08	882.01
Area	7434.40	3843.43	1952.80	11282.89	7439.46
Population Density	1708.38	2880.41	5304.13	1762.92	1185.59

Note: Other than Tokyo and Suzhou's population figures being from 2009, the rest are from 2010 data. Suzhou's jurisdiction area is 8488.42 square kilometers, with 3609 square kilometers in territorial waters. Unit of population in 10,000 persons, unit of area is square kilometer, and unit of population density is persons per square kilometer.

Data source: Tokyo's data is from http://quickfacts.census.gov/qfd/states/36/3651000.html; Shanghai's data is from "Shanghai Statistical Yearbook 2011", the rest are from the respective city's official website and the Sixth Population Census Report.

within Shanghai and Suzhou's boundaries is already equivalent to that of the Tokyo circle, while there is still an obvious gap between the population density of Beijing's jurisdiction and Guangzhou plus Foshan and that of the Tokyo circle. This gap mostly comes from the area outside of the central urban area.[4]

The main concern among urban researchers and policy formulators towards developing mega-cities has to do with the urban ills of congestion, pollution and crime. It is not true, however, that the severity of these urban illnesses is positively correlated with city size. The U.S. history of urban development and congestion shows that although big cities have longer overall commuting times, the steady expansion of the big cities during 1980–2000 did not change the commuting time significantly. If we only look only at those residents who use private vehicles, then the difference between the commuting times of big cities and small cities narrows. An even more important trend is that, during the expansion of big cities, population and jobs are decentralized at the same time, and this makes it unnecessary for many residents in the suburbs work in the city center. The facts are: (a) on average, the commuting time of residents in big cities did not increase significantly; and (b) if only the commuting time of residents that live far from the city center are compared, then the difference between big cities and small cities almost disappears (Kahn, 2010).

China is still in the process of rapid urbanization and the correct policy response should not be restricting population growth to reduce congestion, but to take advantage of the economies of scale generated by the growth in urban population and develop quick and convenient public transportation (especially subways) to alleviate traffic congestion in the city center. At the same time, production and service industries

---

[4] It needs to be mentioned that the source of Chinese urban development is population distribution in the planned economy era. During the process of urban expansion, new population accordingly enters the city while the original population does not sufficiently disperse towards the urban periphery or other areas. If China's future provision of public services between cities and within cities can be further equalized, then a portion of the original downtown population in big cities can disperse towards the urban periphery or other areas and there will still be room in the downtown area to accommodate the newly-increased population.

that do not rely much on urban agglomeration effects should be induced to disperse to the suburbs — promoting the simultaneous decentralization of jobs and housing, and reducing transportation needs to the city center.

Another misunderstanding is that pollution will become more severe as cities grow. This reality is that effective control of urban vehicle density, thereby reduction in exhaust emissions by private vehicles, has been achieved in many cities through the faster expansion of subway networks and the introduction of incentives against car usage, e.g., Hong Kong increased license fees, parking fees, fuel taxes and environmental taxes, and London and Singapore collect congestion fees on certain roads at peak times. After analyzing transportation and travel carbon emissions by residents in 74 Chinese cities, Zheng et al. (2009) found that urban population density displays a significantly negative correlation with taxi and bus carbon emissions. On average, every 1000 person per square kilometer increase will reduce annual household taxi carbon emissions by 0.424 tons and annual bus carbon emissions by 0.837 tons.

In addition, environmental improvement in big cities is mainly brought about by the changes in industrial structure. The industrial structure in big cities is increasingly dominated by services, which emit less pollution. The concentration of manufacturing around big cities is also conducive for reducing overall pollution emissions and pollution control as pointed out by the "National Major Function-Oriented Zone Plan" issued by the State Council: "relative to small scale, dispersed dispositions, concentrated layout of the economy and concentrated residence of population will be greatly conducive to enhancing the level of pollution control."

Recently, Feng, Lovely and Lu (2012) found that, in China, the larger the between-city disparities of industrial output (or secondary industry employment), the lower the industrial pollution emissions per unit GDP. Thus, if the Chinese government actually aggravates the overall environmental cost when it pushes firms to relocate to economically underdeveloped regions; and gives small and mid-sized cities relatively more construction-use land quotas in order to disperse industrial production geographically.

Finally, it is also not true that the crime rate is necessarily linked to urban size, e.g., the U.S. urban crime rate increased in the 1970s and 1980s, but has declined sharply since the early 1990s, especially in the big cities (Kahn, 2010). Soares and Naritomi (2010) have shown recently that the Latin America crime rate is determined mainly by three factors: income inequality, police presence, and incarceration rates. In other words, crime is a public administration issue. If the appropriate policies are employed to narrow inequality and the level of enforcement is strengthened, then crime can be effectively controlled.[5]

3. Balanced Development between Small and Mid-sized Cities and Big Cities

Knowledge is becoming ever more important in the growth of modern economies, and the production and dissemination of knowledge requires interaction among people. As big cities have high population densities and sizes, which are highly conducive to social interaction, big cities become the place where high-skilled people and the engine of national and regional economic growth. Moretti (2004) found in U.S. data that cities with high university graduate ratios see a larger increase in the university graduate ratios. Glaeser and Ponzetto (2010) found that cities with higher proportions of high-skilled professions experience larger increases in the proportion of high-skilled professions. In general, a country's urban system usually exhibits such the following pattern: big cities concentrate more services while small and mid-sized cities develop relatively more manufacturing (which occupies more land, and services the surrounding farms).

We analyzed the two population censuses in 1982 and 2000 and had two major conclusions. The first conclusion is that, in cities with high university graduate ratios in 1982, the magnitude of increase in the university graduate ratio in the following 18 years was higher as well

---

[5] Jiang, Lu and Sato (2012) and Chen, Xu, Liu (2010) have pointed out that if China continues to restrict urban population growth, then the income gap between the indigenous urban residents and new migrants will inevitably widen, an outcome that undermines the construction of a harmonious society.

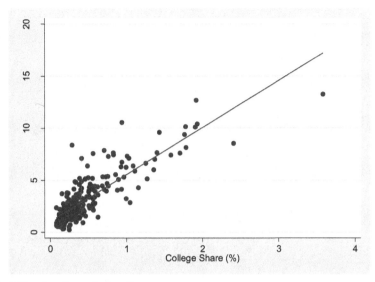

x axis: 1982 university graduate ratio
y axis: 2000 university graduate ratio–1982 university graduate ratio

Figure 1. Growth of University Graduate Ratio (1982–2000).

(see Figure 1). China might display an unusually strong agglomeration of high-skilled labor because China still enforces a rigorous Hukou system and residents with local Hukou enjoy better public services and welfare of all sorts. The better social welfare in the rich cities motivated people to "over-pursue" higher education qualifications in order obtain big city Hukou.

The second major conclusion from the 1982 and 2000 censuses is that there is a positive correlation between the 1982 university graduate ratio and the population growth over the 1982–2000 period (see Figure 2(a)). There is also a positive relationship between the urban population size in 1982 and the subsequent urban population growth in 1982–2000 (see Figure 2(b)). The two scatter plots show that the variance in the data is rather large, and this big variance could be due to the severe restriction on the flow of low-skilled workers into the cities, especially the big cities, hence inhibiting the population agglomeration effect of cities with high educational levels and large populations.

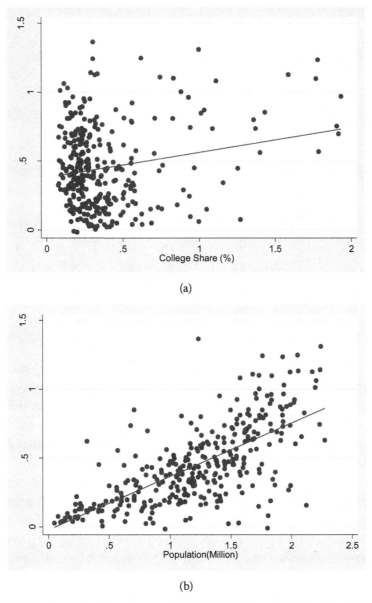

(a)

(b)

x axis: (a) 1982 urban university graduate ratio (%); (b) log(1982 population(in millions) + 1)
y axis: log(1982 to 2000 population growth (in millions) + 1)
Note: The six largest and smallest points in population growth were removed as outliers from the figure.

Figure 2. Urban Population Growth (1982–2000).

Another important phenomenon in China is that the agglomeration of population and land is lagging far behind the agglomeration of economic activity. Since the early 1990s, intercity economic activity agglomeration rose very significantly while the agglomeration of population (whether overall urban population or nonagricultural population) saw a very limited increase. At the same time, since China implemented the quota system to manage construction-use land and prohibited the cross-regional exchange of construction-use land quotas and interregional "balance between occupation and compensation of agricultural land," a severe decoupling between land urbanization and population urbanization has emerged. From 1990 to 2006, the average annual constructed area expansion rate for all city samples was 7.77%, while the nonagricultural population growth rate in the same period was only 4.56%. When we divide the sample cities into eastern, central and western parts, the urbanization of population and land basically is in sync only in the eastern cities. The constructed area expansion rate is almost twice nonagricultural population growth in the central region, and this ratio is almost 3 to 1 in the western region (Lu, 2011). It could be said that restrained interregional production factor reallocation has distorted China's urban system.

As the factor markets are more integrated within a province, will the agglomeration of production factors and economic activity be in sync within a province? We selected 20 provinces that had numerous cities,[6] and calculated the intercity spatial distribution inequality (Gini) coefficient according to intraprovincial intercity GDP, nonagricultural population and constructed area (see Figure 3). We found that, on the whole, the degree of inequality in each province's internal economic activity rose, showing that a trend towards agglomeration in economic development did appear within each province. However, unexpectedly, in each province, the degree of concentration in nonagricultural population and urban area did not increase correspondingly. The degree of

---

[6] We eliminated Beijing, Shanghai, Tianjin and other provinces with not many cities from the sample, as well as Yunnan, which has large variance in data. Chongqing was included in Sichuan and analyzed together. In each of the 20 provinces in the data set, the number of cities in 2009 was between 8 and 19.

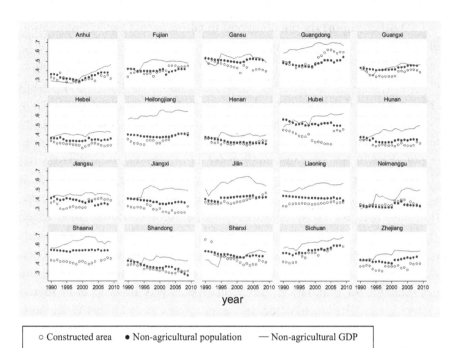

Data source: China City Statistical Yearbook (China Statistics Press, various years) and authors' calculations.

Figure 3. Intraprovincial Spatial Distribution of Economic Activity, Population and Constructed Area (1990–2009).

concentration in nonagricultural population actually declined in 12 provinces; and the degree of concentration in urban land declined in 10 provinces respectively. China is clearly not achieving impressive agglomerated economic development. The dispersed distribution of nonagricultural population in some Chinese provinces may be related to population mobility barriers, and the decline in the inequality of constructed area could be related to the egalitarian allocation of constructed area under the small and mid-sized city development strategy.

Xu, Chen and Lu (2010) found that economic growth between big cities and small and mid-sized cities are linked. Within a range of 300-kilometer distance to regional big cities, the closer the distance to core cities, the faster economic growth is, which is to say, economic growth between big cities and small and mid-sized cities cannot be split artificially. If administrative measures are taken to weaken growth in big cities in order to facilitate growth in small and mid-sized cities, the result may be negative for growth in the latter as well.

4. Agglomeration and Inland Development

Another misunderstanding that blocks China's land and Hukou system reforms is that, if the economy is left to agglomerate and develop on its own, balanced interregional economic development will be hard to achieve. International experience, however, suggests that economic agglomeration and interregional parity are not irreconcilable. Shankar and Shah's (2006) research on the U.S., Chile and Pakistan showed that the convergence in interregional incomes was due to sufficient factor mobility and not to the special regional development policies. Worsening of interregional disparities did occur in the history of U.S. and France, but a continual trend towards narrowing interregional disparities appeared later. World Bank (2008) has argued that only factor mobility and sustained development can eventually narrow interregional disparities. Because interregional fiscal transfer payments are often used to equalize interregional provision of public services, it is instructive to remember that agglomeration is conducive to sustained development, and only a large economic "cake" (generated by fast growth) can generate the fiscal revenues for these interregional transfer payments.

Chen and Lu (2008) and Fan and Zhang (2010) have examined the growth impact of central to local fiscal transfer payments in China. They found that such transfers generated faster economic growth in the short run, but the effect went from positive to negative in the long-run. Central-to-local transfers were actually disadvantageous for the economic growth of underdeveloped regions in China!

What happens when the population cannot move freely, but the economy agglomerates nevertheless? The outcome is a widening of interregional income gaps because, one, the restrictions on the mobility of low-skilled labor means that the population that agglomerates in large cities is highly educated; and, two, the allocation of construction-use land tends to be egalitarian across regions. This is why Figure 4 displays a positive relationship between interregional income gaps and insufficient factor mobility. The more that economic agglomeration within a province exceeds the agglomeration of nonagricultural population, the larger is the intercity per capita income gap in this province.

It is important to stress that there are four reasons why economic agglomeration does not mean that inland regions will have no opportunity for development. First, it is exactly during the process of economic agglomeration that inland labor relocates to the eastern regions on a larger scale and the per capita amount of resources (including land and natural resources) for the inland regions increase. Huge declines in rural population can allow agriculture to be managed on a large scale, enabling the remaining peasants to reap higher yield and embark on the path to greater prosperity.

Second, under free movement of production factors, industrial relocation necessarily concurs with economic agglomeration and specialized production. For industries like finance, the increase in labor

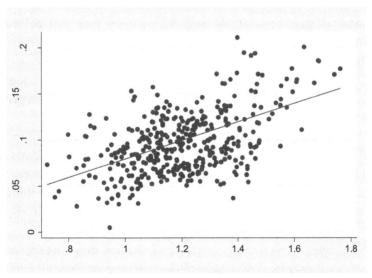

x axis: Ratio of Intraprovincial Intercity GDP Gini Coefficient and Nonagricultural Population Gini coefficient
y axis: Intraprovincial Intercity Employee Wage Gini coefficient
Note: Four outliers due to original data error are not included in the figure.

Figure 4. Deviation of Economic and Population Agglomeration and Its Impact on Income Gaps (1990–2009).

productivity brought by agglomeration will exceed the increase in production factors and these industries will remain agglomerated in big cities. However, some industries, such as common manufacturing, which use relatively more land and labor, will relocate to the suburbs or to small and mid-sized cities, bringing development opportunities to the inland regions. For those regions that are situated in transportation hubs and along the Yangtze golden waterway (e.g., Anhui's city clusters along the Yangtze River), improved coordination in river-sea transportation could reduce logistics costs and improve the prospects for future development.

It must be emphasized that industrial relocation must be distinguished by whether the industrial relocation was in accordance with economic laws or it was the product of artificial promotion. Factor price signals that are distorted by policies will, inevitably, decrease the efficiency of resource allocation.

Third, domestic demand will play an ever more important role in China's future economic development, whether in manufacturing or services, the inland regions will have to form several economic centers that serve regional markets. For example, Bao et al.'s (2011) empirical study based on manufacturing industrial firm data found that local market potential is still an important factor in determining the spatial distribution of Chinese manufacturing firm employment. In manufacturing, several regional "consumption goods production centers" have been constructed to produce consumption goods that are mainly sold locally. Similarly, several regional "services centers" are being constructed to cater to manufacturing, thus, regional "consumption goods production centers" and "services centers" must be in close proximity spatially. Such regional economic centers are city clusters formed around big cities, e.g., Chengdu, Chongqing, Wuhan, and Xi'an. Therefore, taking a broad view, the development of services will not change the trend towards economic agglomeration around coastal regions and inland big cities (Lu, and Xiang, 2012).

Fourth, during the process of globalization, a major reason for the coastal agglomeration of China's economy is the repositioning of the international manufacturing labor division system. Coastal regions are close to ports and thus have lower international trade transport costs.

However, not all goods require shipping by sea. On the one hand, some goods have low unit transport costs and high value-added, e.g., micro-chips, and air transport is more economical than shipping by sea. Such industries are suitable for development in the inland. Similar to micro-chips, software could be "transported" through the internet. The inward migration of these industries saves costs and is a reason for the solid growth in these industries in Chengdu and Chongqing and the sur-rounding areas. There are, of course, some industries that are immobile due to the natural property of production factors (e.g., resource indus-tries, and tourism), and hence are suitable for local development.

As production factors reallocate across regions, the division of labor among different regions and cities will deepen. In contemporary China, although the mobility of production factors still faces numerous restrictions, market forces have deepened the division of labor across regions. Drawing on the data of the population census of 2000 and 2005, Figure 5 shows that the unevenness of interregional employee distribu-tion increased for 14 out of 16 kinds of industries. The two exceptions were "education" and (the non-informative) "other."

Sector analysis within industry displays a similar trend. In the almost 20 years from 1988 to 2006, 18 industries exhibited a trend towards higher spatial concentration. Industries with high degrees of spatial concentration mostly possessed capital and technology intensive features, evident economies of scale, and were relatively more mobile spatially. On the contrary, the electricity, gas, hot water generation and supply industry displays a highly dispersed spatial disposition as it mainly serves local demand and long-distance transportation is often costly (Zhu and Tao, 2011).

The State Council has formulated the "National Major Function-Oriented Zone Plan" as its vision of the interregional division of labor. It needs to be mentioned, however, that if production factors (especially labor and construction-use land quotas) cannot be reallocated freely across regions and local governments continue to employ strategies that maximize the local economic aggregate, then each region will continue to expand the size of industry and services and segment markets between regions. The construction of major function-oriented zones and efficient interregional labor division will face significant impediments.

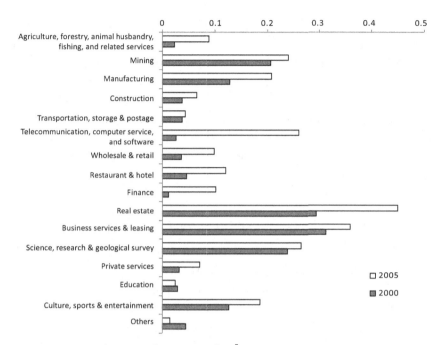

Data source: 2000 and 2005 population census data.[7]
Note: "Others" includes public administration and social organizations; the production and supply of electricity, gas and water; health, social security and social welfare; management for water conservancy, environment and public facilities.

Figure 5. Unevenness of Spatial Distribution (Gini Coefficient) of Employment between Prefectural-level Municipalities.

5. To Achieve Efficient and Equitable Pattern of Urbanization and Regional Development

The Hukou system (household registration system) and the land-use system are the main barriers to urban-rural mobility and interregional mobility of production factors. Because the public services provided by local governments are usually linked with the Hukou status, the public services system also becomes a barrier to labor mobility. The deeper institutional roots of this issue are: (a) the fiscal arrangements between the center and the local (i.e., the division of state revenue and responsi-

---

[7] We thank Lin Nian for allowing us to cite this unpublished data analysis result and Li Lixing for providing the original data with which this analysis was performed.

bilities by the level of government); and (b) the evaluation system of the performance of the local government officials. If local governments must undertake the responsibility of providing local public goods, and must also have the economic growth performance of their districts reviewed by superiors, then local governments will inevitably become barriers to interregional free mobility of production factors. Therefore, if labor mobility is to be facilitated, then a series of parallel reforms must be enacted; and the starting point of these set of reforms is the reformation of the Hukou system.

6. Four Principles to Guide Reform of the Hukou System

The first principle is to start narrowing the disparities in public services created by Hukou Disparities in urban-rural and interregional public services are caused by historical reasons and the different levels of regional economic development; and they are reflected in important areas like education, healthcare, public housing, and social security. The direction of Hukou reform is reduce public services disparities produced by different Hukou identities. From a longer term perspective, the right to obtain local public services should be premised on local residence and taxation (especially property taxes), thereby enabling a mechanism for property taxes to pay for public services, with Hukou gradually evolving into an identity verification and permanent residence registration system.

In order to reduce the appearance of labor migration motivated solely by access to better public services, Hukou reforms should be simultaneously advanced on two fronts. First, the thresholds for non-local population to obtain local urban Hukous should be gradually lowered. Second, steady, moderate equalization in urban-rural and interregional basic public services should be promoted through central fiscal transfer payments.

The second principle in Hukou Reform is to emphasize Hukou reform in the Big Cities. Getting urban Hukou in small and mid-sized cities has become relatively easier but most migrant labor have big cities as their employment destination The amount of permanent non-local labor that does not possess local Hukous has already exceeded a third of total urban population in the big cities of the eastern region, and even exceeds half of urban permanent resident population in Guangdong (Canton). The expansion of city size is an inevitable trend and if Hukou reforms are not accelerated, then the proportion of non-local Hukou population in big cities will necessarily constantly increase. This will result in a new generation of migrant workers (i.e., second generation migrant workers) that finds it hard to settle in the city and hard to return to the countryside, a situation that will create progressively worse social conflicts. Future Hukou reform must therefore be directed towards facilitating Hukou settlement of labor at the location of employment, especially for the big cities.

The third principle in Hukou reform is that the Hukou settlement standards for non-local permanent residents in big cities should be gradually lowered over time. As long as public services and Hukou are somewhat linked, future reforms cannot eliminate Hukous or adopt a free registration system immediately. If reforms are overly radical, this will cause large numbers of migrants to flood the cities in a short period of time, bringing unbearable pressure on the cities, especially big ones. Such a worry has a basis in reality. Yet as long as the Hukou system is not abolished immediately, then there exists the issue of how to formulate Hukou settlement standards. On the issue of who should obtain Hukous the key is to differentiate those who pursue employment from those who pursue public services, and give those that want long term employment and residence in an area priority in obtaining Hukous. Therefore, the standards for Hukou settlement should mainly be employment and social security contribution records, and use years of work and residence in one area as a sequential condition for conferring Hukous. At the same time, the prevalent educational level and professional title thresholds under the current Hukou system should no longer be used as Hukou settlement standards. For university graduates, their actual employment situation should be used as conditions for Hukou settlement and Hukou settlement thresholds based on universities and majors should be not predetermined.

The fourth principle in Hukou reform is that a series of parallel reforms should be adopted in social security and public services. In order to match the abovementioned Hukou reforms, the national social security system should be gradually made transferable across regions, and the link between local Hukou and enjoyment of social security benefits be weakened. The gap between permanent residents with and without local Hukou in terms of the right to enjoy social services should be narrowed through central fiscal transfer payments. Because most of the high quality kindergarten, primary and secondary schooling are concentrated in the downtown area, there should be steady, moderate equalization of education resources among different areas within big cities. Due to historical reasons, most of China's high quality higher education resources are concentrated in the eastern big cities, and these cities give local students larger entrance quotas into these elite universities. The Ministry of Education has already proposed lowering the proportion of local student enrollment — a correct step in weakening the connection between Hukou and social services.

Of course, the correct approach to reduce the gaps between supply and demand for high quality education resource is to increase supply and not to decrease demand. For example, big cities should give incentives to attract high quality foreign education resources (especially, in vocational education), thereby increasing the quality of urban labor and providing high quality and broad choices for the vocational education of the non-local population.

7. Linking of Land Reform and Hukou Reform Will Ensure a Win-win Outcome as Long as Land Reform Is Based on China's Realities

China's urbanization is the process of massive entry of peasants into the cities. During this process, some important fundamental issues that have to be resolved. How to expand the public services resources of population-inflow regions so urban expansion does not elicit opposition from original residents? How should the land system be reformed? How should land (including contracted agricultural land and residential land) owned by peasants that have entered the city be dealt with? How should suburban land appreciation gains from urban expansion be distributed to suburban peasants?

Starting from the current system, we think that the linking of land reform and Hukou reform is the most effective way to solve the above issues. The core of our "linked land and Hukou reforms" proposal is to enable peasants, who are already long-term urban residents, to transfer the construction-use land quotas corresponding with their hometown's rural residential land to the city they are employed at, so that these transferred quotas could be used for urban expansion and to allow the hometowns to increase their reserves of agricultural land through restoring residential land to farmland. The non-local labor wins because giving up the residential land usage rights makes these peasants eligible to obtain urban Hukous. The original residents also win because the some of the gains from the appreciation of suburban land (as they become construction-use land) can be used to fund public services and social security for themselves as well as for the new migrant.

Our reform proposal will separate land usage rights and ownership; and, under unchanged land ownership, will enable land usage rights to become interspatially reallocable assets. Consider the case of a peasant working in the cities, and whose hometown is in an inland region or is in the countryside far from the city. Even if the ownership to residential land in his hometown is given to him, such possession is worthless to him anyway. But if the construction-use land quotas corresponding to his hometown's residential land possession rights are given to him, then the value of this quota can be decoupled from the location of the original residential land, since its value is reflected in its ability to turn suburban agricultural land into construction-use land, thus realizing an appreciation gain from urban land. By turning the construction-use land quota corresponding to his residential land into an asset income, this peasant is made better without making anyone else worse off. After the peasant has sold the construction-use land quota usage rights corresponding to his residential land, his contracted agricultural land can be transferred to the rural collective for a price, or he can continue to enjoy future agricultural profits through subcontracting or sharecropping.

The "land-coupon" trade that is currently undergoing a trial run in Chengdu and Chongqing is essentially a "linked land and Hukou reform" but the extent of its implementation is limited to within the municipality. In comparison, our reform proposal puts a heavier emphasis on solving the issue of migrant workers that enter cities far from their hometown. Under our proposal, policies should allow interprovincial (municipal, regional) "balance between occupation and compensation in agricultural land, that is, pushing forward linked changes in urban-rural construction-use land across regions. Such a proposal is consistent with the majority of migrant worker migration being interregional and the huge disparities in land use efficiency across regions can be utilized to maximize the value of usage rights for construction-use land quotas, achieving an efficient use of labor and land.

Some observers have opposed tradable land usage rights (especially construction-use land usage rights) by claiming that economically developed regions have land that is more fertile than the economically underdeveloped areas in the population-outflow regions. This concern that interregional balance between occupation and compensation of agricultural land undermines food production is unnecessary. During the process of interregional exchange of construction-use land usage rights, residential land area in population-outflow regions that is restored to farmland can be converted to construction-use land in the population-inflow region through a conversion coefficient that equals the ratio of the average yield in the inflow-region to the average yield in the outflow-region.

Some other observers have worried that the exchange of land may lead to unemployment for peasants. The fact is that modern economies are dominated by the secondary and tertiary industries, and agriculture has fallen to about 10% of GDP in contemporary China. The secondary and tertiary industries in China are the main job creators for peasants. If the premise for peasants exchanging their land usage rights is founded on their residence and employment in the city, then allowing them to realize the market value of their land usage rights will not only not lead to unemployment, but will also be beneficial for increasing peasant asset income and obtainment of social security.

In our linked land and Hukou reform proposal, the appreciation gains on suburban land in the population-inflow region are shared among the original suburban peasants, peasants entering the city, suburban land users, the population-inflow region's government and the population-outflow region's government. The suburban peasants in the population-inflow region and the peasants that enter the city both obtain urban Hukous and reasonable compensation. Users of suburban land obtain new space. The population-inflow region's government represents local residents in obtaining a portion of the land appreciation gains while the population-outflow region's government also shares in part of the gains in order to arrange the restoration of abandoned residential land to farmland and provide public services for the population that did not leave. To make this win-win proposal a possibility, there must be interregional reallocation of construction-use land quotas, which maximizes the gains from construction-use land usage rights corresponding to residential land.

Multiple entities share in the gains from appreciation of suburban land in the population-inflow region because the land appreciation gains created by converting the population-inflow region's agricultural land into nonagricultural land are not solely created by local residents, but jointly created with large amounts of non-local labor. From the long term perspective, local residents will benefit from the sustained economic growth generated by urban expansion and also benefit from lower expenditures on defusing social conflicts due to the progression of social integration. Therefore, residents and governments in population-inflow regions should share a portion of land appreciation gains with non-local labor.

It has often been argued that rural land must be used as a safety net for the peasants and hence its usage rights cannot be allowed to be traded. In our proposal, peasants are selling their hometown land usage rights voluntarily to obtain urban Hukous and be eligible to obtain the pension, healthcare, housing and unemployment benefits. At this point, land will no longer need to function as a safety net. In the past, when the countryside lacked a social security system, peasants could only use land as a safeguard. A modernizing country should move beyond using only land as a safety net for peasants and allow land to be used more efficiently as a scarce resource. If land usage rights are a tradable asset, then whether a tract of land is used for agricultural and nonagricultural purposes, which city gets to use the same tract of construction-use land, whether use of the same tract of agricultural land is scattered or scaled, would all be determined by the law of maximum production from scarce resources.

Our linked land and Hukou reform proposal is essentially a mechanism to enable the trading of land usage rights. In such a process, the transaction costs of multiple entities negotiating together are too high and the government still needs to undertake a market simulation role. Forced requisitions and demolition should be avoided during the conversion of urban suburban collective land into urban construction-use land. Under the premise of sufficiently guaranteeing landless peasant interests, a reasonable portion of land appreciation gains should be shared with new migrant entrants.

Our linked land and Hukou reform proposal is really only a marginal reform to the current land system. If clear rural land usage rights are defined for peasants then the nature of land ownership needs not to be changed. When it comes to China's urbanization and land system issues, many academics have placed their hope on land ownership reforms. We do not deny that land ownership reform will ensure efficient allocation of land resources, protect the interests of the peasants, and facilitate industrialization and urbanization. But we must also note that there are three potential problems with land ownership reforms, three problems that are avoided in the trading of construction-use land quotas.

First, it will be hard to push forward Hukou reform under the land ownership reform proposal. If land system and Hukou system reforms are decoupled, then it may lead China to face the awkward situation where the government of the population-inflow region purchases all the land owned by local peasants and convert them to nonagricultural land. Land appreciation gains will mainly be enjoyed by local peasants and not by the numerous migrants, who will also find it hard to settle there.

Second, land ownership reform will expand inequality between rural residents. It must be noted that different geographical locations have experience different amounts of appreciation because geographical location is a primary determinant of the development of industry and services in that location, e.g., next to the coast. Under land ownership reforms, peasants situated in different regions own land with different appreciation potential, and this creates de facto wealth inequality.

Third, the goals of China's construction-use land quota system are consistent with farmland protection. But land ownership reforms may create risks for future Chinese farmland protection goals.

8. Other Parallel (Matching) Reform Measures

For our proposed linked land and Hukou reforms to work effectively, there must also be parallel reforms of the performance review system for local officials and of the fiscal system (especially funding mechanisms for local public services). The performance review system for local government officials should give different weights to aggregate GDP growth and to GDP per capita growth, and that these two weights should be different for different regions.[8] If interregional mobility of labor and interregional reallocation of construction-use land quotas are realized, then the aggregate GDP for population-outflow regions will inevitably grow slower even if GDP per capita were to grow faster. If the performance review for local officials is totally based on the region's aggregate GDP growth performance, then a unified nationwide regional development strategy will not obtain the support of the population-outflow regions. Therefore, China should both GDP per capita growth and aggregate GDP growth into account in the performance review system and accord a different weight to each objective. Furthermore, the more economically developed a region is, the higher the weight for aggregate GDP growth; and the less economically developed a region is, the higher the weight for GDP per capita growth.

The fiscal system needs the following three reforms urgently. First, government taxation as a share of GDP should be decreased in order to allowing market forces more leeway in determining the reasonable scale and interregional layout of cities. Second, the local government's share of taxes under the tax sharing system framework should be increased, and the responsibility of the central government in providing local public goods should be increased in order to lessen the pressure for local governments to increase local taxes. Third, more central-to-local fiscal transfer payments should be directed towards local public services and infrastructure.

---

[8] The "National Major Function-Oriented Zone Plan" also proposes implementing different performance review mechanisms for government officials in different regions, but this is mainly directed at the balancing of economic development objectives and other objectives.

9. Conclusion

Hukou reform and land reform are very urgent in contemporary China. China's actual level of population urbanization is at least 10 percentage points lower than the level it should be at the current level of development (Lu et al., 2008); and obsolete regulations are distorting the distribution of the urban population between regions and between big and small cities. Under such circumstances, China's urbanization has not fully played its role in narrowing urban-rural income gaps. These phenomena are all related to China's Hukou and land systems, which strengthen each other in restricting severely the interregional reallocation of labor and land resources. Unless the land and Hukou systems are reformed, China will not make full use of the economies of scale advantage that a big country should possess. Without free factor mobility, balanced urban-rural and interregional development will be hard to attain; and the lopsided dependence on fiscal subsidies to push forward balanced development will be unsustainable. At the same time, severe social segmentation will deepen between population of different Hukou identities within cities, and steadily undermine social harmony and urban development.

In the next decade, China will endeavor to stride across the "middle-income trap" but this will be difficult to accomplish without adjustments in the urbanization pattern and in the urban system. China must not only abandon the pattern of extensive spatial expansion of the past but must also allow the peasants who are employed in the city to have a safety net, receive reasonable compensation and lead a life of dignity. At the same time, urban-rural and interregional reallocation of production factors also fits the objective laws of agglomerated economic development. This reallocation will give a new impetus to sustain economic growth and reduce the size of the gaps in urban-rural and interregional per capita income. To realize the two goals of sustained economic growth and harmonious social development, the breakthrough point is in the big cities: lowering their thresholds for obtaining Hukou, and implementing linked Hukou and land reforms. To this end, China must prepare for a long hard battle in the adjustment of urbanization and the urban system.

References

Bao, Chengcao, Zhao Chen and Jianfeng Wu, 2011. Chinese Manufacture on the Move: Factor Supply or Market Access. Working paper, CCES, Fudan University.

Chen, Zhao and Ming Lu, 2008. Is China Sacrificing Growth when Balancing Interregional and Urban-Rural Development? In Yukon Huang and Alessandro Magnoli Bocchi (eds.), *Reshaping Economic Geography in East Asia*. The World Bank, pp. 241–257.

Chen, Zhao, Tong Xu and Xiaofeng Liu, 2012. Hukou Identity, Demonstration Effects, and Happiness: Evidence from Shanghai and Shenzhen (in Chinese). *World Economy*, No. 4: 79–101.

Fan, Ziying and Jun Zhang, 2010. How Has China Lost Efficiency when Balancing: From the Angle of Fiscal Transfer (in Chinese). *World Economy*, No. 10: 117–138.

Feng, Hao, Mary Lovely and Ming Lu, 2012. Agglomeration against Pollution. Working paper, Fudan University.

Fujita, Masahisa, J. Vernon Henderson, Yoshitsugu Kanemoto and Tomoya Mori, 2004. Spatial Distribution of Economic Activities in Japan and China. In V. Henderson and J.-F. Thisse (eds.), *Handbook of Urban and Regional Economics*, Vol. 4: 2911–2977.

Glaeser, Edward L. and Giacomo A.M. Ponzetto, 2010. Did the Death of Distance Hurt Detroit and Help New York? In Edward L. Glaeser (ed.), *Agglomeration Economics*. The University of Chicago Press, pp. 303–337.

Henderson, J.V. and H.G. Wang, 2007. Urbanization and City Growth: The Role of Institutions. *Regional Science and Urban Economics*, 37: 283–313.

Jiang, Shiqing, Ming Lu and Hiroshi Sato, 2012. Identity, Inequality, and Happiness: Evidence from Urban China. *World Development*, 40(6): 1190–1200.

Kahn, Matthew E., 2010. New Evidence on Trends in the Cost of Urban Agglomeration. In Edward L. Glaeser (ed.), *Agglomeration Economics*. The University of Chicago Press, pp. 339–354.

Lu, Ming, 2011. The Interregional Reallocation of Construction Land Use Right: A New Impetus of Chinese Economic Growth (in Chinese). *World Economy*, No. 1: 107–125.

Lu, Ming and Kuanhu Xiang, 2012. Geography and Service: Will Domestic Demand Disperse Urban System? (in Chinese). *China Economic Quarterly*, 11(3): 1079–1096.

Lu, Ming, Kuanhu Xiang and Zhao Chen, 2011. China's Urbanization and Adjustment of Urban System: A Review Base on Literature (in Chinese). *World Economy*, No. 6: 3–25.

Lu, Ming, Zhao Chen, Yongqin Wang, Yuan Zhang, Yan Zhang and Changyuan Luo, 2008. China's Development Path as a Large Country (in Chinese). Chinese Encyclopedia Press.

Moretti, Enrico, 2004. Human Capital Externalities in Cities. In *Handbook of Urban and Regional Economics, Volume 4: Cities and Geography*, J.V. Henderson and Jacques-Francois Thisse (eds.), pp. 2243–2291.

Shankar, Raja and Anwar Shah, 2006. Bridging the Economic Divide with Countries: A Scorecard on the Performance of Regional Policies in Reducing Regional Income Disparities (in Chinese). In Anwar Shah, Chunli Shen and Heng-fu Zou (eds.), *Regional Disparities in China*, People's Press, pp. 21–50.

Soares, Rodrigo R. and Joana Naritomi, 2010. Understanding High Crime Rates in Latin America: The Role of Social and Policy Factors. In Rafael Di Tella, Sebastian Edwards and Ernesto Schargrodsky (eds.), *The Economics of Crime, Lessons for and from Latin America*. The University of Chicago Press, pp. 19–55.

World Bank, 2008. *World Development Report 2009*.

Xu, Zheng, Zhao Chen and Ming Lu, 2010. The Core-Periphery Model of China's Urban System, An Empirical Study of Geography and Economic Growth (in Chinese). *World Economy*, No. 7: 144–160.

Zheng, S., Wang, R., Kahn, M.E. and Glaeser, E.L., 2009. The Greenness of China: Household Carbon Dioxide Emissions and Urban Development. NBER Working Paper No. 15621.

Zhu, Xiwei and Yongliang Tao, 2011. Economic Agglomeration and Coordinated Regional Development (in Chinese). In Ming Lu, Zhao Chen, Xiwei Zhu and Xianxiang Xu (eds.), *China's Regional Economic Development, Review and Perspective*. Shanghai People's Press and Truth and Wisdom Press, pp. 29–67.

China 2049: Energy Security and Climate Change[*]

Klaus S. Lackner and Sarah Brennan

1. Introduction

China's energy consumption is skyrocketing and the country recently passed the United States as the world's largest emitter of carbon dioxide (Graham-Harrison and Buckley, 2008; Marland et al., 2008). We believe that China's energy demand will continue to grow rapidly, since energy is a crucial ingredient for economic growth. In addition, China's consumption of gasoline is likely to grow disproportionally fast. Wealthy countries tend to have vastly larger transportation systems than other countries and China is still in a very early stage of developing private transportation. As China's economy grows, we expect to see a very large increase in vehicle ownership per person. As a result, rising demand for

---

[*] This paper was presented at a conference in the Fall of 2008 and finished in December 2008. We have left the text essentially untouched despite publishing delays. Interestingly, two journal articles from 2011 confirm the general trajectory of our hypothesis. A study conducted using MIT's Emissions Prediction and Policy Analysis model estimates that China will produce 450 Mtoes of CTL in 2050 if climate policy is limited to regional cap-and-trade systems (Chen et al., 2011). Our prediction is more aggressive (800 Mtoes), but the MIT analysis suggests that the scale and direction of our estimate is correct, especially considering that current output is essentially zero. The other article provides a survey of the status of CTL projects and policy in China (Rong and Victor, 2011). Shenhua's direct CTL plant in Inner Mongolia is now operational with a capacity of 1 million tons per year. There are also two small indirect CTL plants in operation, with a combined capacity of 320,000 tons per year. Other plants are in the planning stages, with a total estimated capacity of 38.2 million tons per year. The Chinese government is still attempting to slow CTL deployment due to short-term coal price spikes and concerns about water pollution and haphazard development, but the regional governments appear to be effectively pushing for continued CTL deployment. We take comfort in the fact that our predictions from 2008 seem reasonable in 2012 — only 37 more years to go!

vehicle fuel will probably be significantly larger than demand growth in the power sector.

Dependence on oil as a transportation fuel raises difficult issues related to energy security and climate change. The purpose of this paper is to examine China's options for meeting the anticipated increase in transportation energy demand by mid-century. A scenario analysis of transportation fuel supply and demand in mid-century China can contribute to the development of better energy strategies for China and the world at large. An improved understanding of the different options should help minimize future economic and ecological upheaval from supply bottlenecks and environmental constraints that are likely to stress the development of the energy infrastructure. Our goal is to understand the drivers that lead to particular scenarios and their resulting outcomes. At each juncture that we highlight in this scenario analysis, we aim to identify the outcome that is "more likely than not." We have also identified a few critical points where we believe it might be possible to intervene to improve the outcome.

Many climate change scenarios compare two energy paths: business-as-usual and an option that will allow for stabilization at a given ppm-level. In this paper, we have taken an alternate approach, attempting to elucidate what we believe is the most likely path given current political forces and relatively stable factors such as the geographic distribution of fossil fuel resources. We think there is a benefit to examining a scenario that is driven not by the status quo (as in business-as-usual) or by the desire to achieve an optimal carbon dioxide trajectory, but by China's demand for stable economic growth and by its resource constraints. Because these scenarios aim to capture the most important drivers for change, they are more likely to be correct and therefore define a useful starting point for planning.

We believe it is highly likely that China will rely heavily on coal-to-liquid technologies to reduce its dependence on foreign oil. When and how China will mitigate the extremely large carbon dioxide emissions that would be the result of such a strategy is far less certain. However, due to the global distribution of oil, we believe that the scenario developed in this paper is likely, unless the international community incentivizes China to pursue different options. Obviously, we are not fortune-tellers and caveat our conclusions with a recognition of the imperfect nature of information about the oil market from month-to-month, let alone all the way to 2049. That said, we believe that this is a probable future given the geographic distribution of resources and China's growing economy.

2. Economic Growth Will Remain High

Even considering the current economic retrenchment, we consider that it is more likely than not that China's economic growth will continue to remain relatively strong on a decadal timescale. In recent years (1997–2006), China's GDP growth has averaged 9 percent annually; since 1961, it has averaged 8 percent (World Bank, 2008).[1] Going forward, it may be overly optimistic to assume that economic growth will continue at such a high level. In the United States and the OECD, annual GDP growth has consistently averaged around 3 percent. For the purposes of this scenario exercise, therefore, we conservatively assume that China's income (measured as GDP_{PPP}, which is GDP adjusted for purchasing power parity) grows at 5.5 percent per year. This presumed slowdown in growth reflects our expectation that China will gradually transition to a developed country.

In 2006, Chinese GDP_{PPP} per capita was approximately $4,500. Based on the above growth rates, we estimate that GDP_{PPP} per capita will be $43,000 in 2049, assuming 5.5 percent annual growth and the United Nations' medium-variant population projections. This is almost equivalent to present-day GDP per capita in the United States, which was $44,000 in 2006. We therefore envision that in 2049, Chinese living standards will be comparable to those of the present-day United States. Though the United States (assuming 3 percent annual growth continues) will still be wealthier than China, the gap will have narrowed from more than 10 times to less than 3 times China's $GDP_{PPP.}$

This view of the future has at least two significant implications. One, sustaining such a high level of economic growth will require substantial amounts of energy. Even though we believe that China's energy intensity (defined as energy/GDP) will drop significantly between now and 2049,

---

[1] All GDP data from the World Bank's World Development Indicators.

the aggregate amount of energy consumed will increase substantially. Second, the parity between per-capita income in the United States today and the China of 2049 is noteworthy; it suggests that by 2049, China may develop consumption habits similar to those of the present-day United States. We will explore this second conclusion in more detail in the section on transportation demand.

3. China Will Draw upon Its Fossil Fuel Resources

China's total primary energy supply was 1,900 Mtoe in 2006 (IEA, 2008).[2] In 2049, we estimate that primary energy will range between 5,500 (assuming 2.5 percent annual growth in energy consumption) and 12,600 (4.5 percent annual growth) Mtoe.[3] We think it is highly unlikely that energy consumption will grow as fast as economic growth, which would imply 19,000 Mtoe. Although energy intensity has risen over the last few years, the Chinese government has taken steps to put the country back on its long-term declining-energy-intensity path.[4] China's energy intensity decreased almost every year between 1980 and 2002; the average annual decline was 6 percent.[5] We acknowledge, though, that economic growth above 5.5 percent would affect our upper-bound estimate. For the purposes of this paper, however, we will examine the impact of a range of 5,500–12,600 Mtoe per year in energy demand by 2049.

---

[2] From the perspective of 2012, we know that the growth rate of the first few years was significantly larger than the average rate we predicted for 2009–2049, as China's primary energy supply was 2,257 Mtoes in 2009 (IEA, 2011). We believe our long-term estimate is still reasonable, however, as current growth rates are likely to slow down as China reaches the status of a developed country.

[3] As a point of comparison, the IEA predicts that China's primary energy demand will be 3,819 Mtoe in 2035, assuming business-as-usual energy growth (IEA, 2007a).

[4] For example, China's 11th Five Year Plan proposes decreasing the country's energy intensity by 20 percent between 2005 and 2010 (IEA, *World Energy Outlook 2007*, p. 68).

[5] Using constant dollar GDP as the denominator produces an average decline of 5.9 percent, while current dollar GDP is associated with an average decline of 5.7 percent. GDP_{PPP} is associated with an average decline of 8.7 percent.

China has significant coal resources and reserves (Rogner, 1997). Its coal is estimated at 48 Gtoe of proven reserves, 682 Gtoe of resources, and 566 Gtoe of more speculative deposits. Oil is much more limited, with proven reserves of 5 Gtoe and resources of 13 Gtoe. Oil shale, bitumen, and heavy oils like the tar sands represent a large resource of 245 Gtoe. If just half of China's coal identified resources are exploitable by mid-century, the country could use coal to satisfy all of its energy needs for 200 years at the 2006 level and 30 to 70 years at the estimated 2049 level. In contrast, conventional oil reserves plus half of oil resources would last only 12 years, using the rate at which China consumed oil in 2006.

While we cannot estimate the precise rate of technological progress that will translate these resources into proven reserves, it is reasonable to assume that in 2049, China could meet all of its primary energy demand using indigenous fossil fuels, relying mainly on coal, shale and tars. To clarify, we recognize that China is likely to meet some of its energy needs from renewable or nuclear energy sources, depending on the cost of these options relative to fossil fuels. It is also likely that China will import a fraction of the energy it consumes. However, we simply do not believe that there will be a geological constraint on China's coal supply over the next 50 years, and we think it is likely that China will draw upon these resources due to energy security concerns. Though there is a certainly a chance that there will be a breakthrough in alternative energy technologies that could drive their costs down (or perhaps in the case of nuclear, comprehensively addresses safety, waste, and proliferation concerns), we think that it is more likely than not that fossil fuels will remain the low-cost option for at least the next four to five decades.[6]

4. Demand for Transport Fuels Will Increase Significantly

China may pursue environmentally-friendly transportation policies like mass transit, smart urban planning, and high-efficiency vehicles. Yet even if these options are successfully developed, China will still use a

---

[6]From the vantage point of 2012 it also seems likely that shale gas, another fossil fuel, could also become an important player.

massive amount of transportation fuel. At present, the United States has almost 814 vehicles per 1000 people and the OECD as a whole has 668 vehicles per 1000 people; in contrast, China has only 24 vehicles per 1000 people (World Bank, 2008). Even if China uses very high-efficiency cars by 2049, the country will demand a significant amount of fuel if the Chinese people only partially adopt U.S. and European attitudes towards transportation.

If we conservatively assume that China in 2049 has 500 vehicles per 1000 people, this implies that there will be 700 million vehicles on the roads.[7] We assume that each Chinese vehicle is driven 34,000 kilometers (21,000 miles) in 2049, which is our estimate of the amount driven per vehicle in the United States in 2006.[8] We also assume that the average vehicle uses 3×10^{-5} toe/km in 2049 (roughly equivalent to 59 mpg), which will require a doubling of the efficiency of China's automobile fleet. For comparison, the Chinese fleet average economy standard was set to 6×10^{-5} in 2002 and the United States' automobile standard was set to 8×10^{-5} toe/km in 2006 (approximately 24 mpg).[9] These assumptions imply that China will require 800 Mtoe of gasoline to meet its annual transportation needs in 2049, up from 133 Mtoe in 2006.[10]

We note that, for the sake of simplicity, we have included fuel for rail, air, and ocean transport in these calculations, which are meant

---

[7] This estimate fits within the trajectory suggested by other projections, such as 120 million by 2020 (McKinsey Global Institute, 2007), 270 million in 2030 (IEA, 2007a), and 410 million by 2035 (Asian Development Bank, 2006).

[8] The nominal U.S. kilometers per vehicle is calculated as: energy per vehicle (3 toe, calculated as 649 toe of energy consumed in the transport sector divided by 250 million vehicles) divided by the vehicle fuel efficiency standard in the United States in 2006 (8×10^{-5} toe/km). Data from the World Bank and the IEA. This estimate is probably a little high, since "energy consumed in the transport sector" includes rail, air and ocean transport as well as vehicles.

[9] Fuel efficiency standards for China and the United States estimated from IEA, *World Energy Outlook 2007*, p. 303. Converted from liters to toe using conversion factors of 0.7449 grams/cm^3 for the average density of motor gasoline (from IEA, 2004) and 1.07 tons/toe (from IEA, 2008a, p. I.17). Converted from L/100-km to MPG using 235.2/(Y) where Y equals L/100-km (An and Sauer, 2004).

[10] Calculated as: fuel efficiency (3×10^{-5} toe/km) multiplied by the number of vehicles on the road (706 million) multiplied by the kilometers driven per vehicle each year (34,000). We rounded from 720 to 800 Mtoe to leave room for air planes and trains.

to be broad-brush estimates of future demand. The 800 Mtoe estimate implies that transportation sector's energy consumption will grow 4 percent annually between 2006 and 2049, which is toward the high end of our range for energy growth (2.5–4.5 percent) but lower than our estimated income growth (5.5 percent). However, we expect that the transportation sector would show fast growth relative to the other sectors of the economy, because this sector appears to grow rapidly in the later stages of a transition from a developing country to a developed country.

5. China Will Use Synthetic Liquid Fossil Fuels

We think it is likely that the world oil price will continue to stay relatively high — generally over $50 per barrel — over the long term. This does not presume that oil resources are necessarily in decline or that unconventional oil such as Canadian or Venezuelan tar sands will remain unexploited, but simply that the significant additional demand from developing countries such as China will continue apace and keep prices up. The short term drop in oil prices with the recent slowdown of the world economy points to the strong sensitivity of oil prices to fluctuations in demand. If and when the world economy returns to a growth pattern, rapid demand from countries like China will keep upward pressure on the price of fuel. A high cost of oil will exacerbate energy security concerns, which is likely to cause China to abandon petroleum as its primary source for vehicle fuel. This would require breakthroughs in replacement fuels derived from biomass or coal, or novel advanced vehicle technology as hydrogen or electric/plug-in cars. We believe that among these options the development of coal-to-liquid (CTL) fuel is the most likely for two reasons. First, synthetic fuel from coal is already a mature technology, while alternative vehicle technologies (such as batteries and hydrogen storage) require significant research and development (IEA, 2008c). Second, while biofuels such as ethanol are commercially feasible, they place excessive demands on resources that could otherwise be used for food production, and next-generation biofuels do not appear to be on the near-term horizon (IEA, 2008c).

There are two types of CTL technologies — direct and indirect liquefaction — and both produce relatively pure streams of carbon dioxide as a byproduct of the production process. Direct liquefaction occurs when coal is reacted with hydrogen, or hydrogen rich compounds, to form liquid fuels. At the beginning of the twentieth century, Friedrich Bergius developed a hydrogenation process to break the large macromolecules that make up coal into smaller more hydrogen rich molecules that form the constituents of gasoline and diesel. Around the same time, Franz Fischer and Hans Tropsch developed a method to liquefy coal indirectly, by first gasifying coal with steam which produces a mixture of hydrogen and carbon monoxide, and then using iron or cobalt catalysts to transform the gas into liquid hydrocarbons. During the Second World War, German engineers utilized both Bergius and Fischer-Tropsch liquefaction to address gasoline shortages (Andrews, 2007).

After the war, indirect liquefaction technology was not used commercially until the 1970s, when South Africa began using indirect CTL to minimize energy security risks. Direct liquefaction has only recently been commercialized, by China's Shenhua Corporation. Direct liquefaction processes convert coal to liquid fuel more efficiently than indirect liquefaction, but the fuel produced by indirect liquefaction tends to burn more cleanly, with fewer non-carbon dioxide pollutants. In addition, indirect liquefaction can also be used to produce fuels such as methanol and dimethyl ether; these fuels have higher end-use efficiency than gasoline and diesel, largely erasing direct liquefaction's energy conversion advantage (Williams and Larson, 2003).

Of course, significant discoveries of oil or natural gas within Chinese borders could change this liquefaction trajectory. For example, a major find in the Chinese sea could propel China from an oil-dependent to an oil-independent country. In order to make such a transition, the find would have to be of staggeringly large proportions and comparable to Middle Eastern oil fields. The probability of such a discovery is small, especially considering current estimates of China's oil resources (see table below). If such a discovery did occur, China would most likely rely on oil rather than CTL to fuel its transportation sector. It is more difficult to rule out large resources of natural gas (most likely as gas clathrates) or gas shales. Discoveries in both resources might effectively displace coal, but would require similar energy intensive processing to produce liquid hydrocarbon fuels. If natural gas were used, Fischer-Tropsch reactions could again be used to produce synthetic fuels.[11]

Estimated Magnitude of China's Fossil Fuels, Gtoe (Rogner, 1997).

	Proven Reserves	Resources	Additional Occurrences
conventional oil	5	13	na
shale, bitumen, heavy oils	10	42	193
	Total estimated oil: 262		
conventional natural gas	1	12	na
unconventional gas	23	24	36
gas clathrates	na	na	432
	Total estimated gas: 527		
coal	48	682	566
	Total estimated coal: 1296		

We think it is unlikely that intervention could change the predicted outcome at earlier decision points in this scenario exercise. China's economy is going to grow significantly, China is going to use its coal reserves to support that economic growth, and as China becomes wealthier, its transportation patterns will change. At this point, however, we think that meaningful policy intervention could reduce the need for CTL fuels. A significant commitment to vehicle research could speed up the rate of technology development and lessen the comparative advantage of CTL. Without an intentional change in direction, however, we believe that the most likely route is for China to use existing vehicle technology and CTL fuel.

---

[11] Today, in 2012 it is already evident that natural gas in shales represents a large resource for China that could be tapped in producing liquid fuels. This development suggests indirect liquefaction over direct liquefaction as indirect liquefaction via Fischer-Tropsch reactions applies equally to coal and natural gas. Indeed it is possible to convert mixtures of the two to synthesis gas and thus to gasoline and diesel.

6. China Will Use a Significant Amount of CTL Fuels before the Rest of the World

At present, the three countries pursuing CTL deployment most seriously are the United States, China and South Africa (Couch, 2008). South Africa is a leader in the technology for historic reasons, having developed the technology during the economic boycott of apartheid. A South African company, Sasol, has commercialized the technology and currently produces 30 million tons annually, meeting approximately 30 percent of the country's demand for vehicle fuel (Couch, 2008; Vallentin, 2008). Despite the country's first-mover advantage, South Africa's relatively small size suggests that it is not likely to compete with China or the United States, if these countries put serious effort behind the technology. Sasol is expanding its market, however, by partnering with companies in China (WCI, 2006).

We consider it likely that China will produce a significant amount of CTL fuel before the United States. China launched an ambitious CTL research program in the 1980s, which drew increased government support during the mid-1990s as the country became a net importer of oil. China's first CTL plant opened in 1999 and produced 500,000 tons per year; it closed quickly due to problems with the coal feedstock (Qi, 2007). Perhaps in response to this setback, the government expanded its research efforts in 2001 with the "863 program." The following year, the Shenhua Corporation announced that it would built a large direct CTL plant in Inner Mongolia, based upon technology developed by a U.S. company, Hydrocarbon Technology, Inc. (Williams and Larson, 2003). This facility, which is the world's first commercial-scale direct liquefaction plant, has an initial capacity of one million tons per year (with planned expansion to 5 million tons) and is opening in late 2008 (Aldous, 2005; Couch, 2008; Sun, 2008; Zhao and Gallagher, 2007). Numerous indirect CTL facilities are also in various planning stages, some using imported Sasol technology and others using processes developed in China (Zhao and Gallagher, 2007; Adam, 2008; Sun, 2008).

Due to significant investor interest in the technology, the Chinese government has recently restricted CTL deployment to prevent the market from overheating before the technology is perfected. There were approximately 20 CTL plants in the planning stages in 2007, with a capacity of 16 million tons per year (IEA, 2007a). In an attempt to slow uncoordinated deployment by local governments, in July 2007 the central government prohibited CTL plants with an annual processing capacity of less than 3 million tons (Qi, 2007). Then in early September 2008, China placed a moratorium on all CTL plants, aside from the direct CTL plant in Inner Mongolia and one joint venture between Sasol and Shenhua (Jia, 2008). We suspect this is a temporary halt, so that China ensures that the technology is deployed systematically with respect to the mining and water resources needed for CTL production.

U.S. companies are certainly interested in liquefaction technology, though there are presently no commercial CTL plants in the United States. In August 2008, an industry spokesperson claimed that more than 10 companies were planning CTL projects to be built over the next decade (Montgomery, 2008). The recent drop in oil prices will have put all of these projects in question. Despite advocacy from politicians from coal-producing regions, the federal government has not yet provided enough support to counter concern over oil price fluctuations and probable climate change legislation (Vallentin, 2008). There is significant opposition to CTL from the U.S. environmental community, which is better mobilized than their counterparts in China. The environmental community has been able to discourage significant private investment in CTL in the United States, and when Consol Energy announced plans for the country's first commercial-scale CTL facility, the facility included the capture and storage of all its carbon dioxide emissions (Brownstein, 2008).[12] With its higher per capita GDP, and with a stagnant (if not shrinking) demand for oil, the United States is also in a better position to afford expensive oil than China. As a long-time consumer of significant quantities of oil, the United States also has well-established business relationships with major oil suppliers.

If China successfully commercializes CTL, it may benefit from the opportunity to sell the technology to coal-rich countries like the United States, Australia, and India. But there are many risks associated with becoming an energy technology leader. The hallmark of a developed,

---

[12] This plant was cancelled in the fall of 2008 (Greenwire, 2008).

industrialized country is that its advancement is based on creating new technologies, whereas developing nations can still benefit by piggy-backing on existing technologies perfected elsewhere. In a sense, wide-spread deployment of commercial CTL will cause China to become a developed nation, at least with regard to energy technology.

Once a country becomes the leader in a technology that affects a large section of the economy, the rate of economic growth is likely to slow down. An argument can be made that the slower growth in the OECD countries is a direct consequence of having coupled economic growth directly to technological innovation. China will need to carefully manage this potential threat to its economy, just as it will need to respond to the risk posed by high oil prices. This statement is not meant to detract from our earlier assumption that China's economy will grow by at least 5.5 percent annually from 2006–2049. We are simply drawing attention to the fact that the development of CTL will provoke a transition in the Chinese economy that the government will need to address.

The large-scale introduction of CTL is another decision point where policy intervention could change the outcome. For example, a significant commitment to CTL research by the United States would allow for rapid development of U.S.-owned technology. China could use this technology to produce CTL fuel using its indigenous coal resources. Depending upon the terms of the technology transfer, this might address China's energy security concerns while still allowing the country to take advantage of technologies developed elsewhere. Another possible outcome is a joint CTL effort by the largest coal producers in the world — the United States, China and India — to create a measure of oil independence. Russia, even though it is a fossil fuel exporter, might also partici-pate in such an effort using indirect liquefaction of natural gas.[13]

7. CTL Will Complicate Negotiations about China's Role in an International Climate Change Agreement

Given the magnitude of China's contribution to current emissions, it

---

[13] With the boom in shale gas in the United States, GTL (gas to liquid) technologies could play a similar role even without access to coal.

seems likely that the country will eventually accept carbon limitations as part of an international climate change agreement, but the timing and conditions under which this will happen are highly uncertain. Widespread use of CTL fuel, whether in China or the United States, will make climate change much more difficult to address.[14] CTL fuel emits an amount of carbon dioxide from the automobile tailpipe that is essentially identical to emissions from oil-produced gasoline. However, the lifecycle emissions are far larger because the CTL production process emits far more carbon dioxide than the typical refining process. The Sasol CTL plant is the world's largest point source of carbon dioxide and emits 0.44 tons of carbon dioxide per barrel of oil; in comparison, U.S. refineries typically emit only 0.05 tons of carbon dioxide per barrel (Andrews, 2007).

In our scenario, 800 Mtoe of gasoline demand in 2049 would require 1.3–1.9 Gtoe of coal, assuming energy-conversion efficiency of 60 percent for direct liquefaction and 40 percent for indirect liquefaction.[15] This is roughly equivalent to China's current production of 1.2 Gtoe of coal per year (IEA, 2008). This amount of CTL fuel along the whole lifecycle would emit 1.4 to 2.2 Gt of carbon, compared to 0.6 Gt from the gasoline derived from oil.[16] In sum, we estimate that coal liquefaction emits 2 to 3 times as much carbon as traditional gasoline.[17]

---

[14] A full environmental analysis of CTL fuel would examine both its positive attributes (the fuel burns cleanly, minimizing particulate and sulfur dioxide emissions) and all of its drawbacks (e.g., production requires significant amounts of water, see Couch, 2008 and Chan et al., 2006). We have focused on CTL's climate change implications because these appear to be the most significant.

[15] By 2049, both indirect and direct liquefaction will probably be significantly more efficient (see Boardman 2007 for potential efficiency improvements), but to be conservative we have used present-day estimates of conversion efficiency (IEA, 2007a, p. 367; see also Andrews, 2007, appendix).

[16] Carbon-emissions associated with coal and gasoline calculated assuming 1.11 tC/toe from coal and 0.84 tC/toe from crude oil, based upon the following data from the IEA: 26 tC/TJ from coal, and 20 tC/TJ from crude oil, and 41,868 TJ/Mtoe (IEA, 2007b, p. I.24). We use the carbon emission factor for crude oil rather than for gasoline (18 tC/TJ) to account for emissions from processes that refine crude oil into gasoline.

[17] Our estimate is somewhat higher than that given by most of the literature on synthetic fuels, which ranges from 1.6 to 2.5 (Couch, 2008; Hawkins, 2007; Vallentin, 2008; EPA, 2007; Wang et al., 2007), except for one prominent study that places the range from

	Estimated Gasoline Demand	Comparable Indirect CTL Fuel (40% Efficiency)	Comparable Direct CTL Fuel (60% Efficiency)
Mtoes	775	1,938	1,292
Carbon emissions factor (tC/TJ)	20	26	26
TJ/Mtoe	41,868	41,868	41,868
Carbon emissions factor (tC/Mtoe)	837,660	1,108,665	1,108,665
Estimated emissions (tC)	649,112,188	2,148,561,342	1,432,374,228
Lifecycle comparison	1	3.3	2.2

It is worth noting that carbon emissions at the liquefaction plant (approximately 0.8 to 1.6 Gt in this example) could be captured and stored far more easily than the vehicles' tailpipe emissions (0.6 Gt); we will return to this point in the following sections. Using CTL fuel to meet all of China's estimated vehicle demand in 2049 would contribute an estimated 0.4–0.5 ppm per year to atmospheric levels of carbon dioxide (assuming that the emissions are not captured and stored), compared to 0.2 ppm from gasoline alone.[18]

Our estimate of CTL emissions is equivalent to one-fourth of the current annual increase in atmospheric carbon, and suggests that large-scale deployment of CTL in China would greatly complicate international negotiations over climate change. At present, China has refused to

---

2.5 to 3.5 (MIT, 2007). We verified our result by calculating the carbon output of two representative facilities, a NETL 40.5% efficient direct liquefaction plant and a Gulf Oil direct CTL plant with 60% efficiency (Andrews, 2007). The NETL plant produces 2.25 barrels of gasoline per ton of coal. We estimate that this amount of gasoline has 245 kg of carbon, while given that the feedstock coal has a heat content of 14,040 BTU/lb, the CTL fuel has 851 kg of carbon per ton. In this case, the ratio of carbon from CTL/gasoline is 3.5. A similar calculation for the Gulf Oil plant results in a ratio of 2.4. On the other hand, the aforementioned Sasol plant has an implied ratio of about 2. The wide range of ratios suggests that efficiency varies widely from plant to plant. Over time, the ratio will probably decline as the CTL process becomes more efficient.

[18] We assume that each ton of carbon contributes 2.5×10^{-10} ppm of carbon dioxide to the atmosphere. This is admittedly an underestimate, since it ignores an almost equal amount of carbon dioxide that is emitted to the atmosphere and gradually absorbed by the ocean over a number of decades. However, for the purposes of this scenario exercise, we have simplified the analysis to include just the semi-permanent portion of the ppm-contribution.

accept any carbon dioxide limits, and its recent five-year plan has energy-intensity goals but does not explicitly address carbon emissions, nor does it aim to reduce total energy use. China announced a climate change plan in 2007, but this seems unlikely to significantly constrain its emissions. Historically, China has contributed relatively little to the accumulation of carbon dioxide in the atmosphere and its per capita emissions (1.4 tons of carbon per year) are still significantly below those of the United States (5.3 tons). Yet China's per capita emissions are above the world average (1.3 tons), and China contributes more than 20 percent of the world's carbon emissions from fossil fuel combustion (Graham-Harrison and Buckley, 2008; Marland et al., 2008).[19] In order to address climate change, China's emissions will need to be addressed in some way. Even if the world were only attempting to hold carbon dioxide emissions constant, China and the United States would both have to reduce their emissions.

Yet unless climate change impacts become obvious and painful within the country's borders, it is unlikely that China will be eager to risk slowing economic growth by limiting emissions. It is certain, however, that climate stabilization without China is impossible. By mid-century, emissions reductions of between 30–85 percent of 2000 levels are estimated to be necessary in order to stabilize at 350–440 ppm, which is associated with a predicted temperature increase of 2.0–2.8°C and sea-level rise of 0.4–1.7 meters from pre-industrial levels (IPCC, 2007).[20] Stabilization in that range implies that the world's annual ppm-increase would need to drop from around 2 ppm to approximately

---

[19] These calculations are based upon the following data for 2007: China 1.8 GtC and 1,319,983 people; United States 1.6 GtC and 301,621,000 people; and World 8.5 GtC and 6,612,040 people).

[20] A gigaton of carbon emitted as carbon dioxide to the atmosphere raises the atmospheric carbon dioxide level by roughly 0.25 ppm (Broecker, 2007). The precise amount of this increase depends on the time trajectory of the release. However, as long as the time window for emissions is on the order of a century the actual number is fairly insensitive to the precise emission trajectory. Stabilization at 440 ppm would give the world a remaining carbon budget of 55 ppm or 220 GtC. Given that fossil fuel emissions are currently 8.0 GtC/yr (Marland et al., 2008), stabilization requires a continued annual emission reduction of 3.6 percent. In the year 2049 this would result in a world annual emission of 1.8 GtC/yr, a reduction of more than 70 percent from 2000 (6.7 GtC/yr).

0.3–1.3 ppm (IEA, 2007b). Even if the rest of the world's emissions went to zero and China used renewable sources to meet one-quarter of its estimated energy demand, it would still emit roughly 3 to 6 Gt of carbon by 2049, contributing 0.9 to 2.0 ppm of carbon dioxide to the atmosphere each year.

Even in the absence of large-scale deployment of CTL technology, stabilization of carbon dioxide in the atmosphere will be unlikely without the introduction of carbon capture and storage (CCS) technologies. CCS can greatly reduce or even completely eliminate the carbon dioxide emissions from fossil fuel consumption. Combined with direct capture of carbon dioxide from the air, it is even possible to store more carbon dioxide than is emitted due to fossil fuel combustion. Solar energy, nuclear energy, and CCS technologies are the three options that could be scaled up to meet the energy demand of an economically developing world at mid-century. While other types of low-carbon energy, such as wind, hydroelectric, or geothermal energy, will certainly provide a portion of the world's future energy supply, their potential for large-scale deployment appears limited (Lackner and Sachs, 2005).

We consider it more likely than not that by 2049 China is actively engaged in stabilizing the level of atmospheric carbon dioxide. Stabilization will probably require explicit government intervention to raise the efficiency of energy and transportation systems, possibly a transition to plug-in hybrids or electric cars, an active effort to introduce nuclear energy and renewable energy sources, and a large effort to capture and store carbon dioxide. Once China is actively engaged in stabilizing the level of atmospheric carbon dioxide, the current generation of power plants will represent a difficult legacy of large emissions which will be expensive to control.

Given the large resource base of fossil fuels, any strategy that excludes CCS is unlikely to substantially reduce carbon dioxide emissions. Reliance on CTL technology would exacerbate the need for CCS and probably promote its introduction at an earlier date. Comprehensive deployment of CCS would eliminate the major drawback of CTL technologies, though environmental concerns related to water consumption and mining would remain.

8. CCS Can Address Climate Change Concerns

Technologies for carbon dioxide capture at large concentrated sources already exist, though there is still progress to be made on cost and engineering considerations. Although the components of the process have all been proven to work separately, the technologies have not yet been integrated at a large-scale demonstration plant. For this reason, there is still considerable uncertainty about cost estimates, the necessary regulation, and the degree of public acceptance of the technology. China is participating in international efforts to explore CCS technologies and is currently building two power plants that will demonstrate the capture of carbon dioxide from the exhaust stream (IEA, 2007a).[21]

Using current technologies, scrubbing carbon dioxide out of flue stacks of electricity generating units would reduce energy efficiency by about 10 to 40 percent for natural gas and pulverized coal plants, respectively (IPCC, 2005, TS.10). Pricing carbon should spur a concerted effort in technology development that will lead to new advanced power plant designs that fully integrate carbon dioxide capture into the process design and which eliminate virtually all emissions to the atmosphere while greatly improving energy efficiencies (Lackner and Yegulalp, 2005). Similar strategies for the designs of zero emission cement, steel and fertilizer plants would eventually lead to the possible capture of nearly all carbon dioxide emissions from concentrated sources.

There are three storage options currently under development or research — ocean disposal, underground injection, and mineralization — each with varying degrees of safety and permanence. Ocean disposal involves the dilution of carbon dioxide into ocean waters or the collection of carbon dioxide in pools at the ocean floor. Ocean disposal is not currently being pursued aggressively due to concerns over its impact on marine life and the relatively short life-time of this form of storage (Lackner, 2002; IPCC, 2005).

---

[21] The Yantai IGCC plant will generate between 300–400 MW. The Greengen IGCC plant has two phases: a 250 MW IGCC plant and a 400 MW IGCC plant with carbon dioxide separation and hydrogen power. These facilities are expected to open between 2010 and 2015 (IEA, 2007a, p. 347).

In underground injection, carbon dioxide is compressed into a supercritical fluid and then injected into geologic storage spaces, such as oil or gas wells. This process uses technologies currently deployed in oil drilling, though permanent storage will require the development of new technologies to ensure that the carbon dioxide stays in place forever. The total worldwide capacity of such reservoirs is up for debate, with opinions ranging from 80 Gt of carbon to a capacity that exceeds the world's carbon supply. Estimates of China's storage capacity vary widely as well, ranging from 40 to 550 Gt of carbon (IEA, 2007a). In part, the total storage capacity will depend upon the safety and permanence requirements that policymakers deem necessary.

Underground injection under the deep ocean floor is especially promising, since gravity would trap carbon dioxide underneath the ocean floor, greatly lessening the risk of potential leakage (House et al., 2006; Levine et al., 2007). Mineral sequestration, a process in which carbon dioxide is reacted with mineral rocks to create carbonates, would allow permanent and safe storage on a virtually unlimited scale (Goff and Lackner, 1998; Lackner, 2003; Park and Fan, 2004; Kelemen and Matter, 2008). The cost of mineralization is still too high relative to underground injection; additional research will probably make this a cost-effective storage option in the future.

Without CCS, the literature generally suggests that CTL would be cost-competitive when oil is above $35–$50 per barrel (Couch, 2008). Adding carbon capture to the production of CTL fuel is estimated to add 10 percent to the cost of production, raising the cost from $50 to $55 per barrel (MIT, 2007). This translates into $35 per avoided ton of carbon, compared to $92 per ton captured from electricity generation; liquefaction requires the separation of carbon dioxide into a pure stream, thus eliminating a significant component of the capture expense at electricity plants (MIT, 2007).[22] The total cost would also need to include transport

---

[22] The magnitude of this disparity suggests that it might be more cost-effective to power vehicle transport with CTL + CCS + air capture (a technology to be discussed in the following section) rather than coal-fired electricity + CCS. Both routes would be climate neutral.

and storage, estimated at $18 per ton of carbon (MIT, 2007).[23] In sum, however, the exact cost will be uncertain until there is a significant deployment of the technology, as learning-by-doing and economies of scale may drive down the cost. In addition, though China does have an active advanced coal research effort (Zhao and Gallagher, 2007), technology transfer may still be an issue for certain components of the CCS process.

In our scenario, where vehicles use 800 Mtoe of CTL fuel, there are 0.6 GtC emitted from the tailpipe and 0.8–1.6 GtC emitted at the power plant. Adding CCS to CTL production increases the energy requirement by an estimated 30 percent, which leads to additional carbon emissions.[24] As a result, CCS would need to capture 1.0–2.0 GtC from China's CTL plants each year in order to reduce the atmospheric contribution from 0.4–0.5 ppm (lifecycle CTL emissions) to 0.2 ppm (tailpipe emissions). This would cost $53–$106 billion per year, based upon an estimate of $53 per ton of carbon. We note that even if China uses CCS at every CTL plant, it will still be emitting a significant amount of carbon dioxide into the atmosphere just from automobile tailpipes. Recent research suggests that stabilization at 450 ppm will require that the carbon emissions associated with the world's coal resources grow slightly until 2023 and begin to decline in 2025, going to zero by 2050 (Kharecha and Hansen, 2008). If this analysis is correct, stabilization will probably require mitigation of the tailpipe emissions of automobiles.

---

[23] We have relied upon the MIT report, as it includes estimates of CCS at both CTL facilities and electricity plants, but we note that its estimate ($110/tC for CCS at a coal-fired plant) is toward the low-end of the literature. The IPCC's range is $31–$260/tC and McKinsey recently estimated that an early-stage commercial plant would cost $210/tC (IPCC, 2005; McKinsey, 2008).

[24] The energy penalty for CCS at an electricity plant is generally assumed to be 30 percent. We do not have a comparable figure for CCS at a CTL facility, but we imagine it is significantly less than 30 percent given that the estimated capture cost is so much lower. To be conservative, however, we have assumed a 30 percent energy penalty for this scenario exercise.

9. Air Capture Would Allow for Climate-neutral Use of CTL

There is a nascent technology — air capture — that could address tail-pipe emissions of carbon dioxide (Lackner et al., 1999; Zeman and Lackner, 2004; Keith et al., 2006; Zeman, 2007; Lackner, 2008). The process, which captures carbon dioxide directly from the ambient air, mimics flue gas scrubbing but with much lower concentrations of carbon dioxide. Carbon dioxide is a uniformly mixed gas and quickly disperses evenly throughout the atmosphere. For this reason, air capture devices can be located near carbon storage sites, thus minimizing the expense associated with post-capture transport of carbon dioxide.

Although it is often considered difficult to extract carbon dioxide from air because of the low concentration of carbon dioxide, trees and other photosynthesizing organisms perform this task routinely. Industrial air capture devices known as "synthetic trees" can capture carbon dioxide much more efficiently than natural processes and can operate at costs only slightly larger than conventional capture in flue stacks. Synthetic trees are similar to windmills, in that both devices reduce net carbon dioxide emissions to the atmosphere. The windmill displaces fossil fuel consumption, while the air capture device recovers carbon dioxide emissions caused by fossil fuel consumption and thus renders fossil fuels carbon neutral. Synthetic trees, however, are much more compact than windmills for the same carbon impact.[25] We estimate that capturing all 8.5 Gt of carbon released worldwide due to fossil fuels each year would require a collection area the size of the state of Arizona. Several hundred times as much land would be required to generate enough wind power to prevent all carbon dioxide emissions. For this reason, air capture could become more effective in reducing

---

[25] A synthetic tree collects carbon dioxide and thereby directly reduces atmospheric carbon; in contrast, a windmill indirectly reduces atmospheric carbon by displacing fossil fuel consumption. Given basic kinetics, a windmill must be several hundred times larger than a synthetic tree in order to have a comparable carbon impact. This is because the kinetic energy density of air is approximately 20 joules per cubic meter (assuming wind speed of 6 m/s), while the heat of combustion of gasoline that results in the carbon dioxide in a cubic meter of air is approximately 10,000 joules (Lackner et al., 1999; Lackner, 2008).

CO_2 emissions than wind power, though wind is still more cost effective at this point.[26]

Once air capture is commercialized, the cost per ton of carbon should be comparable to point-source capture at a power plant using conventional retrofit scrubbers. Air capture would allow China to use CTL fuel without contributing to climate change. In our 2049 scenario, 0.6 Gt of carbon would need to be extracted from the atmosphere to compensate for the tailpipe emissions from CTL fuel. This carbon could be collected by air capture devices located in China, or near storage sites anywhere else in the world. This siting flexibility could also provide climate negotiators with some additional leeway in determining the terms of an international agreement. We estimate, albeit with a great degree of uncertainty, that it would cost perhaps $120/tC to capture and store these tailpipe emissions.[27]

10. Conclusion

China's energy technology development is currently motivated by three main factors: the desire for rapid economic growth, energy security, and to a growing extent, concern over the health impacts of pollutants such as particulates and sulfur dioxide. Though China has recently become the world's largest emitter of carbon dioxide, climate change is a more distant concern for policy-makers. In some respects, this lack of emphasis on climate change is entirely understandable given China's relatively small historic contribution to the problem. Going forward, however, the world will need to encourage China to reduce its carbon dioxide emissions if it is to prevent catastrophic climate impacts over the next century.

---

[26] For more recent discussions on the topic and a more detailed description of the technology see also (Sarewitz and Nelson, 2008; Lackner, 2009; Lackner and Brennan, 2009; Lackner, 2010; APS, 2011; Lackner et al., 2012).

[27] This estimate is calculated as follows: $110/tC for air capture plus $12/tC for storage or $120/tC after rounding. The air capture figure is based on the author's experience with a prototype of the technology. (See also footnote 26 for additional discussions on more recent cost estimates.) The storage figure is backed out of the MIT (2007) estimate of $18/tC for storage and transport, using the cost ratio of 2:1 for storage to transport from McKinsey (2008).

Given the magnitude of its population and its anticipated economic growth, China will play a key role in stabilizing atmospheric carbon dioxide at a tolerable level.

Because China is already relatively likely to pursue CTL technologies, we are especially wary of policy mechanisms that discourage the use of coal for electricity but leave it available for other uses. For example, the fungibility of China's coal resources suggests that Clean Development Mechanism projects that decrease China's production of coal-fired electricity may simply free up coal for alternate uses, such as CTL. A more effective mechanism might provide nations with incentives to leave carbon in the ground, or for capturing and storing carbon dioxide after combustion. Somewhat analogously, preventing carbon dioxide emissions from deforestation by paying for wood-product substitutes would have the perverse effect of simply freeing up wood for other uses. Therefore, current deforestation and land-use proposals suggest compensating countries for preserving an *in situ* resource, thus preventing the release of carbon dioxide (Gullison et al., 2007). Unless the international community provides compelling incentives, developing countries will use their natural resources — forests and fossil fuels — in order to pursue the type of living standards demonstrated by industrialized countries.

If China follows the path suggested by our analysis of "more likely than not" decisions, we believe it is likely to deploy large-scale CTL due to energy security concerns. In the absence of China's participation in an international carbon agreement, this could be devastating to the climate. Yet our decision-tree analysis also highlights three critical junctures where international policy intervention could shift the trajectory: (1) significant RD&D could lead to a breakthrough in vehicle technology, causing a shift away from liquid hydrocarbons; (2) research on CTL technology could improve its efficiency, thus reducing emissions; and (3) widespread deployment of CCS plus air capture could make CTL climate neutral. While China could certainly accomplish these policy interventions independently, we think it is improbable that China will be willing to finance significant climate change mitigation efforts without international assistance.

References

Adam, D., 2008. Alarm over New Oil-from-Coal Plans. *The Guardian* (guardian. co.uk), February 20, 2008.

Aldous, P., 2005. China's Burning Ambition. *Nature*, 435(30): 1152–4.

American Physical Society, 2011. Direct Air Capture of CO_2 with Chemicals: A Technology Assessment for the APS Panel on Public Affairs.

An, F. and Sauer, A., 2004. Comparison of Passenger Vehicle Fuel Economy and GHG Emissions Standards around the World. Prepared for the Pew Center on Global Climate Change.

Andrews, A., 2007. Liquid Fuels from Coal, Natural Gas, and Biomass: Background and Policy. CRS Report for Congress, RL34133.

Andrews, E.L., 2007. Lawmakers Push for Big Subsidies for Coal Process. *New York Times*, May 29, 2007.

Asian Development Bank, 2006. Energy Efficiency and Climate Change Considerations for On-Road Transport in Asia (www.adb.org/Documents/ Reports/Energy-Efficiency-Transport/energy-efficiency.pdf, accessed on October 29, 2008).

Boardman, R.D., 2007. Statement of Richard D. Boardman, Ph.D., Energy and Environmental Science and Technology Division, Idaho National Laboratory, before the Subcommittee on Energy and Environment, Committee on Science and Technology of the U.S. House of Representatives, September 5, 2007.

Broecker, W., 2007. CO_2 Arithmetic. *Science*, 315: 1371.

Brownstein, M., 2008. A Viable Coal-to-Liquids Project? environmentaldefenseblogs.org/climate411, July 30, 2008.

Chan, M., Duda, J., Forbes, S., Rodosta, T., Vagnetti, R. and McIlvried, H., 2006. Emerging Issues for Fossil Energy and Water: Investigation of Water Issues Related to Coal Mining, Coal to Liquids, Oil Shale, and Carbon Capture and Sequestration. U.S. Department of Energy, National Energy Technology Laboratory (DOE/NETL-2006/1233).

Chen, Y.-H., Reilly, J.M. and Paltsev, S., 2011. The Prospects for Coal-to-Liquid Conversion: A General Equilibrium Analysis. *Energy Policy*, 39: 4713–4725.

Couch, G., 2008. Coal to Liquids. IEA Clean Coal Centre: London, March 2008.

Dalton, M., 2007. Big Coal Tries to Recruit Military to Kindle a Market: Use as Liquid Fuel Is an Aim, But Cost, Pollution Are Issues. *Wall Street Journal*, September 11, 2007.

EPA, 2007. Greenhouse Gas Impacts of Expanded Renewable and Alternative Fuels Use. Office of Transportation and Air Quality. EPA420-F-07-035, April 2007.

Goff, F. and Lackner, K.S., 1998. Carbon Dioxide Sequestering Using Ultra-mafic Rocks. *Environ. Geoscience*, 5(3): 89–101.

Greenwire, 2008. Synthesis Energy Systems Ceases Development of Benwood, West Virginia Synthetic Gasoline Project Due to Current State of Credit Markets, October 23, 2008.

Gullison, R.E., Frumhoff, P.C., Canadell, J.G., Field, C.B., Nepstad, D.C., Hayhoe, K., Avissar, R., Curran, L.M., Friedlingstein, P., Jones, C.D. and Nobre, C., 2007. Tropical Forests and Climate Policy. *Science* 316: 985–986.

Harrison-Graham, E. and Buckley, C., 2008. China Says Greenhouse Gases Catch Up with U.S. *Reuters*, October 29, 2008.

Hawkins, D., 2007. Testimony of David G. Hawkins, Director, Climate Center, Natural Resources Defense Council. Hearing on Benefits and Challenges of Producing Liquid Fuel from Coal. Subcommittee on Energy and Environment, House Committee on Science and Technology, September 5, 2007.

House, K.Z., Schrag, D.P., Harvey, C.F. and Lackner, K.S., 2006. Permanent Carbon Dioxide Storage in Deep-Sea Sediments. *Proceedings of the National Academy of Sciences*, 10.1073/pnas.0605318103.

Intergovernmental Panel on Climate Change, 2005. Special Report on Carbon Dioxide Capture and Storage. Cambridge University Press, New York.

Intergovernmental Panel on Climate Change, 2007. Climate Change 2007: Synthesis Report.

International Energy Agency, 2004. Special Issue Paper 9: Densities of Oil Products. Energy Statistics Working Group Meeting.

International Energy Agency, 2007a. World Energy Outlook 2007: China and India Insights (OECD/IEA: Paris).

International Energy Agency, 2007b. CO_2 Emissions from Fuel Combustion, 1971–2005: 2007 Edition (OECD/IEA: Paris).

International Energy Agency, 2008a. Energy Balances of Non-OECD Countries, 2008 Edition (OECD/IEA: Paris).

International Energy Agency, 2008b. Energy Balances of OECD Countries, 2008 Edition (OECD/IEA: Paris).

International Energy Agency, 2008c. Energy Technology Perspectives 2008: Strategies and Scenarios to 2050 (OECD/IEA: Paris).

International Energy Agency, 2011. Energy Balances of Non-OECD Countries, 2011 Edition (OECD/IEA: Paris).

Jia, H., 2008. China Suspends Coal-to-Oil Projects. RSC Chemistry World (www.rsc.org/chemistryworld/News/2008/September/10090801.asp, accessed on October 29, 2008).

Keith, D.W., Ha-Duong, M. and Stolaroff, J.K., 2006. Climate Strategy with CO_2 Capture from Air. *Climatic Change*, 74: 17–45.

Kelemen, P. and Matter, J., 2008. In Situ Carbonation of Peridotite for CO_2 Storage. *Proceedings of the National Academy of Sciences*, 105(45): 17295–17300.

Kharecha, P.A. and Hansen, J.E., 2008. Implications of 'Peak Oil' for Atmospheric CO_2 and Climate. *Global Biogeochemical Cycles*, 22, GB3012, doi:10.1029/2007GB003142.

Lackner, K.S., 2002. Carbonate Chemistry for Sequestering Fossil Carbon. *Annual Reviews of Energy and the Environment*, 27: 193–232.

Lackner, K.S., 2003. Climate Change: A Guide to CO_2 Sequestration. *Science*, 300(5626): 1677.

Lackner, K.S., 2008. *Thermodynamics of the Humidity Swing Driven Air Capture of Carbon Dioxide*. Author's manuscript, August 9, 2008, updated August 22, 2008.

Lackner, K.S., 2009. Capture of Carbon Dioxide from Ambient Air. *Eur. Phys. J. Special Topics*, 176: 93–106.

Lackner, K.S., 2010. Washing Carbon Out of the Air. *Scientific American*, 302: 66–71.

Lackner, K.S. and Brennan, S., 2009. Envisioning Carbon Capture and Storage: Expanded Possibilities Due to Air Capture, Leakage Insurance, and C-14 Monitoring. *Climatic Change*, 96: 357–378.

Lackner, K.S. et al., 2012. *The Urgency of the Development of CO_2 Capture from Ambient Air*. doi:10.1073/pnas.1108765109

Lackner, K.S. and Sachs, J., 2005. A Robust Strategy for Sustainable Energy. *Brookings Papers on Economic Activity*, 2: 215–269.

Lackner, K.S. and Yegulalp, T., 2005. Thermodynamic Foundation of the Zero Emission Concept. *Minerals and Metallurgical Processing*, 22(3): 161–167.

Lackner, K.S., Ziock, H.-J. and Grimes, P., 1999. Carbon Dioxide Extraction from Air: Is It an Option? *Proceedings of the 24th International Conference on Coal Utilization & Fuel Systems*, Clearwater, Florida.

Levine, J.S., Matter, J.M., Goldberg, D.M., Cook, A. and Lackner, K.S., 2007. Gravitational Trapping of Carbon Dioxide in Deep Sea Sediments: Permeability, Buoyancy, and Geomechanical Analysis. *Geophysical Research Letters* 34, doi:10.1029/2007GL031560.

Marland, G., Boden, T.A. and Andres, R.J., 2008. Global, Regional, and National Fossil Fuel CO_2 Emissions. In *Trends: A Compendium of Data on Global Change*. Carbon Dioxide Information Analysis Center, Oak Ridge National Laboratory, U.S. Department of Energy, Oak Ridge, Tenn., USA.

McKinsey Global Institute, 2007. Leapfrogging to Higher Energy Productivity in China.

McKinsey & Company, 2008. Carbon Capture and Storage: Assessing the Economics.

MIT, 2007. The Future of Coal: Options for a Carbon-Constrained Future.

Montgomery, D., 2008. Liquefied-Coal Industry Gains Energy. McClatchy Newspapers, August 22, 2008.

Park, A.-H. and Fan, L.-S., 2004. CO_2 Mineral Sequestration: Physically Activated Aqueous Carbonation of Serpentine and pH Swing Process. *Chemical Engineering Science*, 59: 5241–5247.

Qi, W., 2007. China Reins in Fast Growth of Coal-to-Liquid Fuel Projects. Xinhua News Agency, July 29, 2007.

Rogner, H.-H., 1997. An Assessment of World Hydrocarbon Resources. *Annual Reviews of Energy and the Environment*, 22: 217–62.

Rong, F. and Victor, D.G., 2011. Coal Liquefaction Policy in China: Explaining the Policy Reversal Since 2006. *Energy Policy*, 39: 8175–8184.

Sarewitz, D. and Nelson, R., 2008. Three Rules for Technological Fixes. *Nature*, 456: 871–872.

Sun, Q., 2008. CTL Development in China Based on Shenhua CTL Projects. Powerpoint for Congressional Noontime Briefing, Washington, D.C. (U.S.-China Energy Center: West Virginia), April 24, 2008.

Wang, M., Wu, M. and Huo, H., 2007. Life-Cycle Energy and Greenhouse Gas Results of Fischer-Tropsch Diesel Produced from Natural Gas, Coal, and Biomass. Center for Transportation Research Argonne National Laboratory, 2007 SAE Government/Industry Meeting, Washington, D.C., May 14–16, 2007.

Williams, R.H. and Larson, E.D., 2003. A Comparison of Direct and Indirect Liquefaction Technologies for Making Fluid Fuels from Coal. *Energy for Sustainable Development*, 7(41): 103–129.

World Bank, 2008. World Development Indicators Online (downloaded on September 6, 2008).

World Coal Institute, 2006. Coal: Liquid Fuels (www.worldcoal.org, downloaded on October 25, 2008).

Vallentin, D., 2008. Policy Drivers and Barriers for Coal-to-Liquids (CtL) Technologies in the United States. *Energy Policy*, 36: 3198–3211.

Zeman, F.S., 2007. Energy and Material Balance of CO_2 Capture from Ambient Air. *Environmental Science and Technology*, 41: 7558–7563.

Zeman, F.S. and Lackner, K.S., 2004. Capturing Carbon Dioxide Directly from the Atmosphere. *World Resource Review*, 16(2): 157–172.

Zhao, L. and Gallagher, K.S., 2007. Research, Development, Demonstration, and Early Deployment Policies for Advanced-Coal Technology in China. *Energy Policy*, 35: 6467–6477.

The Sustainability of Water Resources in China

Ximing Cai and Upmanu Lall

1. Introduction

China's economic development, agricultural growth, and food security are highly dependent on water resources in the country. The Government of China has declared the lack of water resources a serious limitation to the economic and social development of the country.[1] According to an estimate by China's Ministry of Water Resources, the loss of food production due to water stress reached 25–30 million metric tons, and the direct economic loss to agriculture and industry reached about RMB 150 billion (equivalent to US$18 billion) in 2005 (China Economic Herald, 2005), which was a normal precipitation year at the country level. With increasing water scarcity and deteriorating water quality, the competition for available water resources is getting more and more intense among the economic, social and environmental sectors. Since the water needs of the domestic and industrial sectors are economic and social necessities and environmental uses are gaining in acceptance and importance in the country, a radical reduction in the water share of agriculture will be an unavoidable outcome. Several studies found that with business-as-usual water management and agricultural development practices, the current water stress trends are set to worsen in future years given the continued rapid economic development in China combined with continued, albeit low, population growth, and rapidly changing diets, including increased consumption of meats and vegetables (Rosegrant et al., 2002).

---

[1] Report by former Premier Zhu Rongji, National People's Conference meeting, February 2000.

A serious concern has emerged as to whether China can provide the quantity and quality of water needed to meet the demand of all groups, including ecosystem services, in the future. What does a sustainability goal imply for water resources management? There are multiple frameworks under which this question needs to be considered.

First, this question needs to be addressed in the context of the current fundamental national policy — *social harmony*. Under water stress, conflicts in water allocation and the damages to the public environment have intensified, and a pressing concern for "social equity" has appeared in Northern China (Cai, 2008). In the context of resource allocation, social equity refers to a bundle of rights and duties of government, collective, and/or individuals, which are applied to protecting weak and vulnerable populations in society. *Spatial or regional equity* considerations naturally emerge under this criterion. It will be interesting to see how the national policy towards "building a harmonious society" will enhance social equity in water resources management, which should be an essential part of any harmonious society, since water is a key resource for life and production in society.

Second, water resources sustainability is also related to a very traditional and most recently emphasized philosophy of China — *human-nature harmony*. Facing the risk of environmental damage, China is beginning to recognize the spirituality of "human harmony with nature," which is rooted in Chinese historical ethics of Taoism, a philosophy of non-interference, emphasizing education and mastery of natural phenomena, discipline, and social harmony (Li et al., 2004). It is impossible to eliminate human interferences to the natural systems but it is possible to restore and maintain natural integrity to a level that human and natural system would coexist forever. This is a challenge for intensively managed (including urban) watersheds, not only in China but also around the world.

Third, *inter-generational equity* is an oft-cited aspect of sustainability as part of the long-standing debate on development versus conservation (WCED, 1987). The current rate of groundwater depletion in Northern China raises a strong concern on how much water will be left for the next generation. Some deep wells around Beijing must be drilled up to half a mile deep before reaching water. Scientists now estimate with confidence that the aquifers beneath the Northern China Plain will dry up in 30 years if the current water use rate continues. The chronic water shortages have left many cities without adequate drinking water and affected plans for economic development.

Given these three dimensions of water resource sustainability, the still increasing population coupled with rapidly rising per capita consumption of food, water and energy; significant spatial and temporal variability in water availability, and uncertainty as to the impacts of human induced climate change, some macro level priorities articulated by the government of China include drinking water safety, food security, environment protection and ecosystem restoration, and urbanization and regional development. The key question is: Given that all these priorities that compete water resources, how can limited amount of water be allocated to the various sectors of use? Engineering, innovative technology, policy reforms and education and institutional development for water conservation are all needed to develop a solution. However, considering the feasibility, capacity and limitation of all these solutions, there is no single quick solution for resolving the issues discussed above. This study does not attempt to provide a solution but rather to further clarify the problems and call for research and policy debates in order to approach the right solution.

2. Challenges to Sustainability — Problems and Causes

2.1. Water stress — Scarcity

Even as China's rapid and impressive economic development is noted, water stress particularly in Northern China is a widely recognized crisis. Water stress occurs when the demand for water exceeds the available amount during a certain period or when poor quality restricts its use. One of the common indicators of water stress is per capita renewable water. A 1000 m^3 per capita is recognized as a critical level for severe water scarcity (Engelman and LeRoy, 1993). The three major basins in Northern China, Hai, Huai and Huang/Yellow (the 3-H basins), have 520, 470, and 530 m^3 per capita, respectively, which are less than half of the water scarcity threshold (Cai and Rosegrant, 2005). Water stress in the region is also reflected in other indicators. In 1997 the 3-H basins contained about 40 percent of the country's agricultural land and produced 32 percent of the country's GDP, but had less than 8 percent of the country's water resources (CAE, 2001). The higher the withdrawal to runoff ratio, the more intensive the use of water in the river basin, and the lower the water availability and quality for downstream users. Basin-level criticality ratios[2] equal to or greater than 0.4 are considered "high water stress," and ratios of 0.8 "very high water stress" (Raskin, 1997; Alcamo et al., 2000). The world average criticality ratio is 0.09, masking large country and regional differences. In 1995, the ratio of water withdrawal to runoff was 0.89 in the Huanghe Basin, for example, and even higher in the Inland and Haihe basins; while the average for China was 0.26. These already high intensity levels are projected to increase significantly by 2025, with levels exceeding 1.0 for the Inland, Haihe, Huaihe, and Huanghe river basins (Figure 1).

The limited water availability due to low rainfall and runoff and the uneven temporal distribution has been recognized as a natural cause of water stress in Northern China (CAE, 2001). Research has also found that runoff generation in the region shows a declining trend during recent decades. Compared to the annual average during 1956–1979, average precipitation in the 3-H basins decreased by 9.6 percent, runoff decreased by 23.8 percent, and flow to the ocean decreased by 58.6 percent (CAE, 2001). At the regional scale, surface runoff generation within Hebei Province has declined by 65 percent and inflow declined by 72 percent compared to the average in the 1950s (Li and Wei, 2003). The impact of global climate change on water availability in this region needs further monitoring. As in many other regions in the world, the impacts of human activities on runoff generation include deforestation, agricultural and urban development, and groundwater overdraft. According to the assessment of the Chinese Academy of Science (CAS, 2005), vegetation coverage (percentage of the total land) decreased from 38 percent to 32 percent in Northern China during 1988–1999, and urbanized area increased from 5.0–8.2 percent to 6.5–9.5 percent (varying over eastern,

---

[2] The criticality ratio is defined as the ratio of water withdrawals for human use to total renewable water resources.

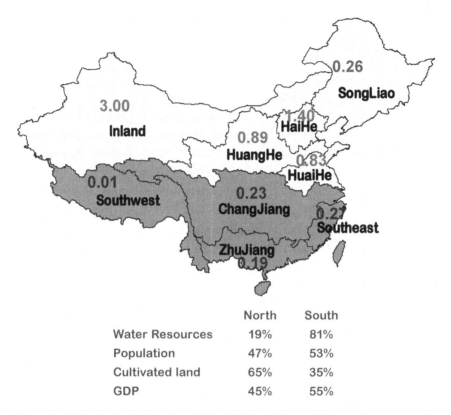

	North	South
Water Resources	19%	81%
Population	47%	53%
Cultivated land	65%	35%
GDP	45%	55%

Figure 1. Major basins in South and North China. The numbers in the map are the ratio of water withdrawal over total renewable water in each basin.

western and central parts). Around urban areas, agricultural land has been converted to urban use. On the other hand, in mountain areas, which were the primary areas of runoff generation, forest and grassland is being replaced by crop land due to growing population in rural area. This land use conversion reduces soil water storage and increases flooding. Moreover, the water stress in Northern China is also a consequence of declining streamflow during the past 50 years, which seems to be related to climate change (Jiao, 2008), as well as upstream storage and diversion. How much is due to climate change and how much due to land use and waterway modification likely varies regionally, and is not well quantified.

Demand growth is of course the major cause of water stress in China. According to the assessment of CAE (2001), between 1980–1999, water use (withdrawal) in Northern China has increased by 41.7 km^3 (CAE, 2001), which is about the average total annual runoff in the Hai River Basin, and 1.3 times of that in the Colorado River Basin. In 2004, the total water withdrawal in the 3-H basins was 137 billion km^3, which was 70 percent of the total annual runoff in the basins. Water demand, particularly municipal and industrial (M&I), will continue to increase. According to a medium projection made by CAE (2001), in the 3-H basins, between 1997 and 2010, water demand will increase by 13.0 m^3 (8%); and between 1997 and 2030, 31.4 km^3 (20%). For the same region, Rosegrant et al. (2002) made a business-as-usual projection of the water demand increase between 1995 and 2025 as 49.0 km^3, close to the high projection of CAE. The continuous increase will make the water supply system more vulnerable.

Like in many other countries and regions, low water use efficiency especially in agriculture, which is the largest water user in Northern China, is a contributor to water stress. In the 3-H basins, agriculture was responsible for 84 percent of total water consumption in the region. This fraction declined in recent years but it is still over 75 percent (Rosegrant et al., 2002). According to the statistics in the Annual Book of Water Resources in China over 85 percent of the irrigation is done through overflow methods and open water channels (MWR, 2004). Starting from the mid 1990s, the Chinese government has greatly increased investment for updating irrigation system. However, the implementation of advanced irrigation technologies faces many technical difficulties (Henry, 2004) and social-economic blocks, which will be discussed later in this chapter.

2.2. Pollution and water quality and ecosystem degradation

Many Chinese researchers believe that water pollution is the biggest concern for water sustainability, in both Northern and Southern China (e.g., Jiang et al., 2004). Due to rapid industrial and municipal development and a large increase in agricultural fertilizer and pesticide use in the past two decades, cases of downstream users receiving polluted water from upstream lands have dramatically increased. During 1980–2004, sewage water discharge doubled in the 3-H basins, and it increased by 160 percent and 140 percent in the Huai and Huang Rivers, respectively, according to the annual water resources bulletins of the 3-H basins. The increasing use of fertilizers and pesticides in agriculture has also dramatically increased non-point source pollution.

Waste water treatment capacity is very limited in China at present. The amount of urban waste water in China wass 35.1 billion m^3 in 1997. The reported treatment rate is only 13% and the actual rate might be lower than 5% (Qian and Zhang, 2001). The water sources in over 90% of the urban areas in the entire country have been polluted to varying degrees and the pollution in over 98 major cities is at a severe level.

Drinking water quality is still a problem in rural areas of China. According to Li et al. (2005), water quality for drinking water in China is worsening due to reasons including the excessive use of chemicals. In those regions where irrigation water is polluted or is largely reduced in quantity, drinking water will be affected in both quantity and quality. The most notorious case is the extremely high cancer rate in a number of villages located along some tributaries of the Huai River. Farmers have used the rivers running around their villages for drinking and irrigation for hundreds of years, but now they find that not only the water directly taken from the rivers, but also the water pumped from wells nearby the rivers, is poisonous (news report, "Visiting a cancer village in the Huai River Basin").

Waste water used for irrigation has caused soil quality problem and may further lead to food quality and health problems. Irrigated areas using waste water increased from 42 thousand hectares in 1963 to 3.6 million hectares in 1998, the majority of which is in Northern China, surrounding large cities such as Beijing and Tianjin (Li et al., 2005). Using waste water for irrigation has brought up a high risk of soil contamination (CER, 1999). Moreover farmers sell most of the agricultural products such as vegetables and fruits irrigated by waste water to urban consumers, which closes the "pollution cycle" between cities and nearby agricultural areas.

So far in North China, the environment, not the farmers, has borne the largest sacrifices from water stress. Environmental water uses form part of instream water uses: they include direct uses for fishing or

wetland harvests, as well as ecological function values, like waste dilution, water storage, flood control, and ecological diversity. For many
rivers, there is not enough water available for pollutant dilution, which
has partially caused the water quality problem, and groundwater overdraft in coastal areas has caused sea water intrusion. Hebei Province,
located north of the Yellow River and covering a major part of the Hai
River Basin, is a typical case of the changed water environment in
Northern China. According to Li and Wei (2003), the province changed
itself from a water-rich region in the 1950s to a water-poor region at
present. Fifty years ago, Hebei had perennial rivers with over 3000-
kilometer long navigation channels, large lakes including the well-known
Baiyangdian Lake, and widely distributed wetlands, and the region suffered frequent disasters of flooding and waterlogging (associated with
land salinization). Today, rivers are dry most of the time, lakes and
wetlands have shrunk and even disappeared (including the Baiyangdian
Lake, "pearl" on the land of Northern China), and the region suffers
damages caused by water shortage every year. Such a change is caused by
excessive water consumption, as well as regional climate variability and
environmental change.

It should be noted that water pollution is a serious problem in many
areas of South China too and wastewater treatment needs large investment. One particular example is the water pollution with the Three
Gorges Dam. Since the construction of the Three Gorges Dam, many
waste water treatment plants have been completed to reduce the water
pollution from the large populated city Chongqing and the suburban
area around it. According to the Ministry of Environmental Protection
of PRC, until April 2007, there were more than 50 waste water treatment
plants installed and the total capacity reached 1.84 million tonnes per
day. However, more treatment facilities might be needed along with the
full operation of the dam in the future.

2.3. The impact of climate change and variability

China's climate is highly heterogeneous spatially and also temporally.
The marked difference between the average annual rainfall and renewable water supply in N. and in S. China was noted earlier. Actually, there

is also considerable variation in seasonality, inter-annual and decadal variability in climate. China has extensive long term written and proxy records of flooding and precipitation that have recently been compiled and analyzed (Jiang et al., 1997; Becker et al., 2006). Evidence for structured inter-annual (3–8 year), decadal (16–20 year) and longer (70–80 year) climate variability from these records is presented. There are four main observations that are worth emphasizing from this literature.

First, in terms of sustainable water resource development, measuring sustainability that use the average annual renewable water available estimated from a 30–50 year recent data set as a basis may not be an appropriate idea, since the climate system can shift to produce dramatically different mean values for the next 30–50 years. Thus, assessments need to be put in the context of the longer term analysis of structured climate variability at the river basin and at the trans-basin scale to develop clearer estimates of what the implications for sustainability are at those scales.

Second, given the pronounced temporal structure in rainfall, persistent multi-year droughts and wet spells are quite likely. The severe drop in streamflow availability in the lower Yellow River basin in the 1990s is almost certainly due to such a structure in climate that was amplified by the human response to multi-year drought in the basin (Becker et al., 2008). Other parts of China were out of phase with this region during this time, i.e., they were wetter. However, to date a systematic investigation of the implications of structured low frequency climate variability on water resource sustainability, reservoir operation, infrastructure design and water allocation does not seem to have been done. Such a spatio-temporal investigation is likely to be very useful in the context of the large scale trans-basin water diversions being envisaged, and also for analyses of food security for the country.

Third, structured climate variability related to larger scale climate teleconnections provides the opportunity for a systematic risk analysis, seasonal to inter-annual prediction of climate inputs, and hence for improved risk management, operation, demand management and resilience of water systems, i.e., for improved water resource sustainability. A limited analysis was done by Xu et al. (2007) of the Yangtze River inflows into the Three Gorges Dam. They identify inter-annual and decadal climate modes that influence these inflows, ocean conditions that likely modulate this variability, and pre-season snow in Western China that seem to be well correlated with monsoon season flows. They develop a simple seasonal flow forecasting model that seems to be quite successful in predicting the reservoir inflows, thus providing an opportunity for improved management. These decadal variations would potentially impact the viability of the SNWT project unless there is large storage available on the Yangtze to carry over flows across multiple years.

Fourth, the presence of persistent low frequency modes makes the attribution of recent trends in rainfall to anthropogenic climate change quite difficult if only trend analysis and correlation is used as the primary tool. Recent trends vary by region, as shown later, and do not necessarily correspond to the direct expectation from intensification of the hydrologic cycle as the planet warms. The ability of the physics based models to reproduce not only the mean annual or seasonal rainfall in each region, but also the nature of long term variability of precipitation in the region needs to be assessed if we are to accept the climate change projections for China for the 21st century in the context of water resource sustainability. Only limited work in this direction has been done so far.

The role of greenhouse gases is dominant in the analysis and projection of human induced global climate change. However, at regional scales, land surface modification may also play a significant role in changing climate, rainfall and hence renewable water supplies. Boucher et al. (2004), Lau et al. (2006), Gordon et al. (2005) among others have noted the marked influence changes in irrigation practices, land cover and dust generation can have on regional climate. The N. China plains and N. India have seen significant changes of this sort in the past century. The potential significance of such changes and future projections of feedbacks as aridity increases or additional irrigation is introduced do not appear to have been studied in detail for China.

The recent trends and model based projections of Greenhouse Gas forced climate change on hydrology and water resources have been extensively studied as summarized by the Research Center on Climate Change Adaptation, Ministry of Water Resources, P. R. China

(Jiao, 2008). During the past 100 years, the average temperature in China increased by 0.14–0.15°C, slightly lower than the global average. The 1990s is one of the warmest periods during the past century (but not hotter than the period of 1920–1940). Many extreme weather events during the recent 20 years seem to be related to global warming. For example, the frequency of large floods and extreme storms have increased significantly over the country such as the floods in the Yangtze Basin, 1998 and 1999 and in the Huai Basin, 2003 and 2007. Severe hurricanes in coastal regions have also occurred more frequently than before. On the other hand, consecutive droughts occurred in Northern China. During the 1980s, the average annual precipitation decreased by 10–15% of the historical average in a wide area of Northern China; during the 1990s, the drought extended to southwest, resulting in a reduction of 5–10% of the average annual precipitation. During the past 20 years, the runoff in the Hai, Huang (Yellow) and Huai ("3-H") basins declined by 25%, 10% and 9%, respectively. The runoff reduction might be a consequence of joint effects of human interferences and climate change.

Numerous studies on the prediction of climate change in China are generally consistent in the increase of both annual average temperature and precipitation. In particular, the daily highest temperature will have a significant increase in South China and the daily lowest in the south of the Yangtze River and the north of the Yellow River. Such changes will have a larger impact on agriculture than other sectors. According to one study which used the prediction result of GCM-MPI, during next 30 years, the annual precipitation may increase by about 11% in the Yellow River Basin including the inland basins north of the Yellow River, but evapotranspiration can increase by 15% (Wang et al., 2003). Most studies from China concluded that the increase of crop evapotranspiration due to the temperature increase may surpass the increase of precipitation and thus rainfed crops may suffer larger water deficit and irrigation water requirement may increase. However, recent assessment shows the opposite results (Cai, 2010). The change in climate as projected may increase rainfed crop yield in all the basins in Northern China; while Southern China may have lower rainfed yield for most crops. Zhujiang may have irrigation water requirement more than double of the current value for all crops with a few exceptions (winter wheat in both up- and downstream, maize and soybean in upstream). For other basins, the change of irrigation water requirement is within 10% of the current value for most crops.

In closing, we reiterate that model based climate change projections need to be viewed in the broader context of long term climate variability, and also need to consider the impacts of land use and irrigation change on regional climate. For climate change adaptation, using scenarios derived from long term climate records and proxies that represent persistent variations in renewable water resources available in different regions of China may be as valuable as the use of the projections from anthropogenic climate change model scenarios for the 21st century. So far, it is unclear that water resource sustainability analyses for China have systematically looked at both factors of change.

3. Water Accessibility

3.1. Infrastructure and physical accessibility

Unlike some developing countries in which the lack of engineering infrastructure is usually a major reason for insufficient water supply, China's water resources engineering development is impressive and has indeed supported growing water demands. However, it is widely believed that there is limited potential left within the country today for engineering solutions. Starting in the early 1950s, the practice of developing engineering facilities to catch and redistribute water has dominated water resources management in Northern China. Huge engineering efforts have been made to catch the precipitation and runoff in the region. In 1995, the reservoir storage of the 3-H basins was 1.6 times their total annual runoff (Rosegrant et al., 2002). Water storage and water diversion and extraction engineering facilities can easily control all renewable water in Northern China. One can understand the scope of the stream flow regulation by imagining that gates crossing many rivers in this region are used to divert flood water for groundwater recharge in the dry floodplains. Since no more water can be caught for use within the region, engineering now turns to trans-boundary water transfer projects. For example, the South-North Water Transfer (under construction), will transfer 38–48 km^3 of water (comparable to the total annual runoff in the Hai River and more than that of the Colorado River) from the Yangtze River in Southern China to Northern China (mainly for the urban and industrial region in the Hai River Basin) over a distance of more than 1,000 kilometers.

China has developed and maintained a huge water supply system. By 1997, there were 84,800 reservoirs with a total storage of 458 km^3 and 5,579 irrigation districts with an area larger than 667 ha. The total irrigated area in the country was 52.3 million hectares, which is 40% of the total crop land. A number of trans-boundary water transfer projects were built such as the projects transferring water from the Yellow River to Tianjin, Qingdao ("Yin-Huang-Ji-Jin", "Yin-Huang-Ji-Qing"); the South-North Water Transfer (transferring water from the Yangtze River to Northern China) project is under construction (Figure 2). The maintenance of the existing facilities faces a great challenge. A large number of projects were built during the 1950s to 1970s with low quality. According to the estimate of China National Academy of Engineering

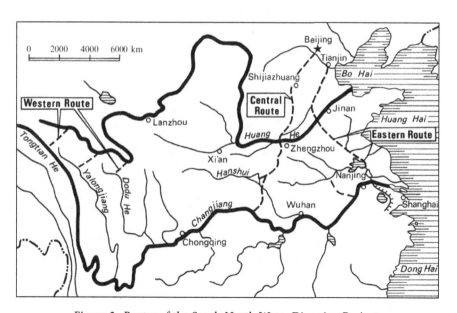

Figure 2. Routes of the South-North Water Diversion Project.

(Qian and Zhang, 2001), the total water supply capacity was reduced by 14% of the designed capacity in 1994. According to a survey of the Ministry of Water Resources, at present, only 70% of the large and medium irrigation districts have compete conveyance and distribution (*pei tao gong chen*), only 50% have well maintained core projects, and one-third of the districts cannot sustain a regular crop yield due to water shortage, waterlogging and soil salinization. More seriously, very limited financial and technical support has been provided to maintain the small-scale irrigation projects distributed over the country, leaving function reduction or total loss to most projects and consequently strengthening agricultural production loss.

A regional and national figure of water system capacity change shows some concerns on water supply sustainability in China. Table 1 provides estimates of the developed surface water, groundwater and total water supply in South, North and entire China, respectively, over a number of selected years from 1980 to 2006. For the whole country, compared to year 2003, water supply in 2006 increased by 20%, 70% and 30% from surface water sources, groundwater sources and the total, respectively; in Northern China, the surface water supply increased by only 1% but groundwater supply by 71%; in Southern China, groundwater supply

Table 1. Annual water supply in North and South China during 1980–2006 (unit: km^3; *Source*: Qian and Zhang, 2001).

Years	Northern China			Southern China			Total		
	Surface water	Ground water	Total	Surface Water	Ground water	Total	Surface Water	Ground water	Total
1980	164.6	54.0	218.6	216.7	7.9	224.6	381.3	61.9	443.2
1993	173.4	75.0	248.4	262.6	12.4	275.0	436.0	86.4	522.4
1997	176.4	90.9	267.3	282.8	12.3	295.1	459.2	103.2	562.3
2000	160.7	93.0	254.4	283.4	13.9	298.7	444.0	106.9	553.1
2001	160.6	96.0	257.4	284.5	13.5	299.4	445.1	109.5	556.7
2002	159.7	93.7	254.2	280.7	13.5	295.6	440.4	107.2	549.7
2003	(n/a)	(n/a)	235.5	(n/a)	(n/a)	296.5	(n/a)	(n/a)	532.0
2004	155.9	89.1	245.7	294.6	13.5	309.1	450.4	102.6	554.8
2005	157.7	90.4	249.1	299.6	13.5	314.3	457.2	103.9	563.3
2006	166.4	92.6	260.2	304.3	14.0	319.3	470.7	106.6	579.5

increased by 77% while the surface water supply by 40%. The ground-water use in both South and North has an increasing trend to the future years. Continuous groundwater depletion in North China will eventually eliminate availability, and experience growing technical difficulty and energy cost in pumping. Also excessive pumping will deplete base flow in rivers, affecting the ecological and other instream water needs. Thus a pressing research need is to identify the sustainable groundwater extraction rate, particularly in river basins in Northern China.

3.2. Human infrastructure: Institution and policy

Current water allocation typically follows the priorities of the local government that are often driven by short-sighted economic profits. There is no formal institution for mediation, so large water disputes between agriculture and other sectors (and also between regions) often are resolved by the government in an ad hoc, case-by-case fashion. In recent years, researchers and government officers in China began to embrace the modern concept of water right and water market (e.g., Wang, 2003; Liu, 2004). In China, water right is a kind of usufruct right and only the nation has the property right of natural resources. There is no clear delineation of the usufruct right, formal and consistent institutional support for water rights does not exist, and thus no mechanism for economically-efficient water rights trading exists. Although the China Water Law approved in 1988 and amended in 2002 provides codes for water allocation and use, current water use rights, both their identification and supervision, are heavily manipulated by the powerful water bureaucracy. Conflict resolution related to water rights is usually handled by administrative measures as individual cases, following some government guidelines such as the Implementation Measures for Water Use Permit Systems (issued by the State Council in 1993). This system, which lacks a consistent legislative framework, may not guarantee the security of water rights and is subject to high transaction costs, as well as social-economic loss with the two sides involved in water allocation. Furthermore, the current water use permit for agriculture is defined as a collective right for farmers in a town or even in a county, and individual farmers need to share the water right within their group. This may add to the difficulty of water right management and affect the efficiency of water right in water allocation. This situation has given rise to grass-root institutions in China, called water users associations (World Bank, 1997). In some rural regions of the country, individual farmers are involved in small pilot trials of water right transfers, which are different from sporadic trades at the village level. Several specific examples of the water right trade developments are discussed by Turner and Hildebrandt (2005) and Liu (2004). Local government is involved in the initial market development, but the challenge remains to build a bottom-up mechanism that allows farmers at the root level to be actively involved.

4. Potential Approaches to Achieve Sustainability

4.1. Engineering and technology development

China has taken a leading role in the development of some of the technologies typically considered for achieving sustainability. These include: 1) Storage infrastructure development — large projects such as Three Gorges and transboundary water diversion systems and also a network of small rainwater harvesting structures; 2) Desalination and wastewater technology development; 3) Efforts towards improvement of on farm irrigation water use efficiency.

The potential impact and scale of these initiatives for future sustainability is briefly discussed here. Biotechnology aimed at drought resistant crops or growing crops in brackish water is another potential factor that could potentially have an impact on water sustainability. However, there is insufficient information at this point as to its potential long term impact. The potential impact of the technologies considered is summarized in Table 2. Considering all optional sources for increasing water supply capacity, such as desalination, rainwater harvesting and wastewater reuse, Qian and Zhang (2001) estimated that these sources would contribute 4.8% and 6.3% of the total water supply capacity in the country in 2030 and 2050, respectively. In other words, these optional sources can only help increase water supply locally or at small-scale and none of these seems to have a critical role in water supply sustainability. Selected items are discussed below.

Table 2. Water Supply in 1997 and Projections in 2030 and 2050 (unit: km^3; *Source*: Qian and Zhang, 2001).

Sources of water supply	Northern China			Southern China			Total		
	1997	2030	2050	1997	2030	2050	1997	2030	2050
Surface water	176.4	167.0	167.5	282.7	361.0	371.5	459.1	528.0	539.0
Ground water	90.8	101.0	103.0	12.3	16.0	18.0	103.1	117.0	121.0
Waste water reuse	0.0	12.0	16.5	0.0	3.0	3.5	0.0	15.0	20.0
Alternative sources	0.7	14.5	20.0	1.9	4.5	5.0	2.6	19.0	25.0
Water transfer in	0.0	32.0	42.0	0.0	0.0	0.0	0.0	0.0	0.0
Water transfer out	0.0	0.0	0.0	0.0	32.0	42.0	0.0	0.0	0.0
Total water supply	267.9	316.5	335.5	296.9	381.5	394.5	564.8	698.0	740.0

Rainwater Harvesting: China is one of the countries where rainfall harvesting has been successfully practiced. Rainwater harvesting is the gathering, or accumulating and storing, of rainwater. Traditionally, rainwater has been harvested in arid and semi-arid areas for drinking water, domestic water, water for livestock and water for small irrigation. Rainwater harvesting was first practiced in Gansu Province of northwest China for the purposes stated above. Since 1995, due to widespread droughts, rainwater harvesting has been promoted by the government as a solution to the problem of water shortages for agricultural production and has been termed rainwater harvesting-based agriculture system (Cook et al., 2000), consisting of collection surface (catchment), runoff channel, sediment tank, storage container and supplemental irrigation system. However, due to a small number of catchment types and poor local economic conditions, the current rainwater harvesting practices in China are still confined to rural family units to supply household water needs and for limited supplemental irrigation purpose, and research is needed to move the practice from small- to large-scale in terms of cost-effectiveness and operational feasibility. The risk of exposure of these technologies to long term climate variations also needs to be understood, particularly where they are the primary mechanism for storage.

Desalination: Today, developing seawater (including brackish water) desalination technology has become a consensus of many countries in the world to solve the water crisis. China has a long coastline of 32,647 kilometers; and the coastal and central and western regions also boast abundant ground brackish water resources. China desalinated 120,000 m^3 of seawater per day in 2005. The Chinese government will accelerate the use of desalinated seawater during the 11th Five-Year Plan period (2006–2010) confirmed by the State Development and Reform Commission (SDRC) by boosting efforts to grasp key technologies, extend water price reform and encourage social capital to invest in the seawater desalination. At present, the development of seawater desalination technology has not led to the wide application of the technology due to high capital investment and operational cost. The current cost of desalinated water is between 4.5 to 8 RMB per m^3 (2 to 4 RMB for brackish water desalination), compared to the average cost of regular water supply, about 1.5 to 2 RMB per m^3 (China Economic Net, 2008). However, according to Qian and Zhang (2001), the capacity of desalination is still limited: desalination and rainwater harvesting together can only contribute 4.0 km^3 and 5.0 km^3 in 2030 and 2050, respectively, in the whole country. The projection is much lower than that from some other sources such as China Economic Net (2008).

Wastewater Treatment: The reuse of treated wastewater has some potential to increase water supply capacity in China, particularly for high value use. According to Qian and Zhang (2001), the estimated amount of industrial and domestic wastewater in China is 85~106 km^3 in 2030 and 110~150 km^3 in 2050 and the urban wastewater treatment rate is projected to be 80% and 95% in 2030 and 2050, respectively. Assuming a recovery of even 15% of the total wastewater being produced, will add 15.0 km^3 and 20.0 km^3 to the water supply capacity in 2030 and 2050, respectively.

Spatial Factors: Transboundary water transfer has been used as an engineering approach to resolve the imbalance of water availability and water need in a region given that extra water is available from a neighboring region. China is now constructing the largest water transfer project in the world ever, which is the so-called South-North Water Transfer project to transfer water from the Yangtze River located in South China to North China. The amount of transfer is 32.0 km^3 by 2030, about 11.4% of the projected water supply in Northern China; the transferring amount will be 42.0 km^3 in 2050; about 14.4% of the pro-jected water supply in North China. The impact of such a large-scale water transfer across different climate zones on the climate and hydro-logic cycle and the environment is worthy of careful examination from a systems perspective, with particular attention on long-term, cumulative environmental changes (Glantz, 1999), although some research has been claimed on the relevant issues.

Water Use Efficiency: Improvement of water use efficiency, particu-larly irrigation water use efficiency has been advocated as a key for water conservation and water stress mitigation. While this is very important, there is only a limited scope for the expansion of renewable supply through efforts towards system level water use efficiency improvement. Water productivity indicators have been proposed to evaluate the food production, economic benefit, or nutrient gain per unit of water use. One definition of water productivity is the crop yield per m^3 of water consumed, including "green" water (effective rainfall) for rainfed areas and both green and "blue" water (diverted water) for irrigated areas. Estimates indicate water productivity ranging from 0.15–0.70 kg/m^3 for irrigated rice, globally, and from 0.40–0.70 kg/m^3 for China. Water productivity for other irrigated cereals is estimated at 0.56 kg/m^3 for developing countries and 0.4–1.4 kg/m^3 for China, with an average of 1.0 kg/m^3. The Chinese average is similar to that of developed countries (Cai and Rosegrant, 2003) and higher than other countries with large agricultural sector such as India (Cai and Rosegrant, 2005). This implies some limitation for increasing water productivity in China, at least compared to other developing countries. However, considering the low level of water use efficiency reported in agriculture (National Bureau of Statistics of China, 2003), there appears to be some indication for agri-cultural water savings through improved water productivity.

Researchers and engineers in China, as well as elsewhere, adopted the projected efficiency of an irrigation district, which represents a frac-tion of water efficiently used for crop growth of the total water with-drawal to the district (Doorenbos and Pruitt, 1977). This concept is appropriate for irrigation system design but it could lead to erroneous conclusions and serious mismanagement of scarce water resources if it is used for water accounting at a larger scale. This is because the return flow is treated as water loss in the context of an irrigation district but it can be reused by downstream users in the context of a basin (Keller et al., 1996; Cai and Rosegrant, 2004). Taking the Yellow River Basin as an example, Cai and Rosegrant (2004) assessed the water use efficiency at the basin scale, adopting a concept called "effective efficiency", which is a ratio of beneficial irrigation water consumption to total irrigation water consumption (Keller et al., 1996). They found the value of the effective efficiency is 0.52, which is much higher than the average projected efficiency estimated by Chinese irrigation experts, 0.3~0.4 (Qian and Zhang, 2001). The effective efficiency takes into account potential reuses of irrigation return flows. Reuses of irrigation return flows have been common in the YRB. According to the estimation of Yellow River Conservation Commission (YRCC, 2002), in the upper reaches (above Toudaoguai), return flow is as high as 35 percent of the withdrawal, which obviously provides a "source" for middle and downstream water withdrawal. However, in the downstream reaches (below Huayuankou), return flow cannot come back to the main channel because of the riverbed is above the ground level. However, water is recycled and reused through the well-developed canal-well systems in the downstream areas. Thus, once system level efficiency is considered the scope for improving water use efficiency is more limited.

4.2. Policy and institutional reforms

The competition across different sectors of use, as well as within each sector, and the spatial and temporal variations in water availability translate into management and regulatory needs to promote efficiency in water use while promoting equity and system reliability. The rapid economic development of China and the accompanying governance changes are generating pressure to identify new paradigms for water system management. A grand experiment towards the use of economic allocation of water appears to be emerging. The role of government interventions is critical for water resources sustainability and the role will be maintained for a long time in China. Some of the mechanisms available to the government are: 1) Financing, construction and operation of large water supply and wastewater treatment infrastructure projects for the common good, including specifically for ecosystem services as part of the human-nature harmony goal; 2) regulated allocation and transfer of water across major users and use sectors, and also management of allocation within a particular use sector; 3) economic incentives, including price, subsidies and technology or information transfer initiatives that target specific use attributes; 4) monitoring of water conditions, planning and preemptive and relief actions where hazards or crisis conditions emerge; and 5) enforcement of regulations and effectiveness of policies. Each of these generally translates into a literature in its own right. Here, we provide some highlights of recent issues that have drawn considerable interest.

4.2.1. The role of government interventions in human-nature interaction management

Several large-scale ecological system restoration projects have recently been developed or are under development. The most high-profile example occurs with the Yellow (Huang) River. Due to excessive river diversion and a prolonged drought cycle, flow cutoffs had been experienced in the main channel downstream from 1972–1998. Flow in the main channel was cut off in 21 of 30 years with both the duration of time and the distance from the river mouth increasing each year. The flow interruption left users in Shandong and Henan Provinces without their traditional sources of surface water, and more seriously, it precluded sediment flushing to the ocean and threatened the downstream ecosystems (Li, 2002). Starting from the year 2000, the Yellow River Conservation Commission (the basin management authority under MWR) has undertaken firm administrative measures to prevent the river cutoffs, including water withdrawal monitoring and more strict execution of the "Water Allocation Programme" with the provinces in the upstream of the basin. The status of the river has since been improved, and there has been no absolute flow cut-off in recent years. Meanwhile, irrigation water withdrawal by the upstream provinces has declined. According to a news report from MWR (MWR, 2005), irrigation districts in Ningxia reduced water withdrawals by 2.2 km^3 during 2001–2005, which is about one-quarter of the total withdrawal by Ningxia in 2000.

Another example of ecosystem restoration has occurred in the Hei
River Basin, an inland basin in northwestern China (Liu et al., 2005).
The Hei River flows from the upstream Gansu Province to downstream
Inner Mongolia region, where the river water feeds the Erjina Oasis and
traditional pasturelands around the Oasis. Starting from the early 1980s,
large expansion in irrigation water diversion in the middle stream of the
basin has resulted in downstream ecosystem degradation including a
shrinking oasis area, declining vegetation coverage, and a complete
dry-up of the outlet lake. The environmental change threatens the home-
land of more than one million people who depend on the pastureland
for livestock breeding. In the late 1990s, the Chinese government initiated activities for the ecological restoration of the region, including
annual flow releases to downstream by administrative order. These
activities followed institutional development including activating the
"Gansu-Inner Mongolia Water Allocation Plan (GIWAP)" approved by
State Council and establishing the Bureau of Hei River Management, an
agency that is authorized to coordinate and supervise the implementation of the new water allocation plan. These releases have prevented
further degradation of the downstream ecosystem.

Two related areas where government will be required to play a major
role in the near term are discussed in the next two sections. The first
relates to policy development as to facilitating water transfers from the
agricultural sector to other sectors, while improving the health of agricultural water management and rural livelihoods. The second relates to
the form of economic incentives that the government could either offer
directly or facilitate through the private sector through appropriate
economic incentives.

4.2.2. Water transfer from agriculture to other sectors

Given the growing supply/demand imbalance in Northern China, it will
be increasingly difficult if not impossible to meet new water demands
from one sector without decreasing supplies to another. Since agriculture
is now by far the largest consumer of water resources and appears to
have relatively low economic output levels, meeting growing industrial
and domestic demands is likely going to mean a reduction in supplies to

the agricultural sector. However, agriculture in China, as in many other countries, holds a special place in rural livelihoods and national food security, so it remains a high priority. Furthermore, the rural agricultural sector is most impoverished and has probably benefited least from recent economic growth. Shifting water away from those already relatively disadvantaged has clear implications for equity and, perhaps, social stability. At the same time, it is industrial growth, which is dependent on increasing water supplies, that is seen as the driving force in powering China's transformation to a modern, world class economy. Therefore, a successful agricultural water transfer to other sectors will be critical for water supply and demand balance in China, particularly in the northern part of the country.

A premise for successful water transfers out of agriculture is that farmers can use less water while food production is not affected. There is no doubt that advanced irrigation technology is needed to replace traditional gravity systems. Starting from the mid-1990s, the Chinese government has significantly increased investment for irrigation system updating, and low-flow irrigation techniques such as drip and sprinkler is now gaining ground in China (Henry, 2004). However, the implementation of advanced irrigation technologies means a higher cost for water, and it is up to farmers to pay at least part of the cost. The question is whether farmers can afford the cost of advanced irrigation technology, and if farmers will and can pay water price that is closer to the true value of water. The answer might be no, if farmers' income is continuously low, and hence they cannot raise the capital to transition from their current usage system to a higher efficiency, higher value system. If water prices cause lower or negative net profits from irrigated agriculture, it may force farmers simply to use less water and give up high crop yields. On the other hand, crop prices may have to increase substantially for a long enough period to allow farmers to develop the capital to make the transition. However, this trajectory could lead to a higher rate of inflation and associated socio-economic pressures.

Alternately, crop diversification, or a shift in crop choice from staples that have low value but high water use to a mix that includes low water use, high cash value crops, could facilitate a transition. However, such a shift will still require investment in irrigation infrastructure, drainage networks, transportation networks and market support/risk management systems to facilitate a transition. Some organic movement in this direction seems to be taking place in China, but a formal role for the government and for the organized private sector (NGOs as well as corporate agriculture) does not yet seem to have emerged. Even at the screening level, it is not clear whether a systematic analysis of "optimal" crop selection and water use/infrastructure mechanisms to support it in a spatially distributed sense in China has been conducted to assess the opportunity for the spatial optimization of water use through appropriate regulation and policy making.

There is thus a "deadlock" with agricultural water management in China, which blocks effective agricultural water savings and smooth water transfers. The deadlock exists with the following conflicts, which are inter-related to each other: 1) farmers are wasting water even as they suffer water shortage themselves and leave increasing industrial and municipal sectors thirsty (Henry, 2004); 2) the society needs agricultural water savings, but farmers may not afford the costs of water savings and due to low profits from crops their willingness-to-pay for water is much lower than the true water value; 3) the national policy of food self-sufficiency requires the maintenance of high crop yields and production that depend on irrigation, even when the government can not maintain the required water for agriculture given the growing requirements of non-agricultural sectors. This deadlock leads to a consequence that may continue to damage the country's growing economy: on one hand, farmers lose water that they once used without appropriate compensation; on the other hand, cities and industries are thirsty and expect to access more water. Both situations have resulted in significant negative consequences to the regional economy and environment. It is not difficult to understand why instream flow and deep groundwater has been depleted and polluted in Northern China given the following facts: although agricultural water savings have not yet been implemented, part of the irrigation water has already been transferred; although M&I has received some water from agriculture, it is still not fully supplied. Therefore both sides, to sustain irrigated agriculture and to maintain fast growth of economy, drive excessive water withdrawal from rivers and aquifers. Note that for local governments, the strong wish for economic development always overrides the responsibility of environment protection. In the short term, it is unlikely that this trajectory will change.

4.2.3. *The role of economic incentives*

When water economies mature — as a result of increasing scarcity values of water — then demand management measures at both the system and basin level increase in importance (Randall, 1981). This is the case in China. The task of demand management is to generate both physical savings of water and economic savings by increasing output per unit of evaporative loss of water, by reducing water pollution, and by reducing non-beneficial water uses. This can be supported through a variety of policy measures, including economic incentives to conserve water use, e.g., pricing reform and reduced subsidies, accompanied by incentives for on farm technologies that save water, but also complementary regulations on water use rights, and policies targeting poor and vulnerable groups, education campaigns, leak detection, recycling, and other technical improvements, enhanced pollution monitoring, and quota and license systems.

Empirical studies or experiments in North China have shown a strong response of the Chinese water economy to economic incentives. Water user associations in a pilot area in Hubei, receiving water from Tie-shan Reservoir, have reduced water use by 30% per ha following the introduction of irrigation water fees (Easter, 2000). Water management reforms, including increased involvement of farmers and village government in irrigation management and increases in annual irrigation water costs from US$4.68/ha in 1972 to US$31.84/ha in 1993 (in 1991 dollars) in Nanyao and Bayi irrigation districts in the Northern China plain contributed to a decline in water applications from 11,000 m³/ha in 1973 to only 4,500 m³/ha in 1993 (Johnson et al., 1995). However, for irrigation pricing to achieve water conservation objectives, clearly defined and legally enforceable water rights or equivalently a water licensing and billing system need to be established, with clearly delineated rights and responsibilities for both irrigators and water authorities. Moreover, in groundwater-irrigated areas, water licensing schemes are called for to effectively limit the volume of groundwater withdrawals (Yang et al., 2003). While many demand management measures have targeted irrigation as the largest water user, municipal and industrial water use fees in China have room for improvement. Rosegrant and Cai (2002) show that water prices can be an effective means to reduce water consumption while increasing environmental water conservation.

The problems of implementing water price reforms and subsidy reductions in China should be noted. Most obviously, equity issues must be addressed so as to provide water to low-income households. Second, measuring and monitoring water use are costly activities, constraining water pricing where institutions and infrastructure are weak. Nevertheless, innovative water-pricing systems can be designed and implemented that have reasonable administrative costs and provide increased incentives for water conservation without reducing incomes, and possibly even enhancing the incomes of the poor (see, for example, Lohmar et al., 2002; Cai, 2008; Ringler and Huy, 2004). In addition to the projected water reallocation from agricultural towards urban-industrial uses, water reallocation within the agricultural sector will likely help conserve water resources in China, particularly in Northern China (Diao and Crook, 2000; Cai and Rosegrant, 2004).

Although formal water markets are still in the experimental stage in China, they are increasingly playing an important role to solve water conflicts (Turner and Hildebrandt, 2005; Liu, 2004). Water researchers and managers in the western world might be curious about the rapid spread of the western economics based water management approaches in China, which have not even been very successful in their countries. Given the extensive studies and practices sponsored by the government of China, the results and impacts might be worth of attention as time goes on. Liu (2005) describes a series of successful case studies using water trading and marketing. Although formal water markets are still in the experimental stage in China, they increasingly play important roles in solving water conflicts; and several pilot transfers in the country are a sign that local governments are starting to develop more formal markets based on traditional informal markets (Liu, 2005; Turner and Hildebrandt, 2005).

A typical example of agricultural water right transfer to M&I in China has occurred in areas along the Yellow River, the Inner Mongolia Autonomous Region and Ningxia Hui Autonomous Region. In these regions, agriculture uses more than 95 percent of the water, with the aged irrigation infrastructure resulting in lower water use efficiency. During the past decade, as many other regions in China, there has been growing M&I demand under rapid economy development, and the total water usage in these regions has reached their allocated quota determined by Water Allocation Programme applied to the main channel of the Yellow River. Therefore, water transfer becomes a critical issue for the economic development in the region. To guide, formalize, and promote water rights transfer, the Ministry of Water Resources issued the Guidelines for Tentative Water Rights Transfer in Mongolia Autonomous Region and Ningxia Hui Autonomous Region along the Yellow River Main Stream. Following the Guidelines, the Yellow River Water Resources Commission formulated the "Yellow River Water Rights Transfer Management Procedures (Tentative)," particularly applied to the upstream regions. The procedures include guaranteeing domestic needs, matching basic ecological water requirements, adapting advanced irrigation systems, and realizing compensations. By May 2004, eight large industrial projects in the two regions have signed agreements of intent for water rights transfer, with a total compensation of 360 million RMB.

Other transfers have occurred between administrative regions. In Zhejiang province, water use right trading was introduced between two cities, Dongyang and Yiwu in 2002. Dongyang is relatively rich in water resource while Yiwu is short in water supply. The two cities, through consultations, signed an agreement on transferring the water use right of Hengjin Reservoir of Dongyang to Yiwu at an agreed-upon price. Another example is with the Zhanghe flowing through Shanxi, Henan and Hebei. The three provinces, have settled their dispute over water allocation through an agreement. Changzhi City in Shanxi province, located in the upper stream of the river, agreed to supply water from its five reservoirs to Hebei and Henan at a mutually acceptable price. Through these demonstration transfers, the involvement of government as a regulator is a sign that local governments start to build up more formal markets based on the informal markets which have existed for long time. On the other hand, it also shows the important role of government in the water transfers between sectors and between regions. Local governments usually act as buyers or sellers in the trades between two administrative regions. Although water markets are certain to develop further in China, there is no doubt for people both inside and outside China that water markets will simply supplement the administrative allocation methods in the foreseeable future before consistent water rights are mature in China. The challenge will be to convert short-term emergency measures into long-term, sustainable water management and regional development plans.

5. Projections for the Future

Drawing on the discussion in the previous sections, water resources sustainability in China is related, but not limited to the following questions: What is the potential for water savings in agriculture? What are the implications for agricultural water use, food security and international food prices from increased environmental water use? What are the options for balancing environmental and food needs in China?

5.1. Baseline projection to 2025

Many studies from China predicted the peak water demand and most critical environmental vulnerability around 2030 (Qian and Zhang, 2001). According to Rosegrant et al. (2002), under a business-as-usual scenario, total water withdrawals in China are projected to increase by 25% between 1995 and 2025, from 680 km^3 in 1995 to 845 km^3 in 2025, which is close to a Chinese projection of new water supply capacity, between 1997 and 2030, of 184 km^3, including surface water supply, groundwater supply, and supply from wastewater treatment (Qian and Zhang, 2001). Non-irrigation water demands, including domestic, industrial, and livestock uses, are projected to grow much more rapidly, from 47 km^3 in 1995 to 98 km^3 in 2025, an increase of 110%. Increases in domestic and industrial water demands are expected to be most rapid in the Huaihe, Inland, Zhujiang, and Southeast river basins. Future water demand in China will be driven, to a large extent, by increases and changes in Chinese food demands. As a result of strong income growth, rapid urbanization, and changing tastes and preferences, Chinese diets will experience further shifts towards higher per capita consumption of meat, milk and milk products, fruits and vegetables, combined with a relative shift in food demand from rice to wheat. In urban areas processed and pre-packaged food accounts for rapidly increasing shares of total food consumption. According to Gale and Reardon (2005), supermarkets have taken over 30% of the urban food market in China, are growing at 30–40% annually, and accounted for about US$71 billion in sales in 2003. Growing meat demand will lead to a strong increase in the demand for maize and other coarse grains for animal feeds. As a consequence, rice demand in China is projected to increase by only 17 million metric tons (mmt), while demand for other cereals is expected to rapidly increase, by 170 mmt during 1995–2025. In terms of water conservation, the changes in demand are favorable, with rice, the most water-consuming crop, being slowly replaced by other cereals. However, rapid increases in total demand, from both food and non-agricultural uses, will put further pressure on Chinese water supplies. Irrigation water requirement is expected to increase by only 8% — because of improved water use efficiency, and a decline in the share of area planted to rice. However, the demand cannot be met as a result of very rapid increases in non-irrigation demands and relatively slow growth in water supply. As a result, irrigation water consumption in China is projected to decline to 231 km^3 in 2025 (6% decrease from 244 km^3 in 1995). Crop yield for both rice and other crops may experience larger deficit due to water shortage, with relative rice yields of 0.82–0.83 for the Haihe, Huanghe, and Inland basins in 1995 drop to 0.65–0.75 by 2025. The fall in the relative crop yield index due to water deficits is a significant drag on future yield growth.

With increased water use efficiency being the main avenue for future water savings, by 2025, water productivity for irrigated rice and other cereals is projected to increase to 0.85 kg/m^3 and 1.53 kg/m^3, respectively, higher than the global averages of 0.53 kg/m^3 and 1.10 kg/m^3. Achieving this level of efficiency increase is a tall order, but within reach for China, which is already undertaking a variety of measures in this direction.

5.2. Implications of increased environmental compliance policies

Environmental water uses form part of instream water uses: they include direct uses for fishing or wetland harvests, as well as ecological function values, like waste dilution, water storage, flood control, and ecological diversity (see Table 3 for the environmental water requirement projections). Water reserved for the environment can help regulate pollution, sustain riparian ecosystems, and maintain existing wetlands, which can have additional positive impacts on the watershed because they can recharge aquifers, digest organic wastes, and store runoff (Johnson et al., 2001). With competition between irrigation and off-stream, non-irrigation water uses already intense and likely to rapidly increase in China, reserving water for environmental uses would put a further strain on water available for irrigated agriculture.

In order to analyze the potential tradeoff between water for food production and water for environmental purposes, three alternative scenarios are analyzed and compared to the BAU: *Environmental Flows* increases the share of water reserved for the environment; *Environmental Flows and Efficiency* compensates increased environmental flows through enhanced water use efficiency; and *Sustainable Groundwater Use* restores sustainable groundwater pumping in those basins in Northern China, where groundwater pumping is above natural groundwater recharge (compared to BAU, by 2025, annual groundwater pumping would be reduced by 30.8 km^3 in Northern China).

Table 3. Projected Environmental Water Requirements (EWR in km^3) by Regions, 2010, 2030, and 2050 (*Source*: Qian and Zhang, 2001).

Regions/Years	2010	2030	2050
Yellow River Basin	22.5	24.0	26.0
Hai River Basin	9.0	10.0	10.5
Huai River Basin	10.0	10.0	10.0
Northwestern inland	41.5	45.0	48.5
Other regions[*]	2.0	2.0	2.0
Total	85.0	91.0	97.0

[*]Requirement for groundwater recharge to prevent aquifer depletion in South China.

Under the Environmental Flows scenario, additional water is freed for the environment by maintaining total irrigation water consumption at 1995 levels, while projected levels of non-irrigation demand are allowed to increase. The total reduction in off-stream uses is 136 km^3, from 844 km^3 under BAU. The Environmental Flows and Efficiency scenario requires an increase in basin efficiency levels from 0.60 under Business-As-Usual to 0.82, in 2025, on average, for all of China. Under the Environmental Flows and Sustainable Groundwater Use scenarios, food demand, supply, and prices are adversely affected compared to Business-As-Usual, while impacts are dampened somewhat if water use efficiency compensates for increased environmental reserve flows. Under the Environmental Flows scenario, annual average irrigated cereal harvested area in 2021–5 declines by 6.4 mha or 10% compared to BAU. If irrigation efficiencies increase, the reduction in irrigated harvested area is 2.9 mha, or 4% compared to BAU. Rainfed area increases slightly under the Environmental Flows and Environmental Flows and Efficiency scenarios by 0.1 and 0.05 mha, respectively. Increased reservation of water for environmental uses also affects irrigated cereal yields. Average irrigated yields during 2021–5 decline by 8.0% and 1.6%, respectively, compared to BAU. As a result, under the Environmental Flows scenario irrigated cereal production drops by 16%, while rainfed production increases by 1% in 2021–5, resulting in a total production decline of 60 mmt. Production declines in China are partially compensated through increases in other countries, leading to a final global production shortfall of 28 mmt. If Chinese water use efficiency levels are raised much faster, the drop is 6% in irrigated production, and an increase in 0.7% in rainfed production; global cereal production would be 11 mmt lower. Under the Sustainable Groundwater Use scenario, the decline in irrigated harvested cereal area is 2.7 mha, and cereal yields are 1.4% below those of BAU. Cereal production in China would be 17 mmt lower, but the decline would be mostly compensated through production increases elsewhere, resulting in a global production decline of only 5 mmt.

The decline in irrigated cereal production in China would also affect China's food trade. While Chinese cereal demand under the alternative scenarios is slightly lower, net cereal imports increase dramatically, by

118% under the Environmental Flows scenario, and 50% and 39% under the Environmental Flows and Efficiency and Sustainable Groundwater Use scenarios, respectively.

5.3. How to balance environmental and food needs

When water economies mature — as a result of increasing scarcity values of water — then demand management measures at both the system and basin level increase in importance (Randall, 1981). This is the case in China. The task of demand management is to generate both physical savings of water and economic savings by increasing output per unit of evaporation of water, by reducing water pollution, and by reducing non-beneficial water uses. This can be supported through a variety of policy measures, including economic incentives to conserve water use, e.g., pricing reform and reduced subsidies, but also complementary regulations on water use rights, policies targeting poor and vulnerable groups, education campaigns, leak detection, recycling, and other technical improvements, enhanced pollution monitoring, and quota and license systems.

Even though further increases in water use efficiency can compensate for enhanced environmental flows, little room exists to improve water use efficiency at the basin scale in severely water-scarce basins, such as the Huanghe and Haihe basins. In these basins, food production and farm incomes could decline significantly if water allocated for irrigation is transferred to other uses, including the environment. Here, alternative interventions may be required to compensate farmers for the negative effects of environmental water diversions. Supporting such farmers requires additional investments in high-value rainfed crops, diversification into less water-intensive crops, and broader economic diversification to reduce the relative role of agriculture over time. Policy reforms, such as raising water prices in the domestic and industrial sectors to slow the growth in water use would be another option to help balance environmental and irrigation water needs. Since farmers are the least able to cope with the policy changes required to rationalize water supply, the focus of Chinese policy needs to be on facilitating changes in the irrigated agriculture sector, while directly supporting the rural poor. The government has started to take steps in this direction.

5.4. Outlook to 2050

China's water and food status beyond 2025 will depend on its status in 2025 regarding the progress of technology in agricultural production, the changes of crop pattern and agricultural structure, infrastructure development oriented for improving water use efficiency and maintenance of existing water supply systems, and the improvement of water management institution. By 2025 it is reasonable to assume that water demand will be stable than the current. Population in China by then is expected to be stable and urbanization development is expected to slow down compared to that before 2025. Therefore, non-agricultural water demand can be assumed to be stable, at least not growing as fast as in the next 20 years, and then there will be less pressure for water transfer from agriculture to non-agricultural sectors. For agricultural water sector, food demand is also expected to be stable and then there will be a smaller requirement for new irrigation development. Moreover, new technology should be more effective in water conservation, waste water treatment, and the development of new sources such as desalinization. Therefore, agricultural water demand beyond 2025 should decline from the level of 2025, leaving more water to non-agricultural sectors and instream environmental requirements, while maintaining the crop production projected up to 2025. In addition, beyond 2025, the South-North Water Transfer project, including the Eastern Route and Middle-Route, is expected to match part of the increased non-agricultural demand, and eliminate the pressure of water transfer from agriculture to non-agricultural sectors.

Using the data from a special project on water resources sustainability in China from China Academy of Engineering (Qian and Zhang, 2001, also see a related report by Liu and Chen, 2001), the water supply and demand projections by 2030 and 2050 are given in Table 4. Water shortage in Northern China in 2050 remains about the same in absolute number as 2030 (about 12.5 billion m^3); but the shortage rate in 2050 is

Table 4. Water supply, demand and deficit (with negative numbers, positive numbers for water excess) in 1997, 2030 and 2050, with low, medium and high demand and deficit projections in 2030 and 2050.

		North China			South China		
		1997	2030	2050	1997	2030	2050
Total water supply (km³)		267.9	317.5	335.5	296.9	381.5	394.5
Water demand-1997 (km³)		273.9			297.5		
Demand Projection (km³)	high		346.9	363.6		410.4	440.1
	medium		330.0	337.1		381.9	394.8
	low		319.1	323.1		368.9	379.6
Deficit-1997 (%)		−2.0			−0.2		
Deficit projection (%)	high		−8.5	−7.7		−7.0	−10.4
	medium		−3.8	−0.5		−0.1	−0.1
	low		−0.5	3.8		3.4	3.9

0.5% compared to 3.8% in 2030. By 2050, water supply basically matches the demand (Table 4).

However, some of the current problems such as resource (groundwater) depletion, water pollution, ecosystem degradation, and water waste just discourage people to have an optimistic outlook to 2025, let alone 2050. It is the time to face those problems and find effective solutions through both infrastructural investment and institution reforms. The country is facing challenges to solve the problems before 2025, but to balance environmental flow requirements and offstream water consumption will be a long-term strategy from generation to generation, and then water conservation, particularly agricultural water saving in China will be a long-term effort. Moreover, the country, as other countries in this planet, is to face the challenge from the emerging global climate change and the change of local climate variability, which could have significant impact on China's water and food, as shown by our preliminary analysis, and deserves a close watch by researchers and policy makers in China.

6. Summary: Scientific and Policy Implications

Extensive studies, including the consultant project conducted by China Academy of Engineering (CAE) (Qian and Zhang, 2001) and numerous more recent projects have provided guidelines for water resources sustainability management in China, which has a national priority in China. We present some suggestions for both the scientific and policy making community for further research.

6.1. Needs for scientific research

6.1.1. *Integrated river basin management*

As early as 1957, an expert panel established by the United Nations proposed integrated river basin management (IRBM): "individual water projects could not usually be undertaken with optimum benefit unless there were at least the broad outlines of a plan for the entire drainage area." While early IRBM measures focused on project planning, today's water resource problems are much more complex, targeting water quality and ecosystem health objectives, as well as water supply. The overall goal of IRBM is to ensure that human societies will benefit forever from the river basin through the development of harmonious relationships between its users and between man and river (Burton, 1995). Managing river basins in a sustainable manner need to resemble a living system in which all resources — social (human), ecological, and economic — are interdependent and draw strength from each other. This is a 3-tiered approach and each leg of the stool is needed because without one leg, the stool collapses.

Nowadays, many river basins in China and elsewhere can be defined as anthropogenically-stressed environmental systems with significant social and environmental problems (UNESCO, 2003), which are symptoms of mismanagement. One can recall the causes of a number of severe water resources and environmental problems occurring in China, such as the flow cutoff in the Yellow River in the 1990s and early 2000s, the long-term problem of eutrophication in Dina-Chi (Lake Dian) and the most recent "blue algae" problem in Tai-Hu (Lake Tai), the shrinkage or disappearance of numerous inland lakes in northwestern China, etc.

IRBM seeks to integrate a framework that reorients the focus from conventional, partial, reductionist science to a more holistic and integrally-informed understanding of natural systems, human subjectivity and social relations (Lopes, 2008). Such a new framework might be particularly useful for water resources research communities in China because of the following observations. First, land and water management, and water quantity and quality management are usually separate, which is probably due to the separated water management institution in China. All the major problems listed above are a result of both land and water management practices. For example, the "blue algae" problem is related to long-term cumulative nutrient load to Lake Tai from the agricultural and urban land uses in the drainage area of the·Lake; while it might be also related to the declining inflow and shrinking storage of the Lake in recent years. Second, water supply and water demand planning and management are usually separated in both research and practice. Since the 1950s, water supply development and management has been oriented by water demand in China, i.e., providing as much as demanded if possible; while in recent years, some Chinese researchers (see the conclusion chapter of a report prepared by Liu and Chen, 2001, sponsored by CAE) recommended the opposite way — water demand should follow supply, i.e., use as much as provided. The demand-oriented approach has already caused numerous water shortage and ecosystem degradation problems in China today. But will the supply-oriented approach work without any problems? Will society accept this approach without causing any socio-economic problems related to fairness and equity as discussed by Shen (2005)? This needs careful studies. Given the water resources problems in China and large inputs for research from the Government in recent years, China is expected to make a contribution to the research and practice of sustainable water resources management, as well as solve her own pressing problems.

The emerging *sustainability science* promises to advance our conceptualization and understanding of river basin sustainability. It seeks to understand the fundamental characters of the interaction between nature and society using a multi-disciplinary systems approach (Clark and Dickson, 2003). Such an understanding must address the questions of *irreversible impact thresholds*: to what degree can a watershed or its components bear the harm caused by the stresses (Turner et al., 2003)? What factors determine the limits of resilience and sources of vulnerability for such interactive systems (Cai et al., 2002)? How do local choices impact the whole system — how do local individual actions (e.g., land and water uses) lead to system output (e.g., water quality, flow regime)? To address these questions, the first need is to depict and quantify the human-nature interactions and biotic-abiotic relationships under human influences; following that is the need to integrate the relationships in emerging models and conceptualizations to form a cohesive, sufficiently detailed and computationally tractable modeling framework.

6.1.2. *Water supply sustainability*

Human interferences and climate change are the two major causes for water supply vulnerability in China and many other countries and regions. The recent impact of extreme events exposes the vulnerability of the water resource system to the cumulative effects of human use and modification in the basin as well as to changes related to greenhouse induced climate change. As illustrated in this chapter, the impact of climate change or structured climate variability at decadal scales on agricultural production and irrigation water demand could be large in the future, which might worsen the water stress situation that is already severe at present. It should be noted that water supply vulnerability is usually not a short-term event but rather a "creeping" environmental change, that is, slow-onset, low-grade, and cumulative (Glantz, 1999). The creeping change starts from a "pre-problem" stage, when the first signs of adverse environmental effects began to appear. If no action is undertaken, a developed stage will follow, when several threshold levels are surpassed, resulting in "irreversible" damages and actions to solve the problem may be too late. The most famous example of such a creeping change is the environmental change in the Aral Sea Basin in Central Asia, one of the world's most notorious environmental disasters (Cai et al., 2002). Similar environmental changes already occurred or are occurring in China, in Northern China and even in Southern China with some large lakes such as Lake Dong-Ting, the second largest lake in South China, which has been rapidly filled by sediment, with its surface area less than half of that one century ago (Li et al., 2003).

The lack of scientific understanding is one of the causes of the ignorance of the pre-problem of large-scale environmental changes, leading to disastrous policy and engineering choices and adverse environmental impacts and irreversible economic failures. River basins are complex systems characterized by the *connectedness* between biotic, abiotic, and human sub-systems and *thresholds* of these sub-systems and the entire system. Identification of the thresholds will provide early warning of irreversible conditions, but this will require quantitative relationships between human interventions and natural processes and between environmental variables (e.g., flow, water quality) and ecosystem health metrics. The understanding of connectedness of physical, biological, and human factors in watersheds and identification of critical system status are core research issues for understanding water supply venerability (USEPA, 2006; Clark, 2007). Related to this research need, notable studies have been published by researchers in China on water resources carrying capacity (WRCC, Jia et al., 2004; Zhu et al., 2005), which can be an important indicator of water supply vulnerability. Further research might be needed to move the study from conceptual or qualitative description to quantitative analysis based on both reliable observations and better understanding of fundamental sciences and policies.

6.1.3. Technology development — from large to small and from centralized to distributed

During the past 60 years, China experienced large-scale, centralized water resource engineering development. As argued before, the social and economic benefit of further development along this line may be marginal or even negative in terms of environmental preservation and social equity. However, small-scale, distributed engineering development within the context of watersheds is promising for sustaining social, economic and ecological values. In literature, best management practices

(BMPs) are often used to describe such development, which is the so-called watershed approach. BMPs have been widely practiced for watershed management such as erosion control, flooding mitigation, groundwater recharge, water use through rainfall harvest, and water quality protection. Actually China has taken a leading role in rainfall harvest in the northwestern China and erosion and sediment control in the Loess Plateau within the Yellow River Basin. In the future the integration of these distributed, small-scale measures with the centralized, large-scale projects can form a complementary relationship for sustainable water and land management. The planning of new centralized projects in any regions may consider an option to use distributed projects that are environmentally friendly, financial flexible and affordable, and socially acceptable.

6.1.4. *Monitoring and information exchange*

As in any other countries, monitoring is a basic measure for environmental sustainability management, since monitoring provides continuous observation of what occurred, which feeds the adaptive management, a systematic process for continually applying collective knowledge to future plans and improving management policies and practices by learning from the outcomes of the real world practices. Moreover, there is also a need to develop monitoring system to watch the creeping environmental changes as discussed above. Like anywhere else in the world, monitoring natural processes has been under development, while monitoring human interferences such as water uses is very limited, which blocks our further analysis of the coupled nature-human systems. Actually, the same issue exists in the U.S.A. As concluded by U.S. National Research Council (NRC), data availability of human activities is limited and water use data (including domestic, industrial sectors, and irrigated agriculture) involve considerable uncertainties; thus water uses are still not yet a major focus of scientific research and the role of water use in the hydrologic cycle is not clear (NRC, 2002).

The role of monitoring will be weakened if monitored and observed data is not disseminated in an effective way. Information exchange is not only necessary for scientific research but also for public participation and education. Unfortunately observation data is usually treated as a "good," formerly or informally, in China, of course not only in China. It might be useful to note that U.S. National Science Foundation (NSF) has been prompting hydrologic and environmental information exchange through cyber-infrastructure development, which is taken as an important measure for sustainable water resources planning and management.

6.2. Implications for policy reforms

6.2.1. *Enable farmers to be able to pay for water*

Water stress in Northern China is characterized by major, inefficient irrigation water use and rapidly growing non-agricultural water demands, as well as limited water quantity and declining water quality. Water use in the region is undergoing transfer from agricultural to municipal and industrial sectors. Currently part of the economic loss and environmental damage due to water stress can be considered as a consequence of water transfer failures, including the current transfers which hurt farmers' livelihood and income, and the needed transfers, which industry and cities have been waiting for but have not received. Successful water transfers in Northern China imply that farmers use less water to produce even more food. However, currently farmers cannot afford the costs of water savings and their willingness-to-pay to water is far below the economic value of water assessed from the gross economy of Northern China.

Policy implications for successful water transfers include the improvement of irrigation systems, the use of feasible water prices, establishment of effective water management institution, delineation of secure and consistent water rights, restoration of environmental flow, and reconsideration of national agricultural policies. These long-term planning strategies allow people in China to take time to perform trial-and-errors. Due to the strong water bureaucracy in China and the need of capacity building in water management, a "smooth" water transfer will take a long time — although some gradual progress can be expected. Whereas some actions are needed right now to avoid serious social instability. First of all, the basic water needs, including those for drinking and ordinary living (Gleick, 1996), should be protected firmly for farmers and also for residents in cities. For this purpose, some transfers that deplete farmers' water below their basic needs should be prohibited, and for the same purpose, some transfers must be undertaken to ensure the basic needs of residents in cities during drought periods. It will be necessary for some government agencies to conduct careful monitoring and quick responses to water transfer events that impact the basic needs of humans.

Some choices must be made. Even if initially painful, properly conceived policies executed correctly can bring tremendous long-term benefits. Since farmers are the least able to cope with the policy changes needed to rationalize water supply, the key solution is then to help farmers to get ready for the changes, which essentially means that farmers *can* and *will* save water. First of all, it is important to replace traditional low-efficiency irrigation systems by advanced irrigation systems, which has been occurring since the 1990s (Henry, 2004). This will strengthen the physical feasibility for farmers to save water while maintaining production. The concern is whether the traditional focus on water supply engineering during the past 50 years can be switched to water management centered on efficient water uses (Boxer, 2001). Second, farmers may not volunteer to save water unless they must pay higher water prices that at least partially reflect the costs of irrigation system updates and the economic value of water. The economic value of water is much higher when water is allowed to transfer between agricultural and other sectors than when water use is constrained within agriculture (Briscoe, 1997). Currently what farmers can afford for water is far below the true economic value of water in Northern China. Under their current income level, farmers are the least able to cope with the price hikes to rationalize water supply. Therefore, agricultural water saving in China is not only a technological problem, but also a socio-economic problem, which is related to national and regional agricultural policies and markets and even the international food markets. For policy makers in China, efficient agricultural water use needs to be considered within the framework of the nation's gross economy. A research question is that at what level of income, farmers' willingness-to-pay for water will match the economic value of water assessed from the gross economy of Northern China. Starting in 2006, the Chinese government stopped levying agricultural taxes. The impact of this change will be positive and broad although it will take time to emerge. It is expected that such measures, if they are stable, will enable farmers to pay a reasonable price for water so that water prices can become an effective economic incentive for water saving.

6.2.2. Establish institution for smooth water transfer

An institutional establishment is needed to allow farmers and other groups to fairly exchange water. The role of government in water transfers has been demonstrated in this paper. At least for now and in the foreseeable future, administrative means of water allocation will take the lead with other means such as water markets as a supplement (Turner and Hildebrandt, 2005). Appropriate governance is still needed to guide and manage the ongoing water transfers. In particular, the mechanism is expected to provide a negotiation and mediation mechanism for officials and representatives from competing sectors to resolve the conflicts, and to protect the benefits of all, especially the weak groups. Many provinces and municipalities are promoting reforms to merge the functions of different water management units into a single authority, called Water Affairs Bureau (WAB). At the root level of irrigation management, the government has been sponsoring the development of water users associations (WUA), who not only take charge of water allocation among individual farmers within a WUA, but also represent a group of farmers (World Bank, 1997).

Delineation of secure and consistent water rights for various water users will be the basis for equitable water transfers among farmers and other groups. According to Wang (2003), implementing water rights and water markets seems to be a long-term target for the so-called "resource-based water resources management" being promoted by the MWR in recent years. Although formal water markets are still in the experimental stage in China, they are increasingly playing an important role to solve water conflicts (Turner and Hildebrandt, 2005; Liu, 2004). Water researchers and managers in the western world might be curious about the rapid spread of the western economics based water management approaches in China, which have not even been very successful in their countries. Given the extensive studies and practices sponsored by the government of China, the results and impacts might be worth of attention as time goes on. The involvement of government and administrative institutions in the markets under development is particularly interesting.

6.2.3. *Act quickly to arrest environmental degradation*

Given the current serious situation of environmental flow depletion, it is critical to restore, at least partially, environmental flow to prevent irreversible environmental disasters. Facing the risk of environmental damage, China is beginning to recognize the spirituality of "human harmony with nature," which is rooted with Chinese historical ethics of Taoism, a philosophy of non-interference (Li et al., 2004). As illustrated by the environmental flow restoration in the Yellow River and the Hei River, projects have been initialized in Northern China. Although current measures under administrative orders impose large transaction costs, they show some positive signs for the restoration of environment. The challenge will be to convert the short-term emergency measures into long-term, sustainable water management and regional development plans (Liu et al., 2005). To balance environmental flow requirements and offstream water consumption will be a long-term strategy in Northern China.

6.2.4. *Consider some optional policies*

Finally, there will be some challenges for national agricultural policies facing unavoidable agricultural water transfer. A major tension behind the water stress is the premise of food self-sufficiency in China, which is important for China with a population of 1.4 billion, but also for the entire world. When there is no way to hit all targets of food production, environment restoration and non-agricultural water demand, a compromise solution must be found. In a preliminary study, Cai and Rosegrant (2004) explored some strategies for sustainable groundwater use in

Northern China given the fact that groundwater depletion is already a serious problem in the region. It was found that to reduce the current groundwater use to a sustainable level by 2025, food production in the Hai and Huang (Yellow) River Basins will decline by 15 and 9 percent, respectively. Although improvements of water use efficiency directed at overdrafting basins could, in theory, compensate the food production declines, they would be unlikely in reality due to technology constraints. In light of this fact, what will be the optional policies of the food self sufficiency, taking into account food production conditions in China, food security, environmental sustainability, as well as international food markets? The international community is now exploring the policy implications of "virtual water flow" (Allan, 1998), which basically means water is transferred from one country or region to another with food export/import. The concept of virtual water links a large range of sectors and issues that revolve around relieving pressures on water resources, ensuring food security, developing global and regional water markets. In the future, higher international food demand may increase food commodity prices, which will hurt poorer countries that must import food. The ideal result of a global strategy of virtual water flow is that more food will be produced in those countries with enough water for crop growth, so that the impact of higher demand (increasing prices) will be balanced by the impact of higher production (decreasing prices) in the international market. Hoekstra and Hung (2002) identified China as one of the top ten countries that import virtual water. Regarding such an international virtual water market, China faces both challenges and opportunities. A better understanding of the role of water in economic growth in Northern China, the trade-offs between equity and efficiency in sectoral water allocation, and the range of possibilities for institutionalizing water allocation decisions would serve to better inform upcoming critical decisions on inter-sectoral transfers.

References

Alcamo, J., Henrichs, T. and Rösch, T., 2000. World Water in 2025: Global Modeling and Scenario Analysis for the World Commission on Water for the 21st Century. Kassel World Water Series Report No. 2. Kassel, Germany:

Center for Environmental Systems Research, University of Kassel.

Allan, T., 1998. Moving Water to Satisfy Uneven Global Needs: Trading Water as an Alternative to Engineering It. *International Commission for Irrigation and Drainage Journal*, 47(2): 1–8.

Becker, S., Gemmer, M. and Jiang, T., 2006. Spatiotemporal Analysis of Precipitation Trends in the Yangtze River Catchment. *Stochastic Environmental Research and Risk Assessment*, March 2006: 1–10.

Boucher, O., Myhre, G. and Myhre A., 2004. Direct Human Influence of Irrigation on Atmospheric Water Vapor and Climate. *Clim. Dyn.*, 22: 597–603.

Boxer, B., 2001. Contradictions and Challenges in China's Water Policy Development. *Water International*, 26(3): 335–341.

Briscoe, J., 1997. Managing Water as an Economic Good: Rules for Reformers. Paper presented to the International Commission on Irrigation and Drainage (ICID), Oxford, UK, 25 pp.

Burton, J., 1995. A Framework for Integrated River Basin Management. *Water Science and Technology*, 32(5–6): 139–144.

Cai, X., McKinney, D.C. and Lasdon, L., 2002. A Framework for Sustainability Analysis in Water Resources Management and Application to the Syr Darya Basin. *Water Resources Research*, 38(6): 1085.

Cai, X. and Rosegrant, M.W., 2002. Global Water Demand and Supply Projections Part 1: A Modeling Approach. *Water International* 27(2): 159–169.

Cai, X. and Rosegrant, M.W., 2003. Water Productivity and Food Security, Current Situation and Future Options. In J.W. Kijne, R. Barker, and D. Molden (eds.), *Water Productivity in Agriculture: Limits and Opportunities for Improvement,* Wallingford, UK: CABI Publishing, pp. 163–178.

Cai, X., Rosegrant, M. and Ringler, C., 2003. Physical and Economic Efficiency of Water Use in the River Basin: Implications for Efficient Water Management. *Water Resources Research*, 39(1): 1013.

Cai, X. and Rosegrant, M.W., 2004. Optional Water Development Strategies for the Yellow River Basin: Balancing Agricultural and Ecological Water Demands. *Water Resources Research*, 40(4).

Cai, X. and Rosegrant, M.W., 2004. China's Water and Food: Future Perspectives in China's Agriculture in 2050. In Tao, C.T. et al. (eds.), Beijing, PRC: Chinese Agricultural Press.

Cai, X. and Rosegrant, M.W., 2005. Water Management and Food Production in China and India: A Comparative Assessment. *Water Policy*, 7: 643–663.

Cai, X. and Ringler, C., 2007. Balancing Agricultural and Environmental Water Needs in China: Alternative Scenarios and Policy Options. *Water Policy*, 9S1: 95–108.

Cai, X., 2008. Water Stress, Water Transfer and Social Equity in Northern China: Implications for Policy Reforms. *Journal of Environment Management*, 87: 14–25.

Cai, X., 2010. The Impact of Climate Change on Rainfed and Irrigated Agriculture in China. Working paper, Department of Civil and Environmental Engineering, University of Illinois at Urban-Champaign.

China Economic Net, 2008. Seawater Desalination to Relieve Water Shortage in China, http://en.ce.cn/Insight/200602/28/t20060228_6217706.shtml, accessed in August 2008.

Chinese Academy of Engineering (CAE), 2001. Water Resources Assessments and Supply and Demand Projections. Vol. 2, Reports on Water Resources Development Strategies/Sustainable Development in China, Beijing, China.

Chinese Academy of Science (CAS), 2005. The Impacts of Human Activities on Droughts in Arid Regions. http://pd973.tea.ac.cn/download/middle/kt4.pdf (in Chinese).

China Environmental Review (CER), 1999. The Development of Soil/Groundwater. *Quarterly Newsletter for China Environment, Health & Safety Managers*, winter issue. http://www.environmental-expert.com/magazine/aer/china/winter/article2.htmS, accessed in December 2011.

China Economic Herald, 2005. Economic Development Considering Environmental Change in River Basins in China. http://www.ceh.com.cn/xiaofei/detail.asp?id=21993&type=99 (in Chinese).

Clark, W.C., 2007. Sustainability Science: A Room of Its Own. In *Proceedings of the National Academy of Sciences USA*, 104(6): 1737–8.

Clark, W.C. and Dickson, N.M., 2003. Sustainability Science: The Emerging Research Program. *Proceedings of the National Academy of Sciences USA*, 100(14): 8059–8061.

Cook, S., Li, F.R. and Wei, H.L., 2000. Rainwater Harvesting Agriculture in Gansu Province, People's Republic of China. *J. Soil Water Conserv.*, 55(2): 112–114.

Diao, X. and Crook, F., 2000. Water Resource in China: Growth Strains Resources. *Agricultural Outlook* (January–February).

Doorenbos, J. and Pruitt, W.O., 1977. Crop Water Requirements. U.N. Food and Agriculture Organization (FAO) Irrigation and Drainage Paper 24, Rome, Italy.

Easter, K.W., 2000. Asia's Irrigation Management in Transition: A Paradigm Shift Faces High Transaction Costs. *Review of Agricultural Economics* 22(2): 370–388.

Engelman, R. and LeRoy, P., 1993. Sustaining Water: Population and the Future of Renewable Water Supplies. Population and Environment Program, Washington, D.C.

Gale, F. and Reardon, T., 2005. China's Supermarkets Present Export Opportunity. Greater China, June 2004. http://www.atimes.com/atimes/China/GF24Ad02.html

Glantz, M.H., ed., 1999. *Creeping Environmental Problems and Sustainable Development in the Aral Sea Basin*. Cambridge, UK, and New York: Cambridge University Press.

Gleick, P.H., 1996. Basic Water Requirements for Human Activities: Meeting Basic Needs. *Water International*, 21(2): 83–92.

Gordon, L.J., Steffen, W., Jönsson, B.F., Folke, C., Falkenmark, M. and Johannessen, A., 2005. Human Modification of Global Water Vapor Flows from the Land Surface. *PNAS*, 102(21): 7612–7617.

Government of China, 2006. Tile from website, http://www.gov.cn/jrzg/2006-05/04/content_273580.htm

Henry, E., 2004. Water Scarcity in the North China Plain: Water Saving Irrigation and Its Implications for Water Conservation, Michigan State University, P.R.E.M.I.U.M. Program.

Hoekstra, A.Y. and Hung, P.Q., 2002. Virtual Water Trade: A Quantification of Virtual Water Flows between Nations in Relation to International Crop Trade. Research report, IHE Delft.

Jia, S.F., Zhou, C.Q., Yan, H.Y., Zhou, H.F., Tang, Q.C. and Zhang, J.B., 2004. Estimate of Water Availability and Carrying Capacity in Northwestern China. *Advances in Water Science*, 15(6): 801–807.

Jiang, J.M., Zhang, D.E. and Fraedrich, K., 1997. Historic Climate Variability of Wetness in East China (960–1992): A Wavelet Analysis. *Int. J. Climat.*, 17: 969–981.

Jiang, R., et al., 2004. A Report on Water Scarcity in China — The Emerging Deadlock of Economic Development, *China Business Weekly*, 8 May 2004, Beijing, China.

Jiao, Y., 2008. Water Safety and Climate Change in China. *China Water Resources*, (2): 10–13.

Johnson, N., Revenga, C. and Echeverria, J., 2001. Managing Water for People and Nature. *Science*, 292(5519): 1071–1072.

Johnson, S.H., III, Vermillion, D., Svendsen, M., Wang, X., Zhang, X. and Mao, X., 1995. Institutional Management and Performance Changes in Two Irrigation Districts: Case Study from Hebei Province. In *Selected papers from the International Conference on Irrigation Management Transfer,* Wuhan, China, 20–24 September 1995. Rome: International Irrigation Management Institute and FAO.

Keller, A.A., Keller, J. and Seckler, D., 1996. *Integrated Water Resources Systems: Theory and Policy Implication.* Research Report No. 3. Colombo, Sri Lanka: International Water Management Institute.

Lau, K.-M., Kim, M.K. and Kim, K.-M., 2006. Aerosol Induced Anomalies in the Asian Summer Monsoon — The Role of the Tibetan Plateau, *Clim. Dyn.*, 26: 855–864.

Li, G.Y., 2002. Regulation of Water Flow and Sediment Flushing in the Downstream of the Yellow River. *Chinese Water Magazine,* 474(12) (in Chinese).

Li, R., Beek, E.V. and Gijsbers, P., 2004. Integrated Water Resources Management for the Yellow River in China: Discussion on Scientific and Ethical Approaches. In *Proceedings of the International Association of Hydrological Sciences Symposium: The Basis of Civilization — Water Science?* IAHS Press.

Li, B., Wang, D. and Zhu, Y., 2005. Causes and Countermeasures of Water Environment Deterioration in Rural Regions of China. *Chinese Hydraulic Engineering Society* (in Chinese).

Li, Y.T., Deng, J.Y. and Sun, Z.H., 2003. A Study on the Flood Storage Capacity in Dongting Lake. *Int. Journal of Sediment Research,* 18(2): 138–147.

Li, Z.Q. and Wei, Z.M., 2003. Water Resources Changes in Heibei Province and Implications for the Development of Western China. *Science and Technology in South-North Water Transfer Project,* No. 1.

Liu, B., 2004. Institutional Design Considerations for Water Rights Development in China. In B. Bruns, C. Ringler, and R. Meinzen-Dick (eds.), *Water Rights Reform: Lessons for Institutional Design.* International Food Policy Research Institute (IFPRI), Washington, D.C.

Liu, B., 2005. Institutional Design Considerations for Water Rights Development in China. In B. Bruns, C. Ringler, and R. Meinzen-Dick (eds.), *Water Rights Reform. Lessons for Institutional Design.* International Food Policy Research Institute (IFPRI), Washington, D.C.

Liu, H., Cai, X., Geng, L. and Zhong, H., 2005. Restoration of Pastureland Ecosystems: A Case Study of Western Inner Mongolia. *Journal of Water Resources Planning and Management,* 131(6): 420–430.

Liu, C.M. and Chen, Z.K., 2001. *Current Water Resources Evaluation in China and the Supply/Demand Trend.* Beijing: Science Press.

Lohmar, B.T., Wang, X., Rozelle, S., Huang, J.K. and Dawe, D., 2002. *China's Agricultural Water Policy Reforms: Increasing Investment, Resolving Con-*

flicts, and Revising Incentives. Market and Trade Economics Division, Economic Research Service, U.S. Department of Agriculture. Agriculture Information Bulletin Number 782.

Lopes, V.L., 2008. Interactive Watershed Science-Linking Science, Policy and Community Participation. http://www.bio.txstate.edu/~watershedlab/pdfs/Interactive_Watershed_Science.pdf.

Ministry of Water Resources of China (MWR), 2004. *The Annual Book of Water Resources in China*. Beijing: China Water Press (in Chinese).

Ministry of Water Resources of China (MWR), 2005. News release, http://www.mwr.gov.cn/index/20060103/63451.asp

National Bureau of Statistics of China, 2003. http://www.stats.gov.cn/tjsj/qtsj/hjtjzl/hjtjsj2003/t20050706_402261014.htm.

National Research Council (NRC), 2002. Estimating Water Use in the United States — A New Paradigm for the National Water Use Information Program. *Natl. Acad. Sci.*, Washington, D.C.

Qian, Z. and Zhang, G. (eds.), 2001. Strategy Study on Sustainable Water Resources Development in China, General Report. Beijing: China Water Resources and Hydropower Press.

Randall, A., 1981. Property Entitlements and Pricing Policies for a Maturing Water Economy. *Australian Journal of Agricultural Economics*, 25(3): 192–220.

Raskin, P. (ed.), 1997. Comprehensive Assessment of the Freshwater Resources of the World. Stockholm Environment Institute.

Ringler, C. and Huy, N.V., 2004. Water Allocation Policies for the Dong Nai River Basin in Vietnam: An Integrated Perspective. EPTD Discussion Paper No. 127, IFPRI, Washington, D.C.

Rosegrant, M.W. and Cai, X., 2002. Market Adaptations to Increased Water Prices in China: The Impact on Water Demand and Rice Production. Invited paper at the First International Rice Congress, Beijing.

Rosegrant, W.M., Cai, X. and Cline, S., 2002. World Water and Food to 2025: Dealing with Scarcity. International Food Policy Research Institute (IFPRI), Washington, D.C.

Shen, D.J., 2005. The Fairness of Water Resources Management in China, *Journal of Hydraulic Engineering*, 1: 1–5.

Turner, et al., 2003. A Framework for Vulnerability Analysis in Sustainability Science. *Proc. Natl. Acad. Sci.*, 100(14): 8074–8079.

Turner, J. and Hildebrandt, T., 2005. Navigating Peace: Forging New Water Partnerships, U.S-China Water Conflict Resolution Water Working Group. *China Environment Series*, 7: 89–98.

United Nations Educational, Scientific and Cultural Organization (UNESCO), 2003. Water for People, Water for Life. United Nations World Water Development Rep., New York.

USEPA, 2006. Principles of Watershed Management. http://www.epa.gov/watertrain/watershedmgt/

Wang, S.C., 2003. *Resource-Based Water Management — Human Harmony with Nature*. Beijing: China Water Press.

Wang, S., Zheng, S. and Cheng, L., 2003. Studies on Impacts of Climate Change on Water Cycle and Water Resources in Northwest China. *Climatic and Environmental Research*, 8(1): 43–51.

Wang, H., Wang, J.H., Jia, Y.W., et al., 2006. Methods for Water Resources System Evaluation in Today's River Basins. *Hydrology*, 26(3): 18–21.

WCED (World Commission on Environment and Development), 1987. Our Common Future ("The Brundtland Report"), Oxford University Press.

World Bank, 1997. *At China's Table*. World Bank, Washington, D.C.

Xu, K.H., Milliman, J.D., Yang, Z.S. and Xu, H., 2007. Climatic and Anthropogenic Impacts on the Water and Sediment Discharge from the Yangtze River (Changjiang), 1950–2005. In: Gupta, A. (ed.), *Large Rivers: Geomorphology and Management*. West Sussex, England: John Wiley & Sons, pp. 609–626.

Yang, H., Zhang, X. and Zehnder, A.J.B., 2003. Water Scarcity, Pricing Mechanism and Institutional Reform in Northern China Irrigated Agriculture. *Agricultural Water Management*, 61: 143–161.

Yellow River Conservation Commission (YRCC), 1998, 1999, 2000, 2002. Yellow River Water Resources Bulletins (1998–2002). www.yellowriver.gov.cn.

Zhu, Y.H., Xia, J., Liu, S.X., Jia, S.F. and Feng, L.H., 2005. Calculation of the Carrying Capacity of Eco-Environmental Systems in the Hai River Basin. *Advances in Water Science*, 16(5): 649–654.

Index